The
BUFFALO SPORTS
CURSE

120 YEARS OF PAIN, DISAPPOINTMENT, HEARTBREAK AND ETERNAL OPTIMISM

GREG D. TRANTER

RIT PRESS
ROCHESTER, NY

Published and distributed by:
RIT Press
90 Lomb Memorial Drive
Rochester, New York 14623
http://ritpress.rit.edu

ISBN 978–1–939125–87–3 (print)
ISBN 978–1–939125–88–0 (ebook)

Printed in the U.S.A.

Book and cover design: Marnie Soom

Library of Congress Cataloging-in Publication Data

Names: Tranter, Greg D., 1957– author.
Title: The Buffalo sports curse : 120 years of pain, disappointment, heartbreak and eternal optimism / Greg D. Tranter.
Description: Rochester, NY : RIT Press, [2022] | Includes bibliographical references and index.
Identifiers: LCCN 2022025687 (print) | LCCN 2022025688 (ebook) | ISBN 9781939125873 (paperback) | ISBN 9781939125880 (ebook)
Subjects: LCSH: Sports—New York (State)—Buffalo—History. | Buffalo Bills (Football team)—History. | Buffalo Sabres (Hockey team)—History.
Classification: LCC GV584.5.B84 T36 2022 (print) | LCC GV584.5.B84 (ebook) | DDC 796.09747/97—dc23/eng/20220708
LC record available at https://lccn.loc.gov/2022025687
LC ebook record available at https://lccn.loc.gov/2022025688

CONTENTS

LIST OF ILLUSTRATIONS   vii

ACKNOWLEDGMENTS   ix

INTRODUCTION   1

1   THE CURSE IS BORN   7

2   BUFFALO BLUES   21

3   THE ALL-AMERICANS ARE BORN   33

4   PRO FOOTBALL COMES BACK TO TOWN   41

5   BUFFALO LOSES A CHAMPIONSHIP – AND THE NFL   49

6   THE BILLS MISS OUT ON HISTORY   63

7   THE MIAMI POUND MACHINE   77

8   THE SABRES LOSE THE CUP   93

9   THE SHORT BUT SWEET TALE OF THE BRAVES   107

10   FERGUSON'S PLAYOFF RUNS SLIP AWAY   123

11   THE BILLS' SNAKEBIT SUPER BOWL RUN   137

12   MLB BID STRIKES OUT   159

13   O.J. SIMPSON'S FALL FROM GRACE   173

14   BILLS GIVE UP A HOME RUN THROWBACK   185

15   NO GOAL!   203

16   THE LEGEND OF "BABY JOE" MESI   217

17   SABRES ON THE BRINK   223

18   A GLIMMER OF HOPE   239

CONCLUSION   263

ABOUT THE AUTHOR   267

BIBLIOGRAPHY   269

INDEX   275

ILLUSTRATIONS

1.   Ban Johnson, American League president   p. 9
2.   James Franklin, Buffalo alderman and Buffalo Bisons owner   p. 11
3.   William F. McKinley, U.S. president   p. 19
4.   Hal Chase, Buffalo Blues   p. 26
5.   Buffalo Blues team photo   p. 29
6.   Buffalo All-Americans team photo   p. 36
7.   Hotel Lafayette, Buffalo, New York   p. 42
8.   Buffalo Tigers Ticket Stub   p. 47
9.   Edgar Jones, Cleveland Browns vs. Buffalo Bills, Dec. 19, 1948   p. 55
10.   Boost the Bills sticker   p. 59
11.   Johnny Robinson, Kansas City Chiefs vs. Buffalo Bills, Jan. 1, 1967   p. 74
12.   Bob Griese, Miami Dolphins vs. Buffalo Bills, Oct. 26, 1975   p. 84
13.   Jim Schoenfeld, Buffalo Sabres vs. Philadelphia Flyers, May 20, 1975   p. 102
14.   Bob McAdoo, Buffalo Braves vs. Boston Celtics, April 26, 1976   p. 110
15.   Ernie DiGregorio, Buffalo Braves vs. Boston Celtics, April 26, 1976   p. 114
16.   Chuck Muncie, San Diego Chargers vs. Buffalo Bills, Jan. 3, 1981   p. 127
17.   Charles Alexander, Cincinnati Bengals vs. Buffalo Bills, Jan. 3, 1982   p. 132
18.   Scott Norwood, Buffalo Bills vs. New York Giants, Super Bowl 25   p. 144
19.   Andre Reed, Buffalo Bills vs. Washington Redskins, Super Bowl 26   p. 148
20.   Don Beebe, Buffalo Bills vs. Dallas Cowboys, Super Bowl 27   p. 152
21.   Thurman Thomas, Buffalo Bills vs. Dallas Cowboys, Super Bowl 28   p. 155
22.   Pilot Field opening-day crowd, April 14, 1988   p. 163
23.   Letter from Buffalo Bisons owners Bob and Mindy Rich, 1990   p. 165
24.   O.J. Simpson, Buffalo Bills   p. 180
25.   Ickey Woods, Cincinnati Bengals vs. Buffalo Bills, Jan. 8, 1989   p. 187
26.   Kevin Dyson, Tennessee Titans vs. Buffalo Bills, Jan. 8, 2000   p. 201
27.   Brett Hull, Dallas Stars vs. Buffalo Sabres, June 20, 1999   p. 214
28.   Joe Mesi vs. Vassily Jirov, March 13, 2004   p. 221
29.   Rod Brind'Amour, Carolina Hurricanes vs. Buffalo Sabres, June 1, 2006   p. 229
30.   Daniel Alfredsson, Ottawa Senators vs. Buffalo Sabres, May 19, 2007   p. 234
31.   Josh Allen and Stefon Diggs, Buffalo Bills vs. Indianapolis Colts, Jan. 9, 2021   p. 249
32.   Stefon Diggs, Buffalo Bills at Kansas City Chiefs, Jan. 24, 2021   p. 252
33.   Jack Eichel, Buffalo Sabres vs. New York Rangers, Feb. 15, 2021   p. 259

ACKNOWLEDGMENTS

This book has been a labor of love and has allowed me to pursue my passion for researching and writing about Buffalo professional sports. I would like to thank several people who were integral in bringing this book to fruition.

I was inspired and encouraged because of Jean Dalbec, a coworker and friend who had confidence that I could put my research and thoughts to paper and people would be interested to read it.

To my sister, Nancy Wright, an English professor at Syracuse University who guided me in my writing and offered many important edits to the manuscript.

A big thank you to Budd Bailey, who edited the complete manuscript. He offered tremendous tips in the utilization of the English language and made the book a more compelling and easier read. He also offered his encyclopedic knowledge of Buffalo professional sports that added many tidbits of information that enhanced the idea of the Curse.

To my wife, Tracy, and son, Bob, for their incredible support of my book pursuits and this manuscript in particular.

A big thank you to Bruce Austin, Molly Cort, and Steve Bradley and all the people at RIT Press for believing in this project and bringing it to a wonderful conclusion with its publication.

INTRODUCTION

Do you believe in curses? Do you think there might be a curse on Buffalo professional sports? This book will make you wonder, and may even convince you that there is. Noted paranormal author Mason Winfield looks at a curse just as many Buffalo sports fans might as he wrote in a story for Buffalo Rising magazine in 2016: "It depresses us with long stretches of failure. It tantalizes us with specific bouts of short-range success. It takes us just close enough to the ultimate prize to have us thirsting it and hungering it. Then on the only stage that counts, it lets us down."

This book was first conceived in 2003 after I had read Roger Abrams' "The First World Series and the Baseball Fanatics of 1903" and realized that the Boston Red Sox really began as the Buffalo Bisons in 1900. Then, later in 2003, the Curse of the Bambino continued in Game 7 of the American League championship series, with a walk-off home run by New York Yankees third baseman Aaron Boone that resulted in the defeat of the Red Sox in stunning fashion. Given that long-ago connection between the Red Sox and the Bisons, I was inspired to research why Buffalo had never won a universally recognized championship in any of the four major professional sports in America: baseball, basketball, football and hockey.

The only claim to a major championship would be the 1964 and 1965 American Football League champion Buffalo Bills; however, the AFL was considered inferior to the National Football League at that time. Thus, the champion of the NFL, not the AFL, was widely considered the best team in professional football.

Buffalo has won championships in major league lacrosse and minor league baseball. The Buffalo Bandits won four lacrosse championships (three in the Major Indoor Lacrosse League and one in the National Lacrosse League) between 1992 and 2008. The Buffalo Bisons minor league baseball team has won several championships over the course of its long history. But those victories, while undeniably significant, have not captured the nation's attention the way the chronic failings of Buffalo's four other major sports teams have.

All of the close calls, blown calls, injuries, deaths, nefarious back-office dealings, maladies, and weird happenings have occurred at just the wrong time to keep Buffalo teams from winning those elusive championships. Buffalo's losing ways are too pronounced to ignore, which gives rise to the idea of a curse. This book analyzes 32 events that convey the significance and expansiveness of the Buffalo Sports Curse.

The Curse began in 1901 and was a confluence of three events involving the Buffalo Bisons, a minor league baseball team that was scheduled to become an original franchise of a new major league, the American League (previously the minors' Western League). However, on Jan. 28, 1901, American League President Ban Johnson double-crossed Bisons owner James Franklin. Instead of establishing an American League team in Buffalo as planned (and virtually promised), Johnson decided on Boston for the new franchise just weeks before the team was to start the season. That new club became the Boston Americans, who would win the first World Series in 1903 and eventually become the Boston Red Sox. The new franchise would win five world championships by 1918. Meanwhile, the Buffalo Bisons retained their minor league status, joining the Eastern League for the 1901 season.

In September 1901, President William F. McKinley was assassinated in Buffalo while attending the Pan-American Exposition. That was followed by the sudden and surprising death of Bisons owner Franklin on Nov. 18.

The Curse began taking shape that fateful January day in 1901 and has continued for 121 years, across eight major league franchises and numerous famous sports moments, including "Wide Right," "No Goal," "Home Run Throwback," and "Agony at Arrowhead." But the Buffalo Sports Curse is much deeper than those four events. It spans four Super Bowls, a fistful of championship games in football and hockey, two runs for the Stanley Cup, countless playoff adventures and several odd personalities and transactions.

The Curse does not cover just Buffalo's current major league teams, the Bills and Sabres, but all of the city's major league teams, of the four major sports, dating to the beginning of the 20th century. (The 19th century wasn't any better than the 20th in those terms. The city had a couple of major league baseball teams, the Bisons of the National League in the 1880s and the Players' League franchise in 1890. Both teams eventually folded without a trace of a championship. But professional sports weren't too organized back then, and you didn't need a curse to lose — just bad management or a lack of money.)

There are stories here of the Buffalo Blues of baseball's Federal League in 1914–15, the Buffalo All-Americans of the early 1920s and the Buffalo Indians/Tigers of the 1940–41 American Football League. We delve into the 1946–49 Buffalo Bisons/Bills team of the All-America Football Conference and we analyze the Buffalo Braves of the National Basketball Association. We even cover the story of boxer "Baby Joe" Mesi, known as the Third Franchise.

We will look closely at moments that lend credence to the curse theory — plays that reversed a team's fortune or were so unbelievable that they can only be explained by a curse. We examine "Wide Right," with Buffalo Bills kicker Scott Norwood missing the game-winning field goal in Super Bowl 25. We explore "No Goal," when the referees allowed Brett Hull's Stanley Cup-winning overtime goal to count, even though he scored the goal with a skate in the crease — a violation of league rules. We chronicle "Home Run Throwback," with the Tennessee Titans defeating the Bills in a playoff game by scoring the game-winning touchdown after an apparent illegal forward lateral. We also examine "Agony at Arrowhead," when the Bills somehow lost to Kansas City after taking the lead with only 13 seconds left. Buffalo inexplicably allowed the Chiefs to kick a game-tying field goal on the final play of regulation and lost the coin toss in overtime, and Kansas City scored the game-winning touchdown without Buffalo ever touching the football.

The history of major league sports teams in Buffalo and the failure to win an undisputed championship in the four major sports is enough to make one wonder what is wrong. But when you add in all the weird happenings at just the wrong time, there is no doubt that the sports teams of Buffalo are cursed — starting on Jan. 28, 1901. By the way, on Jan. 28, 1991, Buffalo held a rally downtown in Niagara Square, thanking the Bills for their great season despite losing Super Bowl 25 two days before. Was that a mere coincidence?!

Buffalo sports fans have suffered for more than a century. They are as dedicated and loyal as any sports fans and care about their teams like few others. The passion for their teams and community are interconnected, and what gets their ire is a perceived lack of respect for either. Many outsiders look down upon the region, making fun of its snow or its continued struggle to overcome economic woes that date to the 1960s or its perceived lack of big-city culture.

Tim Russert, born and raised in Buffalo, was a nationally renowned television journalist as the longest-tenured host of NBC's "Meet the Press" from 1992 to 2008. During his time as host, it became the pre-eminent political television show. Russert was known to display his devotion to Buffalo sports teams on "Meet the Press." Before each of the four Super Bowls, he concluded the show by saying, "Go Bills!"

In his book, "Big Russ and Me," Russert described Buffalo as an underdog city. He said, "There is a special relationship between Buffalo and its football team. Dallas, New York, Atlanta, Chicago — sure, they root for their teams, but in Buffalo it feels different. We are not a high finance city, high fashion, or high rollers. There is a powerful, simple strength to Buffalo, and when the Bills win, it feels like an affirmation of our way of life."

In 1992, when Bills fans were inducted to the team's Wall of Fame, general manager Bill Polian wrote, "You, the Twelfth Man, have become known nationwide as the standard by which fan loyalty and enthusiasm is measured in professional sports." In addition, Bills owner Ralph C. Wilson Jr. wrote, "From the raucous days of the Rockpile to the crowds that have set NFL attendance records and played such a great role in our AFC championships you have been beside us through thick and thin."

Today the Bills Mafia is acclaimed around the country for its dedication and fan loyalty — along with a little craziness. Del Reid, credited with creating the Bills Mafia moniker, said about Buffalo fans, "The Bills aren't just a local team that Western New York roots for. The Bills are part of the very fabric that makes the WNY community what it is. Fanhood is passed down from generation to generation; it's more of a birthright than it is any kind of choice, really." And the same can be said for Sabres fans.

Former Bills standout Steve Tasker said in Sal Maiorana's book "Buffalo Bills; The Complete Illustrated History," there are two things a young football player realizes after coming to Buffalo: "First, for the people of Western New York, being a Bills fan runs as deep as their ethnicity. And second, when you put on a charging buffalo helmet, you become part of a huge extended family, a family that includes a lot of very crazy relatives. ... They believe they are a part of every game the Bills play."

Sabres fans, many of whom share a loyalty to the Bills, have that same degree of passion and enthusiasm and are also known as one of the NHL's best fan bases. Despite not making the playoffs from 2011 to 2022, the team's average attendance during that span was never less than 17,000 per game until 2021 and was at 18,970 in 2012–13. Few cities could match that record of loyalty in the face of such less-than-mediocre play.

Speaking of losing records, Buffalo sports fans have had many more years of pain than glory. And they have never had the opportunity to experience the pure joy of one of their teams winning a major league championship and reaching the pinnacle of their sport.

Will Leitch, founding editor of the sports blog Deadspin, ranked Buffalo Bills fans as the NFL's "most tortured fan base" in 2014. He said the Bills hit the trifecta of pain: 1. They had not made the playoffs in 15 years as of that time (it later stretched to 17). 2. They made it to four straight Super Bowls without winning, the only team ever to do that. (Leitch kindly didn't add that no MLB, NBA or NHL team had ever lost four straight championship finals either.) 3. The fans live in a city that is constantly battling economic woes. "No fan base deserves a Super Bowl win, and has earned one, more," he said.

Buffalo sports fans have suffered, coming *oh so close* to winning that elusive NFL championship, the NHL's Stanley Cup, an NBA title or even the possibility of a World Series champion. They have lost several professional franchises that either moved away, were left out of a league merger or went out of business — and fan support was never the problem in any of those situations. They have also lost professional teams that were on the cusp of coming to Buffalo but pulled out at the last minute.

The fans have gone through long stretches of cheering for losing teams — 17 straight non-playoff seasons for the Bills, 11 consecutive seasons for the Sabres — and have experienced year after year of playoff frustration. Western New York has seen a lot of "close, but not quite good enough."

Buffalo sports fans have adopted different rituals to try to rid their professional sports teams and the city of the Curse. Fans will wear the same clothes, even down to their underwear, when the Bills or Sabres are winning. They will sit in the same chair, eat the same food or follow the same regimen on game day. Some fans have gone as far as asking a priest or a rabbi for divine intervention. When their rituals are not working, they will do just the opposite, hoping something will work and vanquish the Curse. Fans often blame themselves for a loss if they deviate from their routine or when their new ritual does not help. To this point, none of it has helped a Buffalo team win a major championship.

The deep caring of Buffalo sports fans brings consequences of disappointment, frustration and depression when the team does not succeed. Buffalo fans are emotionally scarred from having never experienced the pinnacle of any of the four major professional sports. Their teams have been cursed, and the city and the fans just want to have an opportunity to be at the top one day and let the Buffalo Sports Curse be damned.

Join me on a trip through Buffalo sports history, as this book will show that the Buffalo Sports Curse is real, it is present, it is most pervasive.

Chapter 1
THE CURSE IS BORN

At the turn of the 20th century, Buffalo was a vibrant, bustling, growing city — the eighth-largest in the United States. Location, among other factors, made Buffalo an important city in American commerce, as the Gateway to the West and the second-largest port in the nation. It was preparing to host the Pan-American Exposition as a celebration of Buffalo's inventiveness and importance. The Exposition would establish for Buffalo the title of City of Light, thanks to the harnessing of hydroelectric power from Niagara Falls to provide widespread electric lighting across the city, the first city to accomplish this feat.

The Erie Canal had opened in 1825, changing the course of the city and transforming Buffalo into a major shipping port. The combination of the Erie Canal and the invention of the first steam-driven grain elevator by Joseph Dart propelled Buffalo to become America's primary grain milling center by the 1850s. Two Buffalonians became president of the United States in the 1800s: first in 1850, lawyer Millard Fillmore, and then former Buffalo mayor Grover Cleveland in 1885.

In 1903, one of America's foremost architects, Frank Lloyd Wright, designed his first building in Buffalo, the Larkin Administration Building. He went on to design several additional structures in Western New York, including the Darwin Martin House. By the early 1900s, Buffalo was the country's primary grain supplier, the second-largest port for lumber and the second-largest rail center in the United States. Also in the first years of the new century, Lackawanna Steel moved from Scranton, Pennsylvania, to Western New York, and suddenly Buffalo became one of the country's largest steel centers. The Queen City of the Lakes was clearly enjoying what could be considered its heyday.

At this time, major league sports were just beginning to become important in cities across the country, and teams had begun to insert themselves into American culture. In the first 25 years of the new century, professional baseball would expand from a single National League to add the American League and, in 1903, the first World Series. The American Professional Football Association was created in 1920 and was renamed the National Football League in 1922. The National Hockey League awarded its first Stanley Cup in the spring of 1918. Professional boxing was also a major sport in the 1920s, with Jack Dempsey being celebrated as the reigning heavyweight champion from 1919 to 1926.

In 1894, a newly formed minor baseball league calling itself the Western League was looking for a president. It hired Ban Johnson, a name familiar to many baseball fans. Johnson would serve as the president of the American League from its inception in 1899 until he retired in 1927. The successful establishment of the American League was the direct result of Johnson's fortitude, shrewd business skill, rigorous standards and some good fortune.

Johnson began his baseball career as a catcher and played both college and semi-pro ball with a great fondness for the game. He was the son of a college professor, attending Marietta and Oberlin colleges in Ohio. After college, he became a sports editor for the Cincinnati Commercial Gazette, where he worked for seven years. He secured the Western League job through a relationship he had developed with Charles Comiskey, who recommended him. Comiskey owned the St. Paul, Minnesota, franchise in the Western League and liked Johnson's strong opinions and baseball knowledge. In fact, it was at Johnson's urging that Comiskey would eventually move his team to Chicago to become the White Stockings in 1900.

Johnson saw taking the leadership role in the Western League as a way to implement changes in the game of baseball that he felt were essential for its survival and success. Baseball in the 1890s was a rough and rowdy game with little regard for the umpires. After Johnson became president of the league, he immediately mandated and enforced respect for the umpires. He created an atmosphere at the games that provided family entertainment without the violence or objectionable language present in the National League. Soon the Western League was recognized as the best minor league in all of baseball.

Photo 1. Ban Johnson founded the American League
and served as its president from 1900 to 1927.
(Boston Public Library)

Jim Franklin, a Buffalo alderman, became the principal owner of the Buffalo Bisons baseball club in 1891. When the International League was reorganized into the Eastern Association, Buffalo became a member. Franklin owned a meat market on Niagara Street as well as being a Buffalo politician, and he became known as quite a promoter. On opening day each year, he hired a brass band and had horse-drawn carriages that carried the players. He was also famous for changing managers and being impatient with his ballclub.

The Bisons played in the Eastern Association from 1891 to 1898. Their best finish was second place in 1896. Throughout their tenure in the Eastern Association, the league was unstable and unpredictable. By 1899, Franklin was concerned about the future of the league and decided to join Johnson's Western League. Johnson, in turn, was very pleased with securing the Buffalo franchise. The Bisons opened the 1899 season with high hopes, and the season could not have started better as Chummy Gray pitched a no-hitter. The team won its first four games but then slumped and never regained its winning ways. By the end of the season, the Bisons had fallen to 53–70 and a tie for seventh place in the league.

That October, Johnson decided to rename the Western League, changing the organizational moniker to the American League. He thought the name was more patriotic and would broaden the league's appeal. In addition to the name change, he decided to reorganize the league's franchises, moving two smaller market teams, St. Paul and Grand Rapids, Michigan, to the larger markets of Chicago and Cleveland, respectively. Johnson's power was enormous. He moved franchises, made schedules and signed players.

Franklin, meanwhile, was excited about his team's prospects. He invested significant dollars in the franchise to prepare for its first season in the new league, causing one newspaper to comment, "He is spending money in a way that is astonishing to his friends." The Bisons began the 1900 season strong, again with a no-hitter on opening day, this time fired by Morris "Doc" Amole. However, the thrilling beginning was followed by both winning and losing streaks as the team struggled for consistency. Up and down throughout the season, the Bisons slumped badly at the end, again falling into seventh place with a 61–78 final record.

Despite the disappointing finish, Franklin had other reasons to be optimistic as the first baseball season of the new century came to an end. He knew Ban Johnson was planning on breaking away from the minor league

Photo 2. Buffalo Alderman James Franklin became principal owner of the Buffalo Bisons in 1891 but never saw his dream of running a major league baseball team fulfilled.
(Buffalo Public Library)

system to become an independent major league and planned to go head-to-head with the National League. He was excited that his beloved Buffalo would be part of major league baseball in 1901.

In the fall of 1900, as Johnson positioned the American League, he decided to move three more teams to larger markets. He dropped the Minneapolis, Indianapolis and Kansas City franchises and replaced them with Philadelphia, Baltimore and Washington. In addition to these deals, and unbeknownst to Franklin, Johnson held secret meetings in Boston regarding a potential franchise there, as he believed a Boston team would be necessary to earn full respect for the American League and to compete with the National League. All the while, however, Johnson continued to give assurances to Franklin that "Buffalo was in and not to worry."

Nonetheless, by November Franklin had become uneasy as he kept hearing rumors that Buffalo might be dropped from the American League. He decided to make a trip to the American League headquarters in Chicago to try to get to the bottom of the situation, scheduling a Nov. 20 meeting with Johnson. Franklin and Johnson met throughout the day, with Franklin selling all the benefits of a franchise in Buffalo, including the value of the upcoming Pan-American Exposition. With the Bisons' Olympic baseball park near the fairgrounds, the opportunity to draw many fairgoers to the games seemed too good to pass up. The outcome of the meeting seemed to have been positive, as the Buffalo Evening News reported after the meeting that "it now seems that Franklin's wishes may be respected and that the Bisons will make the eighth club in the circuit."

Another important founding member of the American League was the owner of the Cleveland Indians, Charles Somers. Having made his fortune buying and selling coal mining properties, Somers was a millionaire at the age of 31, so he was also one of the league's chief financiers. Not only was he the owner of the Indians, but Somers helped establish clubs in Chicago and Philadelphia. Somers met with Johnson in Boston on Jan. 4, 1901, proposing to finance and own the Boston franchise. Together, and quietly behind closed doors, they agreed to put a team in Boston despite not having a ballpark to play in.

The Times-Herald in Chicago reported on Jan. 14 that "Ban Johnson of the American League announces that the American League circuit may be made up of ten clubs instead of eight." Johnson went on to say, "We have not completed our plans yet, but I am ready to state that under certain conditions, I favor a 10-club circuit, we already have nine." Johnson further commented that he was not prepared to say that Boston would be in the league in 1901. Buffalo was part of the nine as Franklin had paid the $500 entrance fee securing a spot in the league.

Johnson's comments in Boston presented a somewhat different picture from the one he shared with the Chicago paper, however. On Jan. 16, Johnson told The Boston Globe, "Boston is a good city. It is only a question of time, and unless our plans fail, we will have a club there this year." The next day, Connie Mack, owner of the Philadelphia Athletics, who headed a small group selected by Johnson to find a suitable playing site for an AL Boston franchise, signed a lease for land on Huntington Avenue in Roxbury for the construction of a stadium for the new Boston team. Interestingly Mack had begun his ownership interest in baseball in 1889, while still a player. He invested his life savings of $500 on a Buffalo franchise in the Players League, a new venture that lasted only a single season. Mack played catcher for the Bisons and batted .266. The league lost its battle with the National League and with it Mack lost his money. He then joined the Pittsburgh Pirates as a player and was promoted to manager a few seasons later. He was fired in 1896 and managed in the minor leagues until he joined the Philadelphia Athletics as manager, treasurer and part-owner in 1901.

When land became available in Boston to build a new ballpark, to be known as Huntington Grounds, Buffalo's place in the American League became tenuous at best, unless Johnson went to a 10-team league. And many baseball people felt a 10-team American League was not feasible. On Jan. 20, it was reported by the Buffalo Morning Express and Illustrated that "Boston, it is pretty definitely settled, will take Buffalo's place in the league." Johnson would not confirm the report. It was also reported that Franklin would be compensated with stock in the Boston team in exchange for dispensing his team to Boston.

Somers and Johnson approved plans for the placement of the diamond and grandstands for the Huntington Grounds baseball field on Jan. 23. They were given assurances that the stadium could be ready by April for the start of the season. This was the last of the stumbling blocks for the Boston franchise. Franklin would later surmise that Johnson kept reassuring him of Buffalo's place in the American League because he did not know if he could get the right ownership in Boston and secure a ballpark in time. Thus, Buffalo was kept as a contingency.

The 10-team league fell apart, and Buffalo's opportunity would crumble soon after. On Jan. 28, 1901, Johnson sent out an official announcement, formally establishing the American League, a major league to rival the National League. The announcement also listed the teams that would be included: the Baltimore Orioles, Boston Americans, Chicago White Stockings, Cleveland Blues, Detroit Tigers, Milwaukee Brewers, Philadelphia Athletics and the Washington Nationals. The Buffalo franchise had officially been moved to Boston, and Indianapolis was also deprived a franchise had they adopted a 10-team circuit.

That same day, Franklin, who was shocked and felt double-crossed by Johnson, attended the American League owners meeting, though he was not invited. "Franklin, President of the Buffalo Club, was the sorest man in Chicago tonight," the Buffalo Morning Express reported, "when he was definitely informed that Buffalo had been dropped from the circuit of the A.L." Franklin turned down an ownership stake in the Boston club, and his franchise entrance fee of $500 was returned to him. Boston also offered to buy the Buffalo players, but Franklin turned down the offer as he expected to keep the team together, whatever league they might play in for 1901. In turning down both offers, the Express reported, "Mr. Franklin says, it is very poor satisfaction and that he would much prefer to remain in the American circuit."

Buffalo Bisons catcher Ossee Schreckengost was the only player from the Buffalo team to make the move to Boston and play for the Americans in 1901. He acquitted himself well, appearing in 86 games while batting .304 with 38 runs batted in. The Buffalo franchise returned to the Eastern Association and changed its name to the Pan Ams, after the Exposition of 1901. The team proceeded to finish last with a record of 45–88. Franklin was extremely distraught over his bad fortune. He had lost out on bringing a major league team to his beloved Buffalo, and fans were deeply displeased to see the team land in the minor league cellar.

On Nov. 18, while at Thomas F. Crowley's parlor — coincidentally located on Franklin Street — where he had likely gone to play poker, Jim Franklin died unexpectedly of a heart attack at age 53. The Buffalo Courier reported, while discussing a business matter with parlor owner Crowley, Franklin "leaned back in his chair, heaved a long sigh and fell forward," dying suddenly. The Buffalo Evening News reported the next day, "There is universal regret and not a little genuine mourning in Buffalo today over the death of James

Franklin, President of the Board of Aldermen, and one of the best-known citizens of this city. Mr. Franklin was a member of many local societies and orders. … He was also the baseball magnate of the city." Sadly, with the death of James Franklin, Buffalo's flirtation with major league baseball would not be rekindled for nearly 90 years.

The Boston franchise that moved from Buffalo became the Boston Americans. In one of their first big player moves, they signed star third baseman Jimmy Collins away from the National League's Boston franchise in March 1901. He came to the Americans not only as their starting third baseman but also captain and manager. They paid him handsomely: $3,500 a year guaranteed for three years. This was a significant increase over his salary in the National League.

Collins was born in Niagara Falls in 1870 and his family moved to Buffalo in 1872, where his father was a police officer and would serve for more than 30 years. He grew up in South Buffalo and returned there in 1914 once his baseball career ended. Collins was considered the greatest third baseman of his era and in 1945 was the first third baseman inducted into the National Baseball Hall of Fame in Cooperstown, New York. It is quite ironic that Buffalo lost its opportunity for a major league baseball team to Boston, and then they signed a Buffalonian as the team's star player and manager.

During his first two seasons with the Americans, Collins did not disappoint, swinging his way to a .332 batting average in 1901 and .322 in 1902. He also managed the Americans to a 79–57 record and a second-place finish in 1901. The following season saw the team place third in the league with a 77–60 record.

In 1903, the Boston Americans were the best team in the American League, winning the pennant by 14½ games with a 91–47 record. They played the National League champion Pittsburgh Pirates, led by Hall of Fame shortstop Honus Wagner, in the first World Series. In an exciting and tight series, the Americans beat the Pirates five games to three. Americans pitcher "Big Bill" Dinneen, from Syracuse, New York, struck out Wagner for the final out of the series, giving the world championship to Boston and the upstart American League. Another star player for the Americans on that first championship team was pitcher Cy Young. Young finished the season with a 33–10 record and a 1.62 ERA. He would go on to win 511 games, by far the most in big-league history. Oh, what might have been. Could Buffalo have been the first World Series champion in baseball history? The city could at least take solace in knowing that the first manager to win a World Series was from Buffalo.

The Boston baseball team, known as the Americans from 1901 through 1906, was renamed the Boston Red Sox in 1907 and was the most successful team in baseball until 1919 — a span that included four more World Series victories. The Red Sox opened Fenway Park in 1912 and had the best winning percentage in team history that season, capturing the American League pennant by 14 games with a 105–47 record.

A left-handed pitcher named George Herman "Babe" Ruth joined the Boston Red Sox in June 1914 when he was purchased from the minor league Baltimore Orioles. Ruth made his major league debut on July 11, 1914, defeating the Cleveland Indians 4–3 with his solid pitching. Ruth would lead the Red Sox to three more world championships in the next five years on the strength of his abilities both at the plate and on the mound.

He went 18–6 in 1915, helping the Red Sox to the American League pennant. They beat the Philadelphia Phillies in five games to win the World Series. The following season, Ruth led the league in earned run average by sporting a 1.75 mark to go along with his 23–12 record. The Red Sox again won the pennant and this time beat the Brooklyn Robins in the World Series. In one of the best World Series games ever played, Ruth won an outstanding pitchers' duel 2–1 in 14 innings against Sherry Smith, with both pitchers going the distance. Ruth shut out Brooklyn for 13 consecutive innings after surrendering a first-inning run.

Boston won its fifth world championship in 1918 as Ruth led the league in home runs while also chalking up 13 wins as a pitcher. Carl Mays of the Red Sox defeated the Chicago Cubs on Sept. 11, 1918, to secure that year's World Series for Boston. Ruth pitched a Game 1 shutout and also set a World Series record for consecutive scoreless innings with 29.

Ruth was clearly the star of the Red Sox, and of baseball, in 1919. But Red Sox owner Harry Frazee could not afford to pay him and continue to produce Broadway shows at the same time, so he traded Ruth to a certain team from New York — the rival Yankees. Boston would not win another World Series title until 2004, an 86-year drought, suffering their own curse. They lost the seventh and deciding game of the World Series in 1946, 1967 and 1986. And in 1978, they blew a 14½-game lead and lost to the Yankees in a one-game playoff.

All this wonderful Boston baseball history could have played out in Buffalo, if not for the double-cross of American League founder and commissioner Ban Johnson. The Yankees, meanwhile, would go on to win a record 27 World Series titles.

In 1901, after losing their major league franchise due to Johnson's shenanigans, all eyes in Buffalo were on the Pan-American Exposition. This great world's fair was an opportunity for Buffalo to be in the spotlight across the globe and show off its many innovations. The Exposition advertised as Rainbow City was an incredible display of lights and electricity.

With great anticipation, the Exposition opened on May 1, and it was expected that President William F. McKinley would attend the Grand Opening. However, the president had to postpone his plans as his wife was too ill to travel, though he promised he would attend later in the year. Vice President Theodore Roosevelt attended instead, with the date of the Grand Opening pushed back to May 20.

The vice president, upon arriving at the Exposition, walked through the fairgrounds experiencing many of the wonderful sights, including the Court of the Fountains, the 409-foot cream-colored Tower of Light, the Machinery and Transportation Halls, the Temple of Music and of course the Midway, with some of its death-defying rides like the Aerio-Cycle, which was the most popular. Roosevelt delivered a politically oriented speech to a large crowd on a beautiful sunny day.

After the vice president's visit, Buffalo suffered through a rainy summer, and attendance at the Exposition was well below expectations. However, organizers hoped that they could attract President McKinley and that his visit would provide a surge in attendance before the close of the fair at the end of October. They successfully convinced McKinley to attend, and Sept. 5 was designated President's Day at the Exposition.

McKinley arrived in Buffalo the evening of Sept. 4 and stayed at the Delaware Avenue home of John Milburn, a close family friend. The president and his wife, Ida, spent almost the entire day of Sept. 5 at the Exposition. McKinley delivered his speech with more than 116,000 fairgoers in attendance, the Exposition record for a single day. In his speech, he said, "Expositions are the timekeepers of progress." Overall, his speech was well received by the large throng. He remained at the fair enjoying himself throughout the day, partaking in many of the activities of the Exposition and the special events planned for his visit. He and Mrs. McKinley spent the morning and early afternoon of Sept. 6 touring Niagara Falls. They returned to Buffalo and the Exposition as the president had committed to meet and greet fairgoers beginning at 4 p.m. in the Temple of Music.

Promptly at 4, McKinley began greeting every visitor. He welcomed each person with a smile and a handshake. Everyone was pleased with this glorious day in Buffalo. To this point, things could not have gone better for the president's visit, for the Exposition and for the reputation of Buffalo.

At 4:07 p.m., as more and more people passed by the president, a dark-haired young man with a white bandage over his right arm drew especially close to McKinley and thrust his bandaged right hand into the president's chest. Two sharp popping sounds, like firecrackers, were heard and a thin veil of smoke rose up in front of McKinley. The president clutched his chest and leaned forward, as he had taken two gunshots into his chest. The slumping McKinley was helped into a nearby chair while he bled. Several men wrestled the gun-toting man to the floor, apprehending him. He was later taken to police headquarters and placed in the city jail. Aides rushed to help the president and eventually took him to the hospital on the Exposition Grounds.

The gunman was Leon Czolgosz, an anarchist who came to Buffalo on a mission to stamp out "the evil of government," and he thought he should start at the top. He hated McKinley and his policies. Czolgosz, from Cleveland, was poor, reclusive and often unemployed. He waited in line on Sept. 6 for more than two hours in 80-degree temperatures for his turn to shake hands with McKinley and for his chance to attempt to assassinate the president.

McKinley underwent emergency surgery on the Exposition Grounds to remove the bullets. The surgery was deemed successful, even though surgeons were unable to extract one of the bullets. McKinley slowly improved in the days following the shooting, until Sept. 12. With the hurried surgery and chaos on the Exposition Grounds after the shooting, doctors used several surgical instruments that apparently had not been properly sanitized. Gangrene, which had been quietly forming for a week, was discovered after the president complained of discomfort. McKinley began to deteriorate rapidly, as penicillin had not yet been discovered. The president died early the morning of Sept. 14. Later that day, Theodore Roosevelt was sworn in as the 26th president of the United States at the home of Ansley Wilcox on Delaware Avenue.

Photo 3. President William F. McKinley at the Pan-American
Exposition in Buffalo, shortly before he was
fatally shot on Sept. 6, 1901.
(Buffalo History Museum)

The year 1901, which began in Buffalo with so much excitement, ended with such misfortune. And it is that overall misfortune that gave birth to the Buffalo Sports Curse. The confluence of three events within 10 months of each other originated this Curse, and it is something the city has not been able to shake in 121 years.

Chapter 2
BUFFALO BLUES

In 1914, Buffalo joined the renegade Federal League of Base Ball Clubs, gaining a major league baseball team that was taken away with the move of the team in 1901 to Boston. Though the group was outside the existing structure of Organized Baseball (the American and National leagues), it is still considered major league by historians.

The Federal League was officially founded on March 8, 1913, led by longtime minor league executive John Powers. The league agreed at the time that it would abide by baseball's National Agreement and would be a minor league. The National Agreement was a pact between the American and National leagues signed in 1903 that governed relations between them. It required each league to respect one another's player contracts, and it provided for an annual postseason championship, the World Series, between the two leagues' champions. It also set up a three-person National Commission to settle disputes regarding player contracts.

The Federal League began play that year with six Midwestern teams: Chicago, Cincinnati (represented by Covington, Kentucky), Cleveland, Indianapolis, Pittsburgh and St. Louis. The opening game of the new circuit pitted the Covington Blue Sox against the Cleveland Green Sox on May 3, 1913. Cincinnati moved to Kansas City in midseason. The Indianapolis Hoosiers won the first pennant by a wide margin with a 75–45 record. While the league suffered significant financial losses, bigger plans were ahead.

The Federal League expanded in 1914 to eight teams, and Buffalo was one of the cities added. But the bigger news was that the Federal League decided to break away from Organized Baseball and become a major league of its own, competing directly with the other major leagues. The New York Times reported on Nov. 1, 1913, that "the board of directors of the Federal League here to-night decided to declare war upon the major leagues of Organized Baseball, admitted Buffalo … and Baltimore to the circuit, making it an eight-club organization." Brooklyn was a third new team added, joining five holdovers from the minor league circuit: the defending champion Indianapolis Hoosiers along with clubs in Chicago, Kansas City, Pittsburgh and St. Louis. Cleveland dropped out.

The Federal League went after players in both the American and National leagues, signing them to contracts. The Buffalo Express on Nov. 2, 1913, proclaimed that "Buffalo, New York, would have a Federal League team in 1914, and former major league player and minor league manager Larry Schlafly would be its playing manager."

William E. Robertson was president of the new Buffalo ballclub and put up the money behind the team. In addition to his dollars, local real-estate developers Walter Mullen, Laurens Enos and Oliver Cabana Jr. also bought portions of the franchise, and the team sold stock to the public at $10 for a preferred share. Richard T. "Dick" Carroll, a former minor league ballplayer with a cup of coffee in the majors, was the business manager. He was only 29 years old but was considered very capable and knew his way around Organized Baseball.

The team searched for a place to play, finally determining they had to build a new ballpark. The team selected a tract of land at the old International Fair Association Grounds at Northland Avenue and Lonsdale Road. It would be called Federal League Park. The contractor, Mosier and Summers, broke ground on March 22, 1914, and incredibly the stadium was ready for the team's home opener on May 11. The 20,000-seat stadium was built at a cost of $130,000. Through a name-the-team contest run by a local Buffalo newspaper, the team was nicknamed the Buffeds. Some people had begun calling the team the Buffalo Federals because they were a member of the Federal League. The new nickname was derived from shortening both.

Schlafly went after players in Organized Baseball and was able to lure away pitcher Russell Ford from the New York Yankees, infielder William "Baldy" Louden from the Detroit Tigers and pitcher Earl Moore from the Chicago Cubs. He also secured the services of first baseman Joseph Agler, catcher Walter Blair and center fielder Charles Hanford from the International League. However, the majority of players came through assignment from a central pool by the Federal League. Surprisingly, Schlafly was able to put together a competitive ballclub for the 1914 season.

The Buffeds opened their season in Baltimore on April 13, 1914, and it was an official half-day holiday voted by the Maryland State House because the state was thrilled to have major league baseball back in Baltimore. More than 30,000 fans poured into the stadium. As the Baltimore News reported, "Practically every seat in the great pavilions was filled long before 3 o'clock and the bleachers after becoming overtaxed, turned hundreds into the field. Every inch of the stands are bedecked with red, white and blue streamers, while thousands of American flags made the spectacle one of brilliance."

Moore was the opening-day starting pitcher for Buffalo. The 35-year-old had 13 years of big-league experience, garnering 150 wins along the way.

Buffalo wore unique uniforms on opening day and began a trend that still persists in major league baseball today. They were the first team to wear a road uniform with the city name on the front in script lettering.

Baltimore scored first on doubles by Terrapins pitcher John Quinn and first baseman Harry Swacina in the fourth inning. Baltimore scored two more runs in the inning to take a 3–0 lead. Buffalo bounced back in the fifth as Hanford drove in two runs with a double to cut the lead to 3–2. But Quinn shut down Buffalo for the remainder of the game, and the overflow Baltimore crowd was pleased with the 3–2 victory.

Buffalo played its first 17 games on the road, as its stadium was being completed, going 7–10. The home opener was slated for May 11 against Baltimore. League President James A. Gilmore inspected the Buffeds' new baseball park the day before the scheduled home opener and was pleased with the stadium, saying, "The Buffalo plant is among the best in the league."

Before the opener, the two teams — along with delegations from local commercial and fraternal organizations and marching bands — paraded down Main Street in the drizzling rain to celebrate major league baseball in Buffalo.

Mayor Louis P. Fuhrmann threw out the first pitch from the mound at the brand-new ballpark in front of 14,286 rain-soaked fans. Baltimore scored first with runs in the first and second innings. However, Buffalo responded with the ballpark's first home run off the bat of Hanford in the fourth inning, cutting the lead to 2–1. Baltimore scored another run in the fifth inning, but Buffalo scored single runs in the sixth and seventh innings to tie the game at 3. Buffalo manager Schlafly got heated after the umpires reversed an out call on Baltimore in the eighth inning and he was subsequently ejected for arguing the call. With the score still knotted in the ninth, Buffalo relief pitcher

Gene Krapp loaded the bases on a couple of walks and a base hit, and with two outs walked in the go-ahead run. Buffalo could not muster a rally and lost its home opener 4–3.

Buffalo won its first game in the new park over the Chicago Federals (Chi-Feds) 5–4 on a walk-off, bases-loaded walk on May 14. Louden worked the walk, forcing in Fred Anderson with the game-winning run. Anderson — who had come on in relief of Krapp — was also the winning pitcher.

Buffalo played its best baseball of the season over the next month, winning 19 games and losing 10. On the morning of June 17, the upstart Buffeds were in first place by a half game.

In 1913, Hal Chase of the Chicago White Sox was considered one of the best first basemen in the game. He was an outstanding fielder and a solid hitter. However, Chase was an adventure off the field with a mind of his own. He had a reputation for being lazy, and there were even rumors that he would work to throw a game. He also had tired of the overbearing approach of White Sox owner Charles Comiskey.

The Federal League was trying to get him to sign on with the new circuit. Buffalo pursued Chase throughout the winter, but to no avail. After a spat with Comiskey in June, Chase decided to exercise a provision in his contract that allowed him to provide 10 days' notice and he would be free to sign with another team. Chase notified Comiskey on June 17 that he was serving his 10-day notice. On June 22, the Buffalo Courier-Express reported that American League President Ban Johnson "glibly prophesized that Hal Chase never would play for the Federals."

On June 21, Chase left Comiskey Park with his belongings and drove across town to Weeghman Park to suit up for the Buffeds in their game versus the Chi-Feds. Since it was Sunday, Comiskey and Johnson could not obtain a restraining order, so Chase was able to play for Buffalo. He collected two base hits, including a double driving in the Buffeds' only run, as fans cheered his every move.

Johnson and Comiskey were livid and pursued every angle to keep Chase from playing again for Buffalo. Chase, on the other hand, headed to Buffalo, trying to avoid being served a court injunction. He was expected to play for the team when it returned to Buffalo to open a homestand on June 25. The Buffeds promoted that game as "Hal Chase Day" in honor of his first game in the city. This was Buffalo's first sports superstar.

That morning, Chase was brought into Buffalo from Ontario, still trying to avoid any court-ordered injunctions, by Buffeds business manager Carroll and team vice president Mullen. Later in the day he was smuggled into the ballpark and, instead of going to the clubhouse, was hidden in a tool shed down the right field line.

The crowd was well over 7,000, as reported by the Buffalo Evening News, but the official paid attendance was announced at 6,443 — and they were revved up to greet their new superstar. When fans entered the stadium, they were given booklets with a biography on the life of Chase and a photograph of the star.

The game was delayed 30 minutes, but at 4 p.m., Chase was announced as the starting first baseman and the crowd erupted in cheers. He then came running in from the shed in right field. It was decided to let Buffalo bat first, as the team knew an injunction was going to be served and they wanted Chase to be able to bat. He came to bat with another round of cheers but — with all that was on his mind — struck out on three pitches. At the end of the second inning, Sheriff Fred Becker served the temporary injunction papers to Chase in the dugout and his day was done. Now, he and the team had to wait on a ruling from the court.

Chase and the White Sox squared off in court on July 9 in Buffalo. The case was presided over by Judge Herbert P. Bissell. The White Sox contention was that Chase broke his contract and was illegally playing for another club. Chase's lawyer Keene H. Addington argued that "Organized Baseball is a combination and scheme contrary to common and statute law and a violation of the Sherman antitrust law." His contention was that it illegally restricted movement of players, even when their contracts expired.

Justice Bissell deliberated for 11 days before providing a ruling on July 21. He vacated the temporary injunction restricting Chase from playing with the Buffeds. He declared, "Organized Baseball is as complete a monopoly of the baseball business for profit as any monopoly can be made. It is a contravention of the common law, in that it invades the right to contract as a property right and that it is a combination to restrain and control the exercise of a profession or a calling." With the ruling, Chase was free to rejoin the Buffeds, and he told a Buffalo News reporter, "I am greatly thrilled. I knew I was right and went ahead with the fight."

During the court proceedings, the club slumped, dropping from first to fifth place with a 39–39 record. Once Chase became eligible to play for the

Photo 4. Hal Chase, whom Hall of Famers Babe Ruth and Walter Johnson called the best first baseman ever, played for the Buffalo Blues in 1914 and 1915.

(Library of Congress Bain Collection)

Buffeds, he did not disappoint, batting .347 with 19 doubles, nine triples and 48 runs batted in 75 games. Buffalo improved, going 41–32 to finish the season, but was never able to overcome the contenders in the pennant race. The Buffeds finished with an 80–71 record, good for fourth place, seven games behind the champion Indianapolis Hoosiers.

Buffeds pitcher Ford finished with the best record in the Federal League at 20–6. Krapp was the team's second-best pitcher, finishing with a 14–14 mark. Hanford led the team in home runs with 13. The Buffeds drew a total of 185,326 fans, a very respectable showing for their inaugural season. Despite the solid attendance, The New York Times reported that the club "ran far behind their expenditures."

After the conclusion of the 1914 season, the Federal League was very active with teams signing away players from Major League Baseball. Chi-Feds owner Charley Weeghman was in talks with league leadership about buying the Cubs and reassessing the league's finances.

On Oct. 22, the Federal League's owners met with league president Gilmore. Despite the financial losses of several clubs, the owners were more determined than ever to continue their fight with Major League Baseball and keep the Federal League going. They also decided they needed to help shore up the teams that were the weakest financially, St. Louis and Pittsburgh, and to consider relocating the Kansas City franchise.

Gilmore had convinced the owners that a team in the New York City area was a necessity to effectively compete with Major League Baseball. At first, Gilmore was going to move the Kansas City franchise but instead, after some negotiations, moved the Indianapolis ballclub to Newark, New Jersey. For the 1915 season, the league was intact with the same clubs as 1914, except for that transfer.

On Jan. 15, 1915, the Federal League turned up the heat even more as it filed an antitrust lawsuit against Organized Baseball in U.S. District Court in Northern Illinois. The presiding judge would be Kenesaw Mountain Landis. Gilmore, through the Federals lawsuit "charged Organized Baseball with being a combination, a conspiracy, and a monopoly, in contravention of the Sherman antitrust law." He also claimed it restrained trade and was keeping the Federal League from signing more ballplayers. Judge Landis heard the case later in January but did not render a verdict.

Buffalo was excited for the 1915 season to begin with the team's new moniker, the Blues. They opened the campaign with veteran Boston Red Sox hurler Hugh Bedient on the mound. His opening game did not go well, as the Blues were defeated by Brooklyn 13–9 on April 10. The Blues home opener was no better on April 17, as starting pitcher Al Schulz gave up five runs in the team's 8–4 loss to Brooklyn in front of 18,281, the largest crowd to ever witness a baseball game in Buffalo.

The combination of poor play by the Blues and the terrible weather they encountered in the early part of the season led The Buffalo News to contend that the team was jinxed. A headline in the News on May 20 said, "Schlafly Hopes to Shake Jinx in Game Today." With Buffalo stuck in last place at 8–21 and in St. Louis for a three-game series, the first two games were postponed, prompting the News to report, "The fact that a jinx was on the trail of Larry Schlafly and his Blues had preceded his visit to this city … when the first game of the Buffalo series had to be called off because of the cold and frigid weather, more credence was placed on the jinx idea. But when the ballpark was coated with three inches of snow yesterday afternoon, all doubt of a hoodoo following Schlafly was set aside."

The team continued to struggle and was mired in last place on June 4 with a 13–28 record when Schlafly resigned. Catcher Blair took over on an interim basis and then Harry Lord, the team's third baseman, was named the permanent manager. The Blues showed marked improvement, going 60–47 over the remaining games to end the season with a 74–78 record and a sixth-place finish. But the club was not able to overcome its miserable start and that nascent jinx. The Chicago Whales won the Federal League championship with an 86–66 record, only .001 over the St. Louis Terriers, who finished 87–67.

Chase had an excellent season for Buffalo, leading the Federal League in home runs with 17 and batting a solid .291 with 31 doubles and 89 runs batted in. Former Yankee Schulz led the team with a 21–14 record. But Ford had a miserable season with a 5–9 record and was released in July, then re-signed and released again. Much was expected of Bedient, but he ended the season with a disappointing 16–18 record.

The club's directors had invested an additional $75,000 in the team, but with dwindling attendance, the Blues lost more money in 1915. By the end of the season, according to Daniel R. Levitt in his book, "The Battle That Forged Modern Baseball," "the club was over $50,000 in debt and it was announced that $100,000 would be needed to keep it going."

Photo 5. Buffalo's last major league baseball team, the 1915 Buffalo Blues.

(Baseball Hall of Fame)

During the fall of 1915 and throughout the World Series, Organized Baseball's major leagues and the Federal League were involved in intense negotiations to end the war between them. The Federal League owners proposed having four of their clubs join Major League Baseball, making each of the two existing major leagues consist of 10 teams. It was proposed that Brooklyn, Pittsburgh, Baltimore and Buffalo or Kansas City join. Several National League owners and many minor league owners, who had seen their ranks thinned from 40 teams to 29, were willing to entertain a settlement with the Federal League. However, American League president Johnson was not a proponent of the settlement with the Federals and was resolute in his conviction. After the World Series, rather than continue negotiations, Johnson went home.

In the heat of the back-and-forth negotiations led by Federal League vice president and Brooklyn team owner Robert Boyd Ward, Ward was diagnosed with pneumonia. Less than a week later, on Oct. 18, he died. Upon his death, The New York Times reported, "The death of Robert B. Ward removes from the Federal League one of its staunch supporters. He was ever an active force in promoting the welfare of the league, and on several occasions came forward with loans of money to tide over the difficulties of clubs less firmly entrenched than his own. In view of the position which he held; his death naturally entails consideration of what effect his loss will have on the future of the league."

His death was monumental in the loss of leverage the Federal League had in its negotiations. Almost immediately, Organized Baseball backed off and changed its negotiating posture. The established leagues knew that Ward had the significant money behind the Federal League and now with him gone, they believed their position was much stronger. That turned out to be true as the warring leagues ultimately came to an agreement on Dec. 23, 1915.

The merger terms were much less generous than originally hoped as only two Federal League owners, Weeghman and Phil Ball, were allowed to purchase a major league team, the Cubs and Browns, respectively. A $600,000 financial settlement was agreed upon for the remaining teams to cover losses. In addition, the Federal League agreed to drop the lawsuit in which Judge Landis still had not rendered a verdict. Also, no Federal League teams were absorbed into the majors, a significant disappointment for the remaining clubs.

Buffalo was again left out. The Buffalo franchise filed for bankruptcy on July 21, 1916, listing debts of $89,793, and major league baseball again died for the city.

Chase went back to the majors and played three seasons with the Cincinnati Reds and one with the New York Giants. However, he was allegedly involved in several incidents of throwing games. He also was indicted in the Black Sox scandal, serving as a key middleman between the players and gamblers in throwing the 1919 World Series. However, California refused his extradition. And though Chase was not tried nor found guilty, when the Black Sox scandal trial was completed, Landis, the federal judge who would become the first commissioner of baseball, declared that "no player who threw a game or promised to throw a game would ever be allowed in baseball." That effectively ended Chase's major league career.

Federal League Park was initially converted to a city recreation facility, but that concept eventually failed. The structure was sold by the bankruptcy court for $5,500 and was torn down with the property sold as building lots.

The Buffalo Sports Curse was alive again. Had it not been for the death of Ward, it is very possible the negotiations with Organized Baseball would have ended in a different place for the Federal League. There is a strong likelihood that some teams would have joined the majors and Buffalo could have been one of those clubs. But with his death, that possibility went by the wayside.

Also, Buffalo's first true professional sports superstar joined the team, but the month-long injunction had an impact on the club, putting the Blues into a slump. Maybe Buffalo would have won the first Federal League title had Chase been available from June 17, 1914, on. Another lost opportunity because of the Curse!

Buffalo was again on the verge of a major league baseball franchise, only to be denied because of the surprising and untimely death of the person who had the wherewithal to negotiate an attractive and fair settlement that could have included Buffalo. The city would go 44 years before a potential major league baseball franchise opportunity would present itself again.

Chapter 3
THE ALL-AMERICANS ARE BORN

Buffalo had twice been teased by a potential major league baseball franchise. The first time was back in 1901, when American League President Ban Johnson took the team away to Boston. The second was when Buffalo received a franchise in the rebel Federal League. The ballclub actually played in Buffalo for two years but was lost when the league folded at the conclusion of the 1915 season.

Buffalo finally gained a major league franchise by switching sports. In 1920 the American Professional Football Association was founded in an automobile dealership in Canton, Ohio. Buffalo's major league sports odyssey began with its first full-fledged franchise, the Buffalo All-Americans.

A preliminary meeting of the APFA occurred on Aug. 20, 1920, and a more formal organizational meeting was held at Ralph Hay's Hupmobile showroom on Sept. 17, 1920. At least 10 of the teams were present and many representatives sat on cars' running boards as they organized professional football. Later that fall the APFA kicked off its first season. The league was the forerunner of the National Football League and would formally adopt that name for the 1922 season.

The Buffalo All-Americans were among the inaugural members of the APFA, becoming the first major league football team in Buffalo. The other charter members of the APFA were the Akron Pros, Canton Bulldogs (with Olympic gold medalist Jim Thorpe), Chicago Cardinals, Chicago Tigers, Cleveland Tigers, Columbus Panhandles, Dayton Triangles, Decatur Staleys, Detroit Heralds, Hammond Pros, Muncie Flyers, Rochester Jeffersons and Rock Island Independents.

The All-Americans were formed by Barney Lepper and local businessman Frank J. McNeil. McNeil signed a lease for the team to play its games at Canisius College Villa, which was at Main and Jefferson streets in Buffalo. Also, McNeil signed former Michigan star quarterback Tommy Hughitt as the team's first quality player.

During their first season, Buffalo played a mix of independent teams and members of the APFA. The league was not nearly as organized as professional football is today, and many games were scheduled with little notice. Teams worked on their own to schedule games, and thus in the early seasons, the clubs did not play the same number of league games.

The All-Americans began their inaugural season against four independent teams and handled them all with ease by scores of 32–6, 51–0, 28–7 and 38–0. The stars of Buffalo's first team were running back Ockie Anderson, who scored 11 touchdowns during the season; quarterback and head coach Hughitt, scoring eight touchdowns; back Bodie Weldon; end Heinie Miller; and guard Swede Youngstrom.

The first game the All-Americans played against an APFA member was on Oct. 31 versus the Rochester Jeffersons, earning a 17–6 victory. Weldon, a graduate of Lafayette College, was the star of the game for the All-Americans as he scored the team's first touchdown and kicked a field goal. Buffalo's other touchdown was on a fumble recovery by Bill Brace. The All-Americans defense was stout and held up to bring home the victory.

The following week they played an independent team from Tonawanda and won 35–0. They finished their 1920 slate with five consecutive APFA league games. The All-Americans began that streak with an impressive 43–7 victory on Nov. 14 over the Columbus Panhandles, setting up a visit by the Thorpe-led Canton Bulldogs the next weekend.

Anticipating a large crowd, the game was moved from Canisius' Villa Field to the Buffalo Baseball Park, where it drew the largest crowd of the season — more than 15,000, despite heavy rain before the game. Though Thorpe did not star in the game, the Canton Bulldogs' Al Feeney kicked a field goal late in the contest to hand the All-Americans their only defeat of the season by a 3–0 score. The All-Americans bounced back the next weekend, defeating the Cleveland Tigers 7–0 on a 15-yard touchdown run by Anderson.

Buffalo had a rematch with Canton at New York's Polo Grounds on Dec. 4. It was promoted as the first big game in the new professional football league. The best teams in the first year of the APFA were the Akron Pros, the Bulldogs and the All-Americans. Promoters of the new league were looking for two top teams to provide a demonstration of the higher skill of the pro game for the New York media.

Before 15,000 fans, Thorpe kicked a field goal in the third quarter to give Canton a 3–0 lead. However, Youngstrom, out of Dartmouth College, later blocked a Thorpe punt and ran the ball into the end zone to give the All-Americans a 7–3 lead. The Buffalo defense stiffened and did not allow the Bulldogs to score, giving the All-Americans a huge victory. The New York press praised the efforts of both teams and was extremely impressed with the quality of play and the hard hitting of these professional football players. The APFA's first game in the New York media center proved to be a major success for the league.

The All-Americans traveled back to Buffalo that night and prepared to play the league's only undefeated team, the Akron Pros, the next day. This would be the APFA's inaugural championship game, and it was played at the All-Americans' home field. The headlines of the Buffalo Courier that morning proclaimed, "Buffalo Pros Beat Canton and Play Akron for Title."

The weary All-Americans played their hearts out at the Buffalo Baseball Park but were only able to battle the Pros to a 0–0 draw. Neither team was able to do much offensively in the muddy conditions.

After the game, the Buffalo Times reported, "Akron now has established her claim to the championship of the professional football world having concluded her season without a defeat while Buffalo was defeated once, Canton defeating Buffalo here weeks ago by a 3–0 score when Feeney, a Notre Dame star, booted a field goal within the last few minutes of play." However, Buffalo claimed it should have been awarded the championship because it had more victories than Akron, nine to eight, and Buffalo had avenged its only loss to Canton. Buffalo owner McNeil felt so strongly that his team deserved the title that he purchased gold football charms for each member of the team commemorating the championship. The charm was inscribed with "Buffalo World's Pro Champions."

Akron was awarded the championship by a vote of the league owners at their meeting several months after the conclusion of the season. The session was presided over by Akron owner Art Ranney. Despite their bridesmaid finish, the All-Americans enjoyed a great 1920 season with their 4–1–1 league record and overall 9–1–1 record. Buffalo was well positioned to make a run at the championship in 1921.

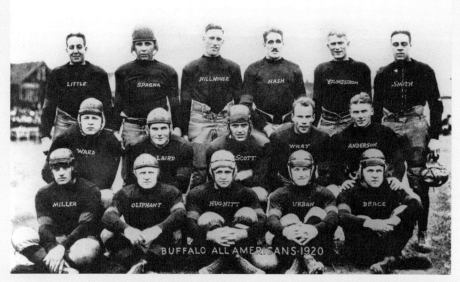

Photo 6. The 1920 Buffalo All-Americans, shown in 1920, finished 9-1-1 in the first year of what would become the National Football League.

(Pro Football Hall of Fame via AP Images)

The All-Americans had an excellent 1921 season, including victories in several big games, and should have been awarded the APFA championship. McNeil added some key players to bolster his team's roster before the season. Running back Elmer Oliphant, a star at Army, and Boston College's Luke Urban joined the team. Also, in the first player transaction in APFA history, the All-Americans acquired star defensive lineman Robert "Nasty" Nash from the Akron Pros. McNeil paid the Pros $300 plus 5% of the gate from a future Akron-Buffalo game to secure Nash.

Buffalo opened the 1921 season on Sept. 25 versus the McKeesport Olympics, an independent team, easily dispatching them 28–0. At the end of the season, the league would not count this victory when it determined who would be the APFA champion because McKeesport was not a league member.

During the next five weeks, playing all APFA opponents, the All-Americans were devastating, outscoring those five teams 169–0. Oliphant led their 17–0 victory over the Hammond Pros with a 10-yard touchdown run, a field goal and two extra points. Anderson scored three touchdowns to lead the All-Americans to a 38–0 win over Columbus.

Buffalo upped its record to 4–0 by drubbing the New York Giants 55–0. Oliphant again had a terrific game, scoring two touchdowns as well as kicking two field goals and seven extra points. Buffalo then shut out Rochester 28–0 and Detroit 21–0 to conclude the streak and defeated the Cleveland Tigers 10–6 in a hard-fought match.

With a 7–0 record, the All-Americans were set to play their toughest games of the season with contests against the defending champion Akron Pros, the Canton Bulldogs and the unbeaten Chicago Staleys. The tough stretch began on Nov. 13 at home against the Pros and the two teams battled through difficult playing conditions on a snow-covered field. The result was the same as the previous year's final game, a 0–0 tie. Buffalo had a couple of good chances to score, but both of Oliphant's field goal attempts were no good.

The following Sunday, the All-Americans played the Bulldogs in Buffalo. However, the All-Americans were without five of their star players. Lou Little, Heinie Miller, Johnny Scott, Butch Spagna and Lud Wray had a dispute with Buffalo owner McNeil regarding unpaid bonuses from the previous season and walked out.

The All-Americans were forced to work with league commissioner Joe Carr to add additional players to ensure that they would have enough for the game. Buffalo picked up five players from the Detroit Tigers as their season had ended. Joining Buffalo were guard Milton Gardner, center Charlie Guy, tackle Clarence "Steamer" Horning, halfback Ray "Waddy" Kuehl and end Walter "Tillie" Voss. These players helped the All-Americans field a complete team, but they were clearly not as good without the five players lost in the dispute.

The All-Americans scored in the first period as Pat Smith had a 5-yard touchdown run. Buffalo's defense was strong throughout the contest. However, late in the game, Guil "Hawk" Falcon of Canton scored on a 2-yard run and Feeney's extra-point kick was good. That final drive earned Canton a 7–7 tie. The result left Buffalo with a 7–0–2 record, setting up a showdown with the unbeaten Chicago Staleys.

The game with the Staleys, owned by George Halas and the predecessors to the Chicago Bears, was played in Chicago on Thanksgiving Day. The Staleys started strong, scoring on their initial drive of the game with a short touchdown run by Ed Sternaman. However, the extra-point attempt failed, giving the Staleys only a 6–0 lead. Neither team scored for the remainder of the first half.

Early in the third quarter, All-Americans quarterback Hughitt lofted a 40-yard bomb to Kuehl for the tying touchdown. Hughitt kicked the extra point, giving Buffalo a 7–6 lead, and the All-Americans defense shut down the Staleys for the remainder of the game, staking their claim to the APFA championship with a solid 7–6 victory.

After the game, the Buffalo Sunday Times proclaimed Buffalo the champions of the APFA. "Back from Chicago with the title of world's professional football champions for the season of 1921, the Buffalo All-Americans are getting set for their tough game with the Dayton Triangles today." The story was headlined, "All-Americans Only Pro Team Undefeated Now."

Despite missing several additional players with injuries, the All-Americans defeated Dayton 7–0. Buffalo's touchdown came on a beautiful 35-yard pass play from Hughitt to Anderson. Again, the All-Americans defense was outstanding, posting its ninth shutout of the season, and with a 9–0–2 record Buffalo earned sole possession of first place.

The Buffalo Evening News ran a headline in its Nov. 28 edition proclaiming, "Undefeated All-Americans Win Championship of A.P.F.A." The story under the headline also reported the All-Americans "will play a number of exhibition games. … The result of these exhibition tilts will not affect Buffalo's title."

McNeil decided to schedule two exhibition games to make some additional money. He assumed the games would not count in the league standings. On Saturday, Dec. 3, the All-Americans defeated the Akron Pros 14–0 to keep their unbeaten streak intact.

The next day, the All-Americans traveled to Chicago and Buffalo lost its first game of the season 10–7. Buffalo finished the season with an overall 10–1–2 record, and McNeil presented his players with tiny gold footballs commemorating the APFA championship.

However, Chicago owner Halas was still pursuing the championship. He quickly scheduled two additional games to try to beat Buffalo's record. The Staleys won and tied those games, leaving them with a 9–1–1 record. Buffalo's record was still one victory better than Chicago's, and thus McNeil still felt comfortable that even if the exhibitions were included, the All-Americans were league champions.

Halas continued his scheming, trying to wrest the league championship away from Buffalo. He convinced the league's executive committee to disallow Buffalo's opening game victory over McKeesport because it was not an official member of the APFA. In addition, he convinced the league owners that his additional scheduled games should count. Halas also asserted that the 10–7 victory over the All-Americans was more significant than the earlier Buffalo victory against his club.

The league amazingly ruled in Halas' favor on all of these questionable issues and awarded the 1921 APFA championship to the Staleys. McNeil was incensed, claiming his team was the true league champion and was being robbed of it by Halas' back-office maneuvering.

Halas had much more power within the league, and his strong influence over many of the other owners clearly led to the league's questionable conclusion. McNeil fought the league's decision for the rest of his life. After his death in 1961, his wife continued for the rest of her life trying to get the ruling overturned. They both failed, and the NFL still recognizes the Staleys as the 1921 NFL champions.

Buffalo had a terrific season and despite losing five key players was still able to finish with a 10–1–2 record, the best in the league. Clearly, the season was part of a great two-year run for the All-Americans, even if they did not have a championship to show for it. The team went 18–2–3 in that span, leading the league in scoring both years. The results, and the way the 1921 championship was "lost," contribute to the Curse.

The core of the 1921 team began to disband in 1922, as the five players the team lost in 1921 over the dispute with the owner never returned. The All-Americans finished 1922 with a 5–4–1 record. The team slowly began to fall on hard times and never approached the standard set by the 1920 and 1921 teams. Buffalo kept its NFL franchise throughout the 1920s, except for a one-year hiatus in 1928. However, it never again came close to competing for the NFL championship.

The team changed its name from the All-Americans to the Bisons in 1924 and in 1926 to the Rangers. It disbanded in 1928 and returned in 1929 as the Buffalo Bisons. At least the franchise went out on a high note: It scored more than one touchdown in a game for the first time that season by beating the Chicago Bears 19–7. It gave Buffalo a 1–7–1 record for the season.

With the stock market crash of 1929 and other financial challenges, the team went out of business for good at the conclusion of the 1929 season. Buffalo's initial NFL franchise ended with an overall 42–37–12 record. And as of 1930, the Curse was alive and well with no championships and no professional football team.

Chapter 4
PRO FOOTBALL
COMES BACK TO TOWN

Buffalo's Hotel Lafayette, at the corner of Washington and Clinton streets in downtown Buffalo, was the place to be on Aug. 4 and 5, 1940, as a new professional football league was born. The six owners representing their cities — William D. Griffith (Columbus), Frank Dalton (New York), Dana King (Cincinnati), Sheldon H. Franks (Boston), George M. Harris (Milwaukee) and Earl "Red" Seick (Buffalo) — along with their lawyers, spent more than 30 hours at the hotel hammering out the details of the new league. For the most part, these men were wealthier than their NFL counterparts, in part because they had outside financial interests to cushion any financial problems. The NFL owners mostly consisted of people who did not have such a cushion.

They negotiated the articles of incorporation, the bylaws, other organizing documents, the officers, the stadiums, the schedule and many other mundane details. It was reported after the meeting that the negotiations had been acrimonious at times. Finally, at 4 p.m. on Aug. 5, the six owners signed an agreement to officially start the American Football League. On Aug. 6, the Democrat and Chronicle of Rochester, New York, proclaimed, "Plans for 6-Team American Pro Grid League Completed at Buffalo."

The new circuit had been announced at a news conference on July 14, but very few details of how it would operate, and what cities would be in, had been finalized. The meeting at the Hotel Lafayette brought it all together. Griffith was named league president, Philip Bucklew — also representing Columbus — was named vice president, and Dalton was appointed secretary

Photo 7. The American Football League was founded on Aug. 4 and 5, 1940, at the Hotel Lafayette in Buffalo.

(Author's collection)

and treasurer. A board of directors was also named with a representative from each franchise.

The owners agreed to a 10-game schedule, five home games for each team, to be played primarily on Wednesday nights and Sunday afternoons. All the teams except Buffalo shared a ballpark with a baseball team and had to work around the baseball clubs' schedules.

The six teams for the inaugural season were the Boston Bears, Buffalo Indians, Cincinnati Bengals, Columbus Bullies, Milwaukee Chiefs and the New York Yankees. Buffalo was thrilled to have a team back in professional football after going through the 1930s without a pro club to call its own.

Buffalo had a burgeoning reputation as a good sports town, especially with the newly opened state-of-the-art Civic Stadium. The new ballpark opened in 1937 with a football game between Colgate University and Tulane University, and the NFL even hosted two games at the field in 1938, drawing excellent crowds.

The new Buffalo franchise was owned by the American Legion, and Seick served as the player-coach and business manager. Seick, who played high school football at Cook Academy in Montour Falls, New York, and at Manhattan College, also competed professionally in the previous AFL, for the Boston Shamrocks in 1936 and New York Yankees in 1937.

Seick concentrated his efforts on signing local football stars, castoffs from the NFL and former players of the recently defunct American Football League. (No relation to the AFL that played in the 1960s. This circuit played minor league football in the Northeast in 1936 and 1937.) He scoured Western New York from Olean across the Southern Tier to Utica, Syracuse and Rochester looking for talent.

Local product Steve Banas, who played collegiately for Notre Dame and professionally for the Eagles and Lions, was signed to play quarterback. Other locals signed by Buffalo were guard Walt Padlo from Olean, end Steve Gilbert and quarterback Steve Hrycyszyn from St. Bonaventure, and center Henry Bogacki and Joe Szur from Canisius. Seick signed other NFL players such as tackle Joe Karp, running back Carl Littlefield, tackle Alex Shellogg and halfback Orlando Nesmith.

On Sept. 6, the Buffalo Indians were introduced at City Hall with a glorious welcome led by Mayor Tom Holling and a band and drill units from the Buffalo Drum Corps. Holling spoke optimistically about the new Buffalo professional team and presented a football to Seick.

Buffalo opened the season two weeks later on Sept. 22, 1940 at Civic Stadium in front of 12,448 enthusiastic fans. The green-and-white clad Indians were without their two starting running backs, Littlefield and Larry Peace, because of injuries. Milwaukee had already played three games, and the combination of its game experience and the loss of Buffalo's two key players led to a 23–0 shutout. Despite the loss, the Buffalo fans and media were impressed with the overall quality of play.

On the same day that the Indians lost their opening game, reports came that a Nazi German submarine had torpedoed and sunk a British refugee ship, killing 293 innocent people. The war in Europe was escalating, and this would be a bad omen for the future of the AFL.

The Indians bounced back 10 days later with a convincing 17–7 win over the Cincinnati Bengals at Civic Stadium before a hardy group of 8,462. Littlefield scored the first touchdown in team history on a 1-yard run in the first quarter. The Indians broke a 7–7 tie in the third quarter on a 35-yard field goal by Alex Drobnitch and then scored a fourth-quarter touchdown on a pass from Szur to Gilbert from 14 yards out, clinching the team's inaugural victory.

The Indians lost a week later to the Columbus Bullies 17–7, starting a five-game losing streak. Buffalo lost back-to-back games with the Boston Bears without scoring a point, losing 10–0 at Civic Stadium and 20–0 four days later on Oct. 20 at Fenway Park. With the club dropping to 1–4, Seick's teammate Orlando Nesmith replaced him as head coach. There was no Nesmith magic, as the Indians were shut out for the third consecutive game by the New York Yankees at Yankee Stadium 17–0 on Nov. 3 and lost the following Sunday to the Columbus Bullies 13–7 at Red Bird Stadium in the pouring rain.

On Nov. 17, the Indians were prepared to host the Yankees at Civic Stadium, however, a snowstorm blanketed the area as well as the tarpaulin protecting the field. Buffalo forfeited the game because the field was deemed unplayable. It was the Indians' final home game of the 1940 season — not a good way to end the home campaign.

The team traveled to Milwaukee on Thanksgiving and was soundly beaten 30–13 by the Chiefs. The final game scheduled in Cincinnati on Nov. 24 was forfeited to the Indians by the Bengals because they lacked enough healthy players. Even with the "gift" win, Buffalo finished 2–8, and only Littlefield scored more than one touchdown for the club, collecting three.

Two Buffalo players — tackle Karp and guard Drobnitch — made the All-League team. The Columbus Bullies were the AFL champions for 1940 with an 8–1–1 record.

The Buffalo American Legion decided to get out of the pro football business and sold the team to coal magnate Fiore Cesare. The new boss named former Green Bay Packer offensive lineman and kicker Paul "Tiny" Engebretsen as the team's new head coach. Engebretsen had been part of a little magic at Civic Stadium in 1938, when he kicked the game-winning field goal as time expired in the Packers' 24–22 come-from-behind victory over the Chicago Cardinals in the second NFL game played there.

Cesare also changed the name of the team from Indians to Tigers. Very few of the Indians' players remained with the team, but he did re-sign Hrycyszyn, Banas and Littlefield. The 1941 AFL season featured five teams instead of six. The Boston franchise disbanded, and the Yankees were sold and became the New York Americans.

The newly minted Buffalo Tigers opened their second season on the road at Xavier University Stadium in Cincinnati on Oct. 5, 1941, and were promptly beaten by the Bengals 29–0. Four days later, at Civic Stadium versus the Americans, the result was similar as the Tigers lost 26–7. Before the game, through a friendship with Buffalo coach Engebretsen, former Green Bay Packers star and future Hall of Famer Johnny "Blood" McNally agreed to play a game for the Tigers. He also brought along two former NFL players from the Kenosha Cardinals, the minor league team he was coaching: end John Dolan and halfback Ernie Wheeler. However, it did not help much as the 4,500 in attendance only saw one Tigers touchdown, an exciting 82-yard fumble return by Joe Ratica in the fourth quarter. McNally carried the football five times in his only game with the Tigers as he returned to Kenosha and did not play again for the club. He is the only Pro Football Hall of Famer to have played in the AFL.

The Tigers rebounded in their return engagement with the Bengals at Civic Stadium on Oct. 19 with a 16–0 win. Newly acquired quarterback Andy Karpus fired two touchdown passes, and the aggressive Tigers defense led the way in their first win of the season.

Buffalo lost its next two games on the road against New York and Columbus, the two best teams in the circuit for 1941. The scores were 31–14 to the Americans and 24–7 to the Bullies. The Tigers returned to Civic Stadium on Nov. 9 and upset the Bullies 14–7. The key play of the game occurred on the second-half kickoff. The Tigers shocked Columbus as Hrycyszyn fielded the kick and lateraled the ball to Karpus, who sprinted 50 yards for the touchdown, putting the Tigers in the lead 14–0. The Bullies scored later in the third period, cutting the deficit to a touchdown. But the Tigers defense shut out the Bullies the rest of the game in handing Columbus its first loss of the season, 14–7.

The Tigers finished the season with back-to-back losses to the Chiefs, 41–14 in Milwaukee at the Dairy Bowl and 14–0 at Civic Stadium. Buffalo ended the season with a 2–6 record and a fourth-place finish. Tigers guard Alex Shellogg was the lone Buffalo player named to the All-League team. The Bullies repeated as champions in 1941 with a 5–1–2 record. The highlight of the Tigers' season was handing Columbus its only loss.

At the conclusion of the season, the AFL owners were optimistic about the future of the league. They had completed the season with five solid franchises and awarded a sixth to Detroit for 1942. The AFL was on firm financial footing as the teams began to plan for 1942. Though attendance was less than the NFL's, it was still encouraging enough for the owners to continue. Buffalo owner Cesare was well-capitalized and felt his team would significantly improve in 1942.

However, on Dec. 7, 1941, the Japanese attacked the U.S. naval base at Pearl Harbor, Hawaii, killing 2,403 Americans. President Franklin D. Roosevelt immediately announced that the United States was entering World War II and joining the Allied forces in their fight against Japan and Nazi Germany.

Throughout the winter and spring of 1942, many players across the AFL, as well as NFL players, were drafted into the armed services. It became apparent that the league could not field enough viable teams, and on Sept. 2, 1942, AFL President William B. Cox announced the suspension of operations until the war concluded. Cox stated that the league had no financial problems, and each team had the money to continue. The AFL never returned, despite having become a formidable competitor to the NFL.

The Buffalo Sports Curse struck again. The AFL had solid financial backing, and the Buffalo owner, Cesare, was well positioned to keep the team and improve its fortunes on the field. As well, the league was founded in Buffalo at the Hotel Lafayette, so continuing would have helped to solidify the city's reputation as a good sports town. However, as fate would have it, the Japanese attack on Pearl Harbor and the United States' entry into World

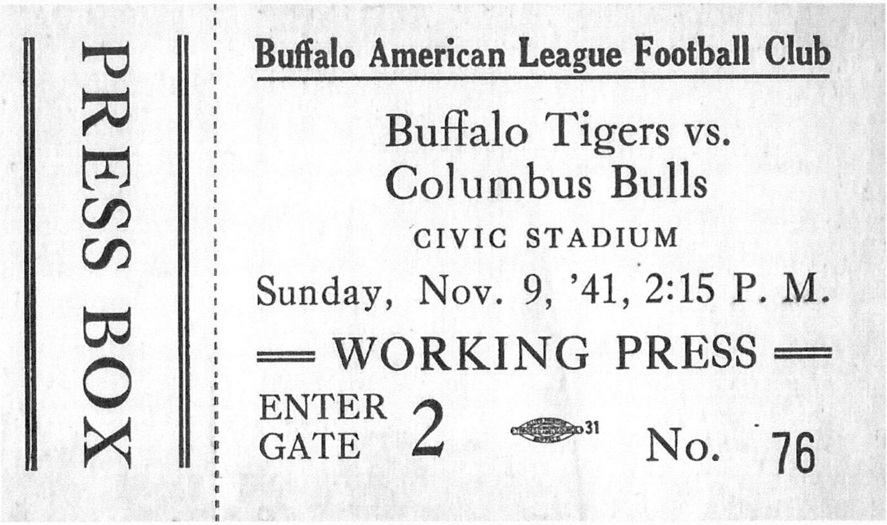

PRESS BOX

Buffalo American League Football Club

Buffalo Tigers vs.
Columbus Bulls

CIVIC STADIUM

Sunday, Nov. 9, '41, 2:15 P. M.

= WORKING PRESS =

ENTER
GATE **2** 31 No. **76**

Photo 8. Buffalo Tigers vs. Columbus Bullies press pass from
the Tigers' 14-7 victory on Nov. 9, 1941.

(Author's collection)

War II spelled the demise of this promising pro football league. The AFL would have likely become a major competitor to the NFL and might have forced a merger.

And at the very least, Buffalo would have had an ongoing pro football franchise to root for every Sunday. If not for the interruption of World War II and the large number of men who joined the service, and with the success of the AFL, Buffalo might be the Canton, Ohio, of pro football today, with the founding documents of the league completed at the Hotel Lafayette.

Chapter 5
BUFFALO LOSES
A CHAMPIONSHIP — AND THE NFL

Another new professional football league was conceived in 1944, a couple of days before D-Day — the June 6, 1944, Allied invasion of more than 160,000 troops on the Normandy beaches that eventually liberated France and was one of the most important military operations during World War II — and Buffalo would have a team in the new circuit. The organizer was Arch Ward, the famous Chicago Tribune sports editor and columnist. Ward also founded the Major League Baseball All-Star Game and the College/NFL All-Star Game and was a publicist for Knute Rockne and Notre Dame football.

With the end of World War II, thousands of servicemen returned home. A new economic burst of homeownership and leisure activities took the nation by storm. It was a perfect time for a new football league to take hold and consume some of that leisure time and money — or at least that's what several millionaire owners thought when they met with Ward.

Buffalo had continued trying to secure an NFL franchise, with an application pending with the league. Sam Cordovano, president of Globe Construction Co., headed a group of Buffalo businessmen who had filed a franchise application with the NFL in January 1944. The NFL reviewed applications from three cities for potential expansion: Los Angeles, San Francisco and Buffalo. The league met on Jan. 14 and tabled the decision on expansion. The $25,000 franchise deposit fees were returned to the Los Angeles and San Francisco groups, but they kept the Buffalo deposit. That left Cordovano and his group very optimistic about getting a team for the 1944 season.

After hearing the news from the league, Cordovano said, "The city wants and will support a professional team and I'll give it to them, even if the only opposition they ever meet is composed of fellow squad members. … We have everything but the franchise. … We have complete support of the mayor, board of supervisors and other city officials. We have a first-rate football stadium that isn't used for any other sport. And, we already have football men scouting the country recruiting players." Cordovano's enthusiasm for an NFL franchise would be short-lived. On April 21, 1944, the NFL voted to table all expansion franchises until after the war.

Once Ward heard that the Buffalo franchise in the NFL had been deferred, he approached the ownership group of Cordovano and Jim Breuil about his new league. Cordovano also was an assistant football coach at Columbia University and a former NFL player. He teamed up with Breuil, owner of the Frontier Oil and Refining Co. and a longtime Buffalo sports booster, along with two other local businessmen who worked at Frontier Oil with Breuil, treasurer William Bennett and sales manager Clayton Maxwell. Breuil was the biggest investor behind the club.

At the All-America Football Conference's first organizational meeting in June 1944, Buffalo — with the ownership group led by Cordovano — was granted a charter franchise. They soon adopted the all-too-common nickname of Bisons. The home field was set to be Civic Stadium at the corner of Best Street and Jefferson Avenue on Buffalo's East Side. The Bisons would play their first game in the new league in 1946 because the circuit was not completely finalized until January of that year. Between those initial meetings in 1944 and the kickoff of the league in 1946, several owners pulled out and were replaced.

Finally, the league decided on its inaugural teams. In addition to the Bisons, the other teams in the Eastern Division were the New York Yankees, the Brooklyn Dodgers and the Miami Seahawks. The Yankees and Dodgers would play in the same stadiums as their baseball counterparts: Yankee Stadium and Ebbets Field. Miami would call Burdine Stadium home, in 1959 the name was changed to the Orange Bowl. The Western Division comprised the Cleveland Browns, the San Francisco 49ers, the Los Angeles Dons and the Chicago Rockets.

The AAFC's first commissioner was Jim Crowley, one of the most famous names in football as one of the renowned Four Horsemen of Notre Dame in the 1920s. The new circuit was a direct competitor and threat to the established NFL.

Bisons owner Breuil named Cordovano the team's first head coach and general manager, but Cordovano resigned on May 28 before he ever coached a game for the team. Red Dawson, who had been successful as Tulane University's head coach, was named to replace Cordovano and led the team through its first three years. Dawson also had coached Tulane in the first game played at Civic Stadium (then known as Roesch Stadium), defeating Colgate 7–6 on Oct. 16, 1937. Francis W. Dunn, a former Buffalo Times sports reporter and director of public relations at Bell Aircraft Corp., was named general manager.

The league was creative and dynamic as it moved west with two of its franchises, Los Angeles and San Francisco. The NFL had been reluctant to go west until the AAFC made that bold step. The AAFC also signed Black players, again pressuring the NFL to do the same. The Browns signed Marion Motley and Bill Willis in 1946. Both players became stars in the AAFC and ultimately reached the Pro Football Hall of Fame after very distinguished careers. The signing of Willis, the first Black player in pro football since the 1920s, beat the much more heralded signing of Jackie Robinson in baseball by a year. Willis and the other Black players who signed in 1946 faced the same type of discrimination Robinson encountered in baseball.

The AAFC debut drew the largest crowd ever to see a regular-season pro football game until that time. On Sept. 6, 1946, 60,135 fans witnessed the Cleveland Browns' game versus the Miami Seahawks at Cleveland's Municipal Stadium. The Browns won 44–0 to start a streak of unprecedented dominance. The Browns would go on to win all four AAFC championships, and upon entering the NFL in 1950, they won three more league championships in 1950, '54, and '55 and won Eastern Division championships from 1950 through 1956.

The Bisons' first season in 1946 was not what Breuil or the fans in Buffalo hoped it would be. The team struggled to a third-place finish in the Eastern Division with a 3–10–1 record. The Buffalo fans supported their team with consistently excellent attendance, averaging 16,851 per game. The average attendance across pro football in 1946 was 14,681 per game, with Buffalo comparing favorably.

The Bisons boasted the league's third-leading rusher with Vic Kulbitski running for 605 yards. The quarterbacking was shared among four players, none playing with the consistency a winning team must have. George Terlep played the most, attempting 123 passes while completing only 39%. He also tossed 14 interceptions. The team's best receiver was Fay King with 30 receptions. The Bisons defense was among the most porous in the AAFC allowing 370 points, an average of 26.4 points per game.

Buffalo's most impressive game was a 17–14 victory over the 9–5 San Francisco 49ers. This was the Bisons' first victory after starting the season 0–6–1. Dawson's crew also secured a 17–14 victory over the Brooklyn Dodgers, avenging an opening-day 27–14 home loss. Their other victory was a 49–17 thumping of the Chicago Rockets. The Bisons' two most brutal losses among the 10 defeats were a 42–17 drubbing by the league champion Browns and a 62–14 shellacking by the Dons. Still, the Bisons' first season was successful despite its dismal record, and Buffalo football fans were happy to have a pro football team back in town and looked optimistically to a more successful 1947 season.

Before the start of the next season, the team decided to change its nickname, and thus the original Buffalo Bills were born. Buffalo owner Breuil conducted a "name-the-team" contest to differentiate the football team from the hockey and baseball teams that also had Bisons as a nickname. The most popular names submitted included Blue Devils, Nickels and Bullets. The winning entry was the Bills, after the legendary William "Buffalo Bill" Cody, who earned his nickname because of his skill as a buffalo hunter and became famous for his traveling "Wild West" show, which spread lasting images of the American West around the world.

The team was significantly strengthened as George Ratterman from Notre Dame became the new starting quarterback, and the team added stud running back Chet Mutryn, wide receiver Al Baldwin and star defender "Buckets" Hirsch. These players elevated Buffalo's game dramatically and made the team a contender in the league.

The 1947 Buffalo Bills challenged the New York Yankees for the Eastern Division crown. With excellent quarterbacking from Ratterman and the powerful running of Mutryn, the Bills posted an 8–4–2 record. Ratterman was third in the league's quarterback rating, as he passed for more than 1,800 yards and 20 touchdowns leading Buffalo to second place in the Eastern Division. Mutryn rushed for 868 yards, fourth in the league. King and Baldwin were the team's leading pass catchers, hauling in 26 and 25 passes, respectively. The Bills defense improved significantly, allowing 288 points — 82 fewer than in 1946.

Buffalo opened the season with an impressive 28–24 win over the 1946 East Division champion Yankees. They lost to Cleveland twice, 30–14 and 28–7, but had key victories over Los Angeles, 27–25 and 25–0, to go along with two wins over rival Baltimore, 20–15 and 33–14, and a 35–7 victory over Brooklyn. Late in the season, the Bills had a chance to overtake the Yankees and win the division. Buffalo invaded Yankee Stadium on Nov. 30, boasting an 8–3–1 record to play the 9–2–1 Yankees. The Bills were not up to the task that day as they were drilled by the Yankees 35–13, keeping them from winning the Eastern Division crown and a shot at the AAFC championship versus Cleveland. The Yankees completely dominated the line of scrimmage, rushing for 254 yards and four touchdowns.

Cleveland went on to win its second consecutive AAFC championship by beating the Yankees 14–3. Though the Bills lost the division championship to New York, it was a successful season as the team almost doubled its attendance, had an excellent record and created great anticipation for 1948 with its nucleus of young players.

The 1948 season was dominated again by the Browns as they finished the AAFC's regular season with a 14–0 record to win the Western Division. Meanwhile, the Bills battled the Baltimore Colts for Eastern Division supremacy. The Colts were led by rookie quarterback and future Pro Football Hall of Famer Y.A. Tittle. He was the league's top passer and helped Baltimore tie the Bills with identical 7–7 records.

The Bills were again led by Ratterman, who passed 335 times for 2,577 yards while throwing 16 touchdown passes in his second season. The team had an outstanding one-two rushing punch as Mutryn compiled 823 yards and 10 touchdowns, while Lou Tomasetti ran for 716 yards with seven touchdowns. Wide receiver Baldwin had a stellar season, hauling in 54 passes for 916 yards and eight touchdowns. Mutryn topped the league in scoring with 16 overall touchdowns for 96 points. The Bills offense was among the league's best, scoring 360 points for the season. However, the defense was the team's Achilles' heel, allowing 358 points, the primary reason Buffalo finished the regular season with a .500 record.

The Bills started the season slowly with three losses in their first four games. They were beaten twice by San Francisco, 35–14 and 38–28, and were also drubbed by Cleveland. The Bills were only 2–5 at midseason. However, they bounced back with quality wins over Los Angeles 35–21, Baltimore

35–17 and New York 35–14. They lost the season's final game at Baltimore 35–15, forcing a playoff game the following week.

The Bills played the Colts at Municipal Stadium in Baltimore on Dec. 12 for the Eastern Division championship and the right to meet the undefeated Cleveland Browns for the AAFC title. The Colts opened the game with a flurry, jumping to an early 17–7 lead. Heading into the fourth quarter, the Colts were still leading by 10 points. However, the Bills battled back as Ratterman began to click. He passed 66 yards to halfback Bill Gompers for a touchdown, cutting Baltimore's lead to 17–14, and on the next possession, Ratterman tossed a 35-yard touchdown pass to Baldwin, giving the Bills a 21–17 lead.

The Buffalo defense was impenetrable in the fourth quarter, and its offense scored another touchdown to give the Bills a 28–17 victory in the only divisional playoff game in AAFC history. The win secured the Eastern Division title and a spot in the championship game. The Bills were now set to play the Browns for all the marbles — the first championship opportunity for Buffalo since the 1921 lost title!

Buffalo had lost both games to Cleveland during the regular season by scores of 42–13 and 31–14, so few people gave the Bills a chance in the game. However, the Buffalo players were confident they could pull off an upset.

In front of 22,981 in Cleveland Stadium, the teams battled for the championship on Dec. 19. The Bills defense was tough early in the game. Cleveland running back Edgar "Special Delivery" Jones ran 3 yards for a touchdown late in the first quarter, giving the Browns a 7–0 lead. This touchdown followed a turnover, a Tommy James interception and 30-yard return.

The Buffalo offense struggled throughout the game, committing six turnovers. The second turnover, a fumble by Rex Bumgardner, was returned by Cleveland defensive end George Young for a touchdown in the second quarter and a 14–0 Browns lead. Ratterman had his worst game as a professional, completing only five of 18 passes with three interceptions and only 24 passing yards. He was pulled in the second half and replaced by backup Jim Still, who contributed two additional interceptions.

The Browns blew the game open after halftime by scoring two touchdowns in the third quarter and three more in the fourth period. Three of Cleveland's five touchdowns in the second half were a direct result of Buffalo turnovers. The Bills finally got on the scoreboard with a 10-yard touchdown pass from Still to Baldwin in the third quarter, cutting the deficit to 28–7.

Photo 9. Edgar "Special Delivery" Jones (90) of the Cleveland Browns scores
a touchdown in the AAFC championship game on Dec. 19, 1948, at Cleveland
Municipal Stadium. Cleveland defeated Buffalo 49–7.

(AP Photo/Football Hall of Fame)

But the Browns tacked on three more touchdowns, capped by Lou Saban's 39-yard interception return, and went on to win the championship 49–7. It was by far the largest margin of victory in an AAFC championship game. Motley starred for Cleveland, rushing for 133 yards and three touchdowns. The Browns became the first professional football team to complete a season undefeated and untied at 15–0.

The AAFC was struggling for survival heading into the 1949 season. The financial war with the NFL was taking a toll on the AAFC, as many teams were losing money, even forcing the Brooklyn Dodgers and New York Yankees franchises to merge. The league only fielded seven teams in 1949. The top four teams would qualify for the playoffs.

The Bills again had a potent offense and a poor defense as new head coach Clem Crowe led the club. Buffalo finished the season with a 5–5–2 record, qualifying for the fourth and final playoff spot. The Bills' biggest accomplishment in 1949 was tying the Browns both times they played, 7–7 and 28–28. They became the only team in AAFC history not to lose to the Browns in a regular season. Buffalo also had impressive victories over San Francisco 28–17 and the New York Yankees 17–14. But they lost to last-place Baltimore 35–28, providing the Colts their only win of the season, and were later routed in their rematch with San Francisco 51–7.

The Bills' offensive stars of 1948 also had excellent seasons in 1949. Ratterman was the second-most prolific quarterback, passing for 1,777 yards and 14 touchdowns. Mutryn finished second in the league, rushing for 696 yards, and Baldwin snared 53 passes for 719 yards.

Buffalo met Cleveland in the divisional playoff game, looking to upset the Browns and keep them from winning their fourth consecutive AAFC championship. However, Cleveland was too good. The Bills lost to the Browns 31–21 — although they certainly played better than they had the year before in the championship game.

The Browns jumped to a quick 10–0 first-quarter lead. The Bills battled back and took a 14–10 halftime lead on two Ratterman touchdown passes. The teams traded scores in the third quarter in the back-and-forth game, but Otto Graham fired a 49-yard touchdown pass to Dub Jones, putting Cleveland back in front 24–21 heading to the fourth quarter.

Early in the final frame, the Bills drove into Cleveland territory, but their attempt at a tying field goal failed. Late in the quarter with the Bills still trailing 24–21, they were driving for the potential go-ahead score when misfortune struck. Ratterman fired an ill-advised pass that was intercepted by Warren Lahr and returned 52 yards for the clinching Browns touchdown.

It was a crushing defeat for a Bills team that played Cleveland toe-to-toe, but two turnovers decided the outcome in the Browns' favor. Ratterman passed for 320 yards and three touchdowns, but his two interceptions were the difference in the game. This contest would be the last in the Bills' history. The Browns beat the San Francisco 49ers the next week 21–7, securing their fourth consecutive AAFC title.

While Cleveland was winning another championship, the AAFC was negotiating a merger with the NFL. The league knew it would not be able to continue in the financial war that had been escalating since 1946. Since the AAFC was struggling financially, its negotiating position was weak and the NFL dictated most of the terms of the merger.

The merger agreement allowed only three of the seven remaining members of the AAFC into the NFL, with the other four clubs disbanding. The Browns and 49ers were the first two teams chosen and neither was a surprise, as they were the most successful teams both on the field and at the box office.

The third team admitted was a shock. Most observers felt the Bills would be the other franchise selected. They had qualified for the playoffs in each of the two previous seasons and had an overall winning record along with a second-place finish in 1947. They also had drawn excellent crowds at Civic Stadium, averaging more than 26,000 fans per game in 1949.

The NFL passed on the Bills and took the Baltimore Colts, who were coming off a 1–11 season and had lower attendance than Buffalo. George Preston Marshall, owner of the Washington Redskins, had always been opposed to a Baltimore franchise and did not want them included in the merger talks — even more reason it seemed Buffalo would be the final team selected. However, some back-office maneuvering was going on. Baltimore owner Abe Watner agreed to pay Marshall $50,000 and helped convince the Washington owner that the two cities, only 40 miles apart, would make for natural rivals. Marshall, with his palms greased, went along and agreed to have Baltimore be the third franchise to join the NFL, leaving Buffalo out.

Several prominent Buffalonians, led by Pat McGroder, a liquor store owner and Buffalo's parks commissioner, tried to save the Buffalo franchise. They put together a detailed presentation for NFL commissioner Bert Bell, outlining all the reasons why Buffalo should be admitted to the league. The group also sold 15,000 season tickets, which at that time was quite significant.

In addition, they sold $5 shares in the Buffalo Bills football club and made some other capital investments totaling $252,170.

The NFL owners met on Jan. 19, 1950, to reconsider Buffalo's bid for a team. Bell outlined two stipulations: The bid had to receive unanimous approval from the owners, and they would have to fit into a league schedule, though with the league at 13 teams, the schedule part seemed easy. At the meeting, Marshall supported the inclusion of Buffalo and made the motion to accept Buffalo's bid. Watner seconded the motion. Each NFL owner was then individually requested to vote yes or no on whether Buffalo should be accepted into the league. The first six owners voted yes. Dan Reeves, Los Angeles Rams owner, was the first dissenting vote, followed by a no vote from Halas, thus killing Buffalo's chances. Kenneth Crippen reported in his book, "The Original Buffalo Bills," that Reeves later said, "I felt it was silly to vote in a new city without first having a good idea where my team would play and when."

Commissioner Bell had committed to the Buffalo contingent to draw up a schedule including them, though he never did. In the end, nine owners voted in favor and four opposed. There definitely were some back-office she-nanigans among Reeves, Halas and Bell that denied Buffalo an opportunity it deserved. It was a terrible decision, and Steelers owner Art Rooney said years later, "It was a sad mistake to not include Buffalo." Again, the city's profes-sional football team was lost to the political jockeying among the NFL's brass.

The NFL's poor decision was reinforced at the end of the 1950 season, as the Baltimore franchise disbanded because of serious financial losses, forcing the club to be sold back to the league and shut down.

The Curse that plagued the first Buffalo football franchise in the early 1920s reared its ugly head again in the AAFC. The Bills lost a lopsided cham-pionship game in 1948 through their own errors, dropped the 1949 divisional playoff game on two interceptions and were denied admittance to the NFL — even though they were deserving!

Despite Buffalo being kept out of the NFL in 1950 with the folding of the AAFC, the league still knew it was a fertile ground for pro football. It began playing preseason games at Civic Stadium again, as it had before the AAFC was formed. Throughout the 1950s, the NFL played nine such games in Buffalo. Those contests featured the Bears, Browns, Cardinals, Colts, Lions, Packers, Redskins and Steelers. League officials also promised multiple times that Buffalo would receive an NFL franchise by the end of the decade.

Photo 10. Boost the Bills promotional sticker from 1949.

(Author's collection)

On Sept. 13, 1953, the defending champion Detroit Lions defeated the Washington Redskins 31–17 in a preseason game at Civic Stadium. The game drew 23,088 fans in a chilling rain. After the game, Marshall — still owner of the Redskins — and Lions general manager Nick Kerbawy were so impressed with the fan turnout and the overall game experience, they committed to play again in Buffalo in 1954.

Cy Kritzer of the Buffalo News reported that Marshall went so far as to say, "We'd like to play a preseason game here every September until Buffalo has its own team. The outlook is that you will have one within the next three years at the very latest." The NFL continued to play preseason games in Buffalo as Marshall had said. However, the city did not get a franchise as promised.

Later in the decade, Lamar Hunt had been in touch with the league when he was pursuing an NFL expansion franchise for Dallas. On March 15, 1959 he had another call with Bell. In the conversation, Hunt brought up the likelihood of an expansion team in Dallas. Michael MacCambridge wrote in his book, "Lamar Hunt; A Life in Sports," that "Bell reiterated that he couldn't consider it until resolving the Cardinals situation (whether they should remain in Chicago or move), but added that owners were not at all impressed with Dallas, because of the poor performance of the Texans in 1952, and that their first commitment was to the city of Buffalo."

Hunt then reached out to Halas and was told that expansion was probably a long way off. After being frustrated at every turn by the established league, "Lamar decided to move forward with his idea and began to seek out his potential partners for the new league," Cambridge reported in his book.

The NFL never delivered on its promise to bring a franchise to Buffalo by the end of the 1950s. The league played its last game at Civic Stadium on Sept. 28, 1958, and Buffalo made NFL history as the league chose to have the first game of its regular season played at a neutral site. Buffalo hosted the opener between the Chicago Cardinals and the New York Giants. The game drew a crowd of 21,923 as the Giants defeated the Cardinals 37–7 behind three touchdowns by Frank Gifford and two by Alex Webster.

Buffalo was definitely cursed with the NFL, as repeatedly a franchise in the league seemed almost a certainty but was always denied. Either internal NFL politics among the owners kept a team away, or the timing was never right, or expansion left the city behind.

It was not until 1959, when Detroit businessman Ralph C. Wilson Jr. called Lamar Hunt, that professional football would return to Western New York.

Chapter 6
THE BILLS MISS OUT ON HISTORY

Ralph C. Wilson Jr., a serial entrepreneur from Detroit, became interested in the American Football League in August 1959 when he was in Saratoga Springs, New York, during the horse racing season, and read an article in The New York Times. He noticed that Texas oil magnate Lamar Hunt was creating a new professional football league so that he could place a team in Dallas. Hunt had made several attempts to get an NFL franchise in Dallas but continued to be turned away. Therefore, he gave up trying to convince the NFL and decided to start a new football league.

Hunt rounded up seven other millionaires who would risk their money to start a new league and go head-to-head with the entrenched NFL. Wilson originally was interested in placing his team in Miami. However, when he met with Miami city officials, the idea of a pro football franchise was not welcome. He could not negotiate a lease for use of the Orange Bowl to play the games and thus the Miami franchise fell through.

Hunt, upon hearing the news of Wilson's failed attempt in Miami, encouraged him to consider five other cities: Atlanta, Buffalo, Cincinnati, Louisville and St Louis. Wilson talked with a few colleagues who suggested he look at Buffalo. Eventually, Wilson met with Paul Neville, managing editor of the Buffalo Evening News, who talked with him about the successful attendance Buffalo had in the AAFC, how rabid Buffalo football fans were and how disappointed the city was when it lost out on entering the NFL in 1950.

Neville did a great job of selling Wilson on the merits of Buffalo and finally convinced him to give the city a chance and place his team in Buffalo for three years. Wilson invested $25,000 to join the AFL, which at the time was a lot of money but seems like a pittance to have paid for the franchise, considering the value of franchises today. On Oct. 17, 1959, a story ran in the Buffalo Evening News with the headline, "Buffalo to Have Team in Pro Football Next Fall."

By Jan. 30, 1960, the original eight AFL clubs were finalized as Oakland was added after Minneapolis had decided a few days earlier to join the NFL instead of the fledgling AFL. Members of the "Foolish Club," as the original eight AFL owners were dubbed, were Billy Sullivan (Boston), Wilson (Buffalo), Bud Adams (Houston) and Harry Wismer (New York) in the East Division, with Lamar Hunt (Dallas), Bob Howsam (Denver), Barron Hilton (Los Angeles) and Wayne Valley (Oakland) in the West Division.

With the formation of the AFL, pro football returned to Buffalo, and though it would not gain real major league status in the eyes of most until 1966, the town was thrilled to have its own pro football team. However, entry into the AFL would not give the Bills the opportunity to end the Curse until the merger with the NFL and the first world championship game between the two leagues at the conclusion of the 1966 season.

Buffalo was scheduled to play its home games at Civic Stadium (about to be renamed War Memorial Stadium), returning to the field the AAFC Bills had played on. Because Wilson had been a minority owner of the Detroit Lions, he hired an assistant coach from them, Buster Ramsey, to be the team's first head coach. Also, the team sported silver and blue uniforms with silver helmets — similar colors to the Lions'.

The Bills' first draft pick was Richie Lucas, an All-American quarterback from Penn State, and they also netted defensive end Tom Day from North Carolina A&T in that initial draft. On June 19, 1960, the AFL signed a contract with ABC, ensuring that the league's games would be shown on television.

Buffalo sold more than 5,000 season tickets for its inaugural campaign. The first training camp was conducted at Seymour Knox's polo fields in East Aurora, and the team's headquarters were set up at the Roycroft Inn. There was tremendous interest in the team as more than 100,000 fans lined Main Street in Buffalo for a welcome parade on July 30, as reported by Scott Pitoniak in his book, "Buffalo Bills Football Vault." That night, the Bills hosted the first AFL game, playing the Boston Patriots in a preseason contest. The game drew 16,474 curious fans. Buffalo lost to the Patriots 28–7 as running back Maurice Bassett scored the Bills' only touchdown.

Buffalo opened its first regular season on the road at the New York Titans. On Sept. 11, 1960, at 2 p.m. in the Polo Grounds, Tommy O'Connell leaned under center to take the snap, and the first chapter in Buffalo Bills football history began to unfold.

The Bills went on to lose 27–3 as O'Connell and Lucas were injured. Though the Bills scored first on Darrell Harper's 35-yard field goal, they could not sustain the momentum after the injuries to their two best offensive players and lost the game.

Buffalo's first regular-season home game was Sept. 18 in front of 15,229 enthusiastic fans. The Bills led the game 21–20 in the fourth quarter. With less than 10 minutes left, Denver Broncos defensive back Johnny Pyeatt intercepted an O'Connell pass and returned it 40 yards for the winning touchdown. The Bills lost 27–21. The team's first victory came in Week 3 as they shut out the Patriots 13–0 at Boston University. Their first home victory came in Week 6 over the Oakland Raiders 38–9.

Overall, the Bills had an up-and-down 5–8–1 first season, finishing with the league's best defense and worst offense.

Wilson lost an estimated $175,000 in the inaugural season, but it was much less than most of the other AFL owners. However, Wilson was quoted as saying that the Bills would have to sell 25,000 season tickets by 1963 if the team were to survive in Buffalo, as reported by Sal Maiorana in his book, "Relentless; The Hard-Hitting History of Buffalo Bills Football."

Buffalo continued to struggle on the field in 1961, finishing its second consecutive losing season with a 6–8 record. Its troubles were accentuated by poor quarterback play. The team coaxed O'Connell out of retirement and acquired Warren Rabb and M.C. Reynolds. None of these quarterbacks were the answer as each of their completion percentages was below 46%. The Bills also used Lucas and Johnny Green at the position with similar results. At the conclusion of the 1961 season, Ramsey was fired as Buffalo's head coach.

The Bills drafted Syracuse University's 1961 Heisman Trophy winner Ernie Davis and pursued him aggressively. Davis was a two-time first-team All-American running back, the first Black player to win the Heisman, and as a sophomore led Syracuse to an undefeated 11–0 season and the school's only football national championship. The Bills competed very strongly with the NFL's Cleveland Browns to secure his services, feeling that Davis would be a great draw for the team and would significantly upgrade their rushing attack. Buffalo offered Davis more money, but he signed with the Browns. However,

Davis died tragically from leukemia at the age of 23 in 1963 and never played a down of professional football. The Bills added some future star players in the 1962 AFL draft as they selected linebacker Mike Stratton, defensive tackle Tom Sestak and defensive back Ray Abruzzese. They all became starters for several seasons on the Bills' successful teams of the mid-1960s.

Lou Saban was hired in early 1962 as the Bills' new head coach. Saban had played four years of pro football as a linebacker with the Cleveland Browns from 1946–1949, winning four AAFC championships under the tutelage of legendary head coach Paul Brown. Upon retiring as a player, he immediately went into college coaching at Ohio's Western Reserve University in 1950. He garnered tremendous success at his fourth coaching stop at Western Illinois, leading the Leathernecks to a 9–0 record in 1959. That success catapulted him to become head coach for the newly christened Boston Patriots in the AFL in 1960. He had mixed success with the Patriots and was fired five games into the 1961 season after leading the club to a 7–12 overall record.

Once he became the Bills head coach, Saban immediately upgraded the coaching staff and went about acquiring more talent for the squad. He signed tight end Ernie Warlick and running back Cookie Gilchrist from the Canadian Football League to help solidify the offense.

Despite what appeared to be an improved team from the prior two seasons, the Bills lost their first five games in 1962. During the losing streak, Buffalo acquired quarterback Jack Kemp off waivers from the San Diego Chargers. This was a very fortuitous happening, as San Diego had made a mistake by putting Kemp on irrevocable waivers after the middle finger of his throwing hand was broken in a game against the Titans. The Bills claimed him, and he became their answer at quarterback for the rest of the decade. Kemp was an AFL All-Star with the Bills from 1963 to 1966 and in 1969. He was also the Associated Press AFL Player of the Year in 1965. After his retirement from pro football, Kemp had a highly successful political career. He served in the U.S. House of Representatives from 1971 to 1989, was George H. W. Bush's Housing Secretary from 1989 to 1993 and became the Republican nominee for vice president in the 1996 election as the running mate of presidential candidate Robert Dole. Kemp was posthumously awarded the Presidential Medal of Freedom by President Barack Obama in 2009.

Saban captured his first victory as the Bills' head coach on Oct. 13 with a 35–10 win over the San Diego Chargers as Buffalo rushed for a team-record 303 yards. The Bills won four of their final five games of the season to finish with their first winning record, 7–6–1. Kemp led the team's final two victories after his broken finger healed up. The Bills defeated the New York Titans 20–3 on the season's final day to secure their winning season.

By 1963, the Bills had a team talented enough to compete for the AFL's Eastern Division championship. The Bills came off their first winning season in franchise history, Saban signed a contract extension to coach the team, the city agreed to add 14,000 seats to War Memorial Stadium, and the Bills acquired quarterback Daryle Lamonica and safety George Saimes in the draft while also trading for linebacker Harry Jacobs. Saban decided to release Rabb and go with Kemp and Lamonica as his quarterback tandem.

Buffalo got off to a slow start with a 1–3–1 record, hardly what the Bills faithful had expected. The Bills front office continued to upgrade the team, adding wide receiver Charley Ferguson and defensive end Ron McDole, both of whom had been cut by the Minnesota Vikings. It helped. The Bills won four of their next five games and the season's last two to tie Boston for first place in the Eastern Division.

The Bills drew their largest crowd in team history on Nov. 17, 1963, when 38,592 fans attended their losing 23–13 effort versus San Diego. President John F. Kennedy was assassinated on Friday, Nov. 22 in Dallas, Texas. The nation was in shock and went into national mourning for several days and the AFL cancelled its games scheduled for Nov. 24. The NFL went ahead and played its schedule and Jeff Davis wrote in "Rozelle; Czar of the NFL," that it "was the one thing he (Rozelle) regretted" as commissioner. The president was laid to rest on Nov. 25.

The Bills game was rescheduled for Dec. 1 at Fenway Park in Boston and Buffalo lost to the Patriots 17–7. In the Bills' Dec. 8 victory over the Jets, Gilchrist ran for a pro football record 243 yards while setting an AFL record by scoring five touchdowns as the team manhandled the Jets 45–14. With Buffalo's Dec. 14 win over the Jets, the Houston Oilers' loss on Dec. 15 and the Patriots' loss to Kansas City, the Bills and Patriots tied atop the East with identical 7–6–1 records. The tie set up a divisional playoff game, and the winner would qualify for the AFL championship game against the Western Division champion San Diego Chargers.

The Bills hosted the Patriots on Dec. 28 in front of 33,044 in wintry conditions at War Memorial Stadium. Buffalo received the opening kickoff, Elbert Dubenion fumbled the return and Boston recovered. The game went downhill from there for the Bills. Boston led 16–0 at the half behind three Gino Cappelletti field goals and a touchdown on a 59-yard swing pass from Babe Parilli to Larry Garron. The Bills' lone bright spot for the day was a 93-yard touchdown pass from Kemp to Dubenion in the third quarter. That touchdown cut Boston's lead to 16–8, but the Bills would get no closer as the Patriots added 10 fourth-quarter points to win 26–8.

The Bills were outplayed as they committed six turnovers to assist the Patriots in their decisive victory. The following week, Boston went to San Diego and was routed 51–10 in the AFL championship. Despite the Chargers' dominating victory, the NFL champion Chicago Bears were considered the world champions of pro football. Among the national media, it was not even a question. It was not a consideration at the time that the ragtag AFL would be on par with the established NFL.

In preparation for the 1964 season, the Bills front office put the final pieces in place to position Buffalo to be the best team in the AFL. They signed rookie placekicker Pete Gogolak on April 12 and punter Paul Maguire on July 22 — two days after he was cut by San Diego.

The Bills were the class of the AFL in 1964. They began the season on Sept. 13 at War Memorial Stadium and proceeded to explode for 31 points in the first quarter on their way to a 34–17 triumph over Kansas City. They opened the season by reeling off nine victories in a row.

In Week 3, the Bills routed the defending AFL champion San Diego Chargers 30–3 in front of a Buffalo record crowd of 40,167. They stretched their record to 5–0 with a 48–17 drubbing of the Houston Oilers. The Bills amassed a team-record 565 yards in total offense, including 405 passing yards — 378 from Kemp, another team record.

Buffalo lost its first game of the season on Nov. 15 to bitter rival Boston. The Patriots handed the Bills a 36–28 setback in front of a record War Memorial Stadium crowd of 42,308. Buffalo won three of its next four to enter the final regular-season game 11–2, the best in franchise history. However, Boston continued to win and entered the Dec. 20 showdown at Fenway Park with the Bills at 10–2–1. The winner of this pivotal game would capture the Eastern Division championship. Emotions ran high, and some trash-talking during the week of the game by several Patriots players only added to those feelings. The first snowstorm of the season hit Boston the morning of the game, dumping 3 inches of snow and making the field conditions sloppy for the biggest game in Bills history to that point.

The Bills' Gilchrist set the tone for this game on the first play from scrimmage, taking a handoff from Kemp and rambling 9 yards — knocking out Patriots safety Chuck Shonta on the play. Gilchrist got up from the run, looked at the fallen Shonta, stared at the rest of the Patriots defense and as reported by Jeffrey Miller in "Rockin the Rockpile," Gilchrist said, "Which one of you mother------s is next?"

Buffalo responded to Gilchrist's explosive run and the pressure of the game with an impressive performance. The Bills held the Patriots to 33 yards rushing. Boston scored a meaningless late touchdown to make the final score a slightly more respectable 24–14. The Bills rushed the ball effectively, amassing 96 yards, and made big plays in the passing game. The highlights included a 57-yard Dubenion touchdown, a 45-yard pass to Ernie Warlick to set up a touchdown run by Kemp, and a 33-yard pass to Glenn Bass that led to a Gogolak field goal.

With a league-best 12–2 record, the Bills hosted the defending champion Chargers the day after Christmas for the AFL championship. An AFL playoff record crowd of 40,242 was on hand to witness the fifth AFL championship game. It was a mild December day, 49 degrees, that started poorly for Buffalo as the Chargers quickly took a 7–0 lead. San Diego's Keith Lincoln ran 38 yards on the first play from scrimmage, ran for 5 more yards and caught a pass for 11 yards, setting up San Diego at the Bills 26-yard line. Tobin Rote then threw a perfect 26-yard pass to Dave Kocourek streaking through the Buffalo secondary, and the Bills trailed only 2:11 into the game.

However, a little more than four minutes later, the momentum of the game changed for good. Lincoln was awaiting a swing pass from Rote when Mike Stratton hit him with a crunching tackle, breaking his ribs and laying him out on the turf for several minutes. The tackle is famous in Bills history and became known as the "Hit Heard Round the World."

The Bills quickly moved the ball 61 yards to set up a Gogolak field goal to close the gap to 7–3 at the end of the first quarter. Buffalo scored 10 points in the second quarter, on a 4-yard run by Wray Carlton and another Gogolak field goal for a 13–7 halftime lead. The third quarter was scoreless as the Buffalo defense remained stout, ultimately forcing three San Diego turnovers for the game. The Bills put the game away six minutes into the fourth quarter as Kemp hit Bass on a 51-yard pass to the San Diego 1-yard line. Kemp scored two plays later to make the score 20–7 in favor of Buffalo, and that's how the game ended.

The Bills brought the first-ever championship to the Queen City. However, at the time, the AFL was considered well below the NFL in caliber of play, and thus the NFL champion Cleveland Browns were considered the true champions of professional football. The Browns ran through the NFL season with a 10–3–1 regular-season record and routed the Johnny Unitas-led Baltimore Colts 27–0 for the NFL championship.

The Browns had pro football's greatest-ever running back in Jim Brown, an impressive passing attack of Frank Ryan throwing to wide receivers Paul Warfield and Gary Collins, a superior offensive line anchored by Gene Hickerson and Dick Schafrath, and a stout defense. It added up to an outstanding team. Sports Illustrated reporter Tex Maule, commenting before the Colts had lost to Cleveland, said the Colts would beat the Bills 48–7 if they played. This was the sentiment of the vast majority of the pro football media.

The NFL had supremacy over the upstart AFL in attendance, TV ratings, the size of cities with franchises and national media coverage. During the AFL's first six years, the league's average per-game attendance was 22,366, compared with the NFL's average of 42,720. The television contracts of each league also showed significant disparity. In the AFL's first five years of existence, its television revenue was $2.125 million per season. The NFL's comparable revenue was $4.65 million through 1963 and jumped to $14.1 million per season in 1964 and 1965. The AFL solidified its survival with its 1965 television deal with NBC for $36 million over five years, a still-paltry amount compared with the NFL. The disparity in the largest media markets was even greater. Of the NFL's 14 teams, at the time, nine were in cities among the top 10 markets in the country. The AFL had only two of its eight teams in top 10 markets: New York and Houston.

Despite the lack of recognition for the Bills and the AFL, Buffalo sports fans were still thrilled with their winning football team. The Bills' 1964 team was Buffalo's strongest during the AFL years but was still not considered on par with the NFL's better teams.

Buffalo was ready to defend its AFL title heading into the 1965 season. However, the Bills would have to do it without Gilchrist who was traded in the offseason because of his penchant for bad behavior. Saban had grown tired of his antics and felt the Bills would be a better team without him.

Buffalo opened the 1965 season with four consecutive victories, including an impressive season-opening win over Boston 24–7. In Week 3, Buffalo hosted the New York Jets and rookie quarterback Joe Namath, who made the first regular-season start of his career that day. He passed for 282 yards and two touchdowns, but it was not enough to outshine the Bills' quarterback. Kemp passed for 292 yards, leading the Bills to a 33–21 victory. Buffalo piled up 408 total yards of offense along the way.

Buffalo's first loss of the season was a 34–3 shellacking by San Diego at War Memorial Stadium. The Bills committed six turnovers and gained just 150 yards of offense. Despite several key injuries, including the loss of wide receivers Dubenion and Bass for the season, the Bills won four of their next five games, including another impressive win over the Patriots 23–7. The Eastern Division race in 1965 was decided early as Buffalo was the class of the division with no other team finishing with a winning record. The Bills concluded the regular season with a 10–3–1 record and had to travel to the 9–2–3 Chargers to defend their 1964 AFL championship.

San Diego entered the championship game with the league's best offense, best defense, best record, home-field advantage and the league MVP, halfback Paul Lowe. However, none of that mattered as the Bills pitched a masterful shutout, 23–0.

The Bills defense was superb as it dominated the powerful San Diego offense and shut the Chargers out for the first time in more than four seasons. Buffalo opened the scoring as Warlick hauled in an 18-yard touchdown pass from Kemp with less than five minutes left in the first half, giving the Bills a 7–0 lead. Two and a half minutes later, the turning point in the game occurred as Buffalo punt returner Butch Byrd fielded a kick at his own 26-yard line and with great blocking ran untouched for 74 yards and a touchdown. The electrifying play broke the spirit of the Chargers and gave the Bills a 14–0 lead. Buffalo added three Gogolak field goals in the second half as the defense continued to dominate.

The NFL, however, was still considered the superior league. The Green Bay Packers won their third NFL championship under Vince Lombardi with an impressive 23–12 victory over the 1964 defending champion Cleveland Browns. This Packers team had the NFL's best defense, allowing only 224 points, and was led on offense by quarterback Bart Starr.

The American Football League would finally reach parity with the NFL, at least legally, on June 8, 1966, as the two circuits announced plans to merge into one professional football league. The AFL and NFL immediately began with a common draft of players and a single championship game, with each league's winner squaring off in a world championship game — which soon became known as the Super Bowl. Even though the leagues would not fully merge and play a common interlocking schedule until 1970, the world championship game would begin after the 1966 season. The Bills now had their chance to prove to everyone that the 1964 and 1965 AFL championships were legitimate professional football titles, and they could do that by winning the first world championship game between the AFL and NFL. The defending AFL champions had the opportunity to play for an undisputed NFL championship for the first time since the early 1920s and end the Curse, if they could win a third consecutive AFL title.

The Bills would have to do it without two vital cogs from their two previous titles. On Jan. 2, 1966, Saban resigned to become the head coach at the University of Maryland. Defensive coordinator Joel Collier was promoted to replace Saban and, at the age of 33, became the youngest head coach in pro football. Also, Gogolak played out his option and on May 17 signed a lucrative contract with the NFL's New York Giants.

Buffalo did not open defense of its two previous AFL titles in championship form. The Bills lost their first two games, to San Diego 27–7 and Kansas City 42–20, and the Bills were only 3–3–1 at midseason. Buffalo finally rediscovered its winning ways as it reeled off five victories in a row, capped off with an impressive 31–10 Thanksgiving Day shellacking of the Oakland Raiders. The win streak propelled the Bills into first place with an 8–3–1 record. However, Buffalo could not stand prosperity and lost a showdown to the second-place Boston Patriots 14–3, a victory that lifted the Patriots into first place. The Bills and Patriots both won the following week. Buffalo had concluded its season with a 9–4–1 mark, and Boston entered its final game with an 8–3–2 record. With a victory over the Jets, the Patriots would capture the AFL East Division championship. However, with Namath playing an outstanding game, the Jets upset Boston 38–28, propelling Buffalo to the title. The Bills would host the AFL championship game on New Year's Day 1967 against the Western Division champion Kansas City Chiefs.

Buffalo was prepared to defend its championship and become the AFL's representative in Super Bowl 1. The stakes for this game were the biggest for any AFL game played to this point. However, the Curse entered the fray. The Bills and Chiefs had split the season series with each team winning once. The

Bills were confident that they would win their third consecutive AFL championship, especially because of their experience in big games and having home-field advantage.

Then the game started. Buffalo won the coin toss to receive the opening kickoff. The kick was a high, floating, short boot that reserve defensive tackle Dudley Meredith tried to handle, but he fumbled the ball and the Chiefs' Jerrel Wilson recovered, giving Kansas City outstanding field position at the Bills 31-yard line. Two plays later, Chiefs quarterback Len Dawson lofted a 29-yard pass beyond the reach of Bills defensive back Byrd and into the waiting arms of Fred Arbanas for a touchdown. The Chiefs quickly led 7–0.

The Bills responded decisively with a 69-yard touchdown pass from Kemp to Dubenion to tie the score at 7. The Chiefs answered early in the second quarter following a 42-yard punt return by running back Mike Garrett. A few plays after the punt return, Dawson hit Otis Taylor on a 29-yard touchdown pass and the Chiefs regained the lead 14–7.

On Kansas City's next offensive possession, the Bills had a golden opportunity to tie the game when Dawson fired a pass intended for Garrett at the Chiefs 23-yard line. Buffalo safety Tom Janik cut in front of Garrett for a sure interception and six points, as nobody was between Janik and the goal line. However, he inexplicably dropped the certain interception, and a tying touchdown was not to be.

The feisty Bills battled back again, driving deep into Kansas City territory near the end of the first half. Buffalo was on the Chiefs 10-yard line with a chance to tie the game before intermission. Kemp attempted a pass to Bobby Crockett, but Kansas City defensive back Johnny Robinson stepped in front of Crockett, picking off the pass at the goal line. Robinson then raced 73 yards with the interception, setting up a critical last-second field goal by Kansas City's Mike Mercer. Sal Maiorana reported in "Relentless" that after the game, Kemp said of the interception, "He made a great individual play. We thought we had him occupied elsewhere." However, as the Democrat and Chronicle reported, "What happened was that one Buffalo pass receiver slipped and fell in the mush, which left Robinson available to make his move." This was a brutal blow to the Bills. Instead of going into the half tied at 14, they instead trailed 17–7.

The third quarter was dominated by Kansas City as it had wrested the momentum from the Bills. Even though the Chiefs did not score in the third

Photo 11. Johnny Robinson (20) returns a first-half interception against the Buffalo Bills in the AFL championship game on Jan. 1, 1967, at War Memorial Stadium in Buffalo. Kansas City went on to win 31–7 and play in the first Super Bowl.

(Photo by Robert L. Smith, Orchard Park, New York)

quarter, they had effectively worn down the Buffalo defense heading into the final period.

Early in the fourth quarter, the Chiefs marched 63 yards for a touchdown. The Bills had stopped Garrett three times on running plays inside the 2-yard line. On fourth down and a foot to go for the touchdown, Bills defensive end Ron McDole had Garrett stopped for no gain, but Garrett's second effort propelled him into the end zone and a 24–7 Chiefs lead.

On the Bills' next offensive series, Kemp was sacked and fumbled the ball, and Chiefs defensive back Bobby Hunt scooped up the ball, returning it to the Buffalo 2-yard line. A few plays later, Garrett made an amazing run. He zigzagged through Bills defenders, changing direction from one side of the field to the other and scampering into the end zone for the Chiefs' final touchdown in their 31–7 victory. The Associated Press reported that Bills coach Collier summed it up best in the locker room after the game: "We started out poorly with the fumble and got progressively worse."

The Curse had struck again. With so much at stake for Buffalo, its miscues — the opening kickoff fumble, the dropped interception, Kemp's last-second interception at the end of the half in the end zone caused by a key player falling down — certainly helped keep the Bills from getting to Super Bowl 1 and having a chance to win the city's first major championship.

The Chiefs, a solid AFL team, went on to Super Bowl 1 and were beaten soundly by the NFL champion Packers 35–10. The Bills were probably a better matchup against Green Bay with their solid defense. Buffalo likely would have given the Packers a better game, but it was not meant to be. Most importantly, the Curse continued to thrive and deprive the city of a championship.

Chapter 7
THE MIAMI POUND MACHINE

After the loss to Kansas City in the 1966 AFL championship, the Bills endured three down seasons as the 1960s came to a close. The 1970s brought renewed hope for Buffalo fans, but the Miami Dolphins would prove to be a thorn in their side throughout the decade.

The Dolphins will always be remembered and loathed by Bills fans for "The Streak." Buffalo lost 20 consecutive games to Miami during the 1970s — an NFL record for futility against a single opponent.

Miami entered the American Football League as an expansion franchise in 1966. The Dolphins joined Buffalo in the Eastern Division and thus would play a home-and-home series with the Bills each season, immediately creating a rivalry between the two teams. The Dolphins did not have much success in their first four seasons in the AFL, finishing in last place twice and having losing records all four years. Their best season was 5–8–1 in 1968. However, Miami hired Don Shula to be its head coach in 1970, and its fortunes changed immediately.

Miami won its first AFC East title that year, went to its first Super Bowl at the conclusion of the 1971 season, and won back-to-back titles in 1972 and 1973, going 17–0 in '72. During the 1970s, the Dolphins won five AFC East titles, three AFC championships and two Super Bowls. Clearly, supremacy in the AFC East went through Miami after Shula became coach. The Dolphins' dominance haunted the Bills on many occasions.

A multitude of Buffalo fans think the Bills were jinxed in the 1970s against the Dolphins — or maybe the Curse was at play throughout the decade. The Bills came close to beating Miami many times but could never win. There were several strange plays and moments that always went the

Dolphins' way. The bizarre nature of some of the defeats leaves an eerie, haunting nature to "The Streak."

The constant losses to Miami involved coaches from John Rauch to Harvey Johnson to Lou Saban to Jim Ringo to Chuck Knox. They haunted the O.J. Simpson years and the Joe Ferguson era. Without the ability to beat the Dolphins, the Bills were not able to win an AFC East title throughout the 1970s, and they only qualified for the playoffs in a single season (1974).

Buffalo defeated Miami in the teams' final meeting of the 1960s on Nov. 16, 1969. The Bills manhandled the Dolphins 28–3, scoring a touchdown in every quarter, with Simpson catching two touchdown passes. Both teams finished the season with poor records: the Bills at 4–10 and the Dolphins in last place at 3–10–1. There certainly was no indication from the results of 1969 of what was to unfold in the 1970s, which featured the Dolphins' complete domination and the Bills' misfortune.

Buffalo's first game versus Miami in 1970 came on Oct. 18. It was Shula's first visit to Buffalo as coach of the Dolphins. The Bills were very obliging hosts as they committed six turnovers with four fumbles and two interceptions in addition to eight penalties, and the Dolphins rolled to an easy 33–14 victory at War Memorial Stadium. Despite the Bills out-gaining Miami by 89 yards, they were never in the game. This result set the tone for the two teams for the next 10 seasons. Miami routed Buffalo in the 1970 rematch at the Orange Bowl in Miami, 45–7. The Dolphins jumped to a 21–0 first-quarter lead and by halftime the score was 31–0, ultimately giving Miami its first playoff berth.

The Dolphins beat the Bills 29–14 in their first meeting in 1971. After a 46-yard touchdown run by Simpson, Buffalo trailed Miami only 19–14. However, early in the fourth quarter as Buffalo was moving the ball to take the lead, Miami safety Dick Anderson intercepted quarterback Dennis Shaw's pass and returned it to the Buffalo 47-yard line. Three plays later, Dolphins quarterback Bob Griese fired a 23-yard touchdown pass to Paul Warfield to clinch the game.

In their second meeting of 1971, the Dolphins smashed the Bills 34–0. The Bills fumbled the ball three times in Miami territory and quarterback James Harris threw two interceptions, including one in the Dolphins' end zone. Despite the Bills gaining 364 yards, they were blanked by the Dolphins in Miami's first shutout.

The Bills' Oct. 22, 1972, loss to Miami was a bitter 24–23 defeat. The Bills had a 13–7 halftime lead as kicker John Leypoldt booted two field goals — one followed a failed fourth-down gamble by Miami, the other a result of a Dolphin turnover. The Buffalo touchdown was Ken Lee's 16-yard interception return.

However, the Bills' good fortune turned in the second half. Miami defensive lineman Manny Fernandez stole a handoff from Shaw, leading to Larry Csonka's 10-yard go-ahead touchdown run. Miami blocked Buffalo's punt on the next series, setting up a very unlikely 54-yard Garo Yepremian field goal. Using a gale-force wind to his advantage at War Memorial Stadium, he made the longest kick in Dolphins history.

With Miami holding a slim 17–16 lead, Dolphins running back Mercury Morris sprinted 15 yards for a touchdown. The touchdown probably should have been called back, as Miami tackle Norm Evans committed an obvious holding penalty that sprung Morris for the score, but the officials failed to call the infraction. The Bills responded with a touchdown to pull within a point, but they could not overcome their mistakes and the Yepremian wind-aided field goal and lost a heartbreaker.

The 1972 season was when Miami posted the 17–0 record, the only undefeated, untied team in the Super Bowl era. That 24–23 victory was the closest Miami came to being beaten.

The Bills' misfortune continued in their second game with the Dolphins that season as they played Miami tough again, but a couple of miscues cost them dearly. The Bills trailed 16–6 late in the second quarter when Bills safety Tony Greene intercepted a pass from quarterback Earl Morrall and raced 39 yards for a touchdown. It sliced the Dolphins' lead to 16–13. The Bills had a chance to tie the game at the end of the first half, but coach Lou Saban gambled and decided to go for the touchdown and the lead. Shaw was intercepted by Miami safety Tim Foley, ending the drive with no points for Buffalo.

Early in the second half, the Bills' bad luck continued with Leypoldt's 27-yard field-goal attempt going awry after center Remi Prudhomme botched the snap. The Bills continued to shoot themselves in the foot as later in the third quarter, they appeared to have stopped the Dolphins on a third-and-2 play when John Pitts came up from his cornerback position and nailed power back Csonka short of the first down. When the officials gave Miami a very generous spot of the ball, Bills defensive lineman Jerry Patton swore at the officials resulting in a 15-yard penalty and an automatic first down for Miami. It took Morrall only four plays to make Buffalo pay dearly for its errors, hitting tight end Marv Fleming with a 7-yard touchdown pass to give Miami a 23–13 lead.

The Dolphins clinched the game in the fourth quarter when safety Jake Scott intercepted Shaw's pass, setting up Miami for another score to wrap up the 30–16 victory. Saban was incensed after the game, feeling that the penalty against Patton was unwarranted and was the deciding factor in the game.

Buffalo was the surprise team of the NFL at the start of the 1973 season. Simpson rushed for an NFL-record 250 yards on opening day as the Bills trounced rival New England 31–13. The victory propelled the Bills to a 4–1 start, and Week 6 brought a first-place showdown with the Dolphins at the Orange Bowl on Oct. 21. Buffalo took an early 3–0 lead but was no match for the Dolphins on this day. The Bills had no first downs in the first half, their quarterbacks were sacked nine times and Simpson was held to a season-low 55 yards rushing as the Dolphins manhandled Buffalo 27–6.

Four weeks later, the Bills hosted the rematch at Rich Stadium in front of a raucous sellout crowd of 77,138. Fullback Jim Braxton and Simpson each rushed for more than 100 yards, the first time in 45 games that the Dolphins had allowed a single 100-yard rusher, let alone two in a game. Incredibly, the Bills were shut out by Miami, 17–0. Buffalo has the dubious distinction of being the only team in NFL history to have two 100-yard rushers in one game and get shut out! The Bills' miscues haunted them in a game in which they outplayed Miami but lost.

Leypoldt missed a 23-yard field goal in the first quarter, and Braxton was stopped on a fourth-and-goal play from the 1-yard line in the second quarter. In addition, Simpson let a pass bounce off his hands and Dolphins linebacker Mike Kolen intercepted. He returned it 25 yards, setting up a touchdown that built the Dolphins' lead to 17–0 in the second quarter. That turned out to be the final score. Miami went on to win its second consecutive world championship, dominating Super Bowl 8 with a 24–7 trouncing of Minnesota.

The 1974 season brought much anticipation for Buffalo football fans. The team was coming off a highly successful 9–5 season in 1973, just missing the playoffs despite Simpson's historic 2,003-yard rushing season. They had added some key new players in the offseason: tight end Reuben Gant and linebacker Doug Allen, who arrived through the draft, and wide receiver Ahmad Rashad, who came to the Bills in a trade for Dennis Shaw.

The Bills opened the 1974 season on "Monday Night Football" in Rich Stadium before 79,876 geared-up fans. The overflow crowd was treated to a visit from the Oakland Raiders — and one of the most exciting games in Buffalo's history.

With the Bills trailing 20–14 late in the fourth quarter after Art Thoms returned a fumble for a Raiders touchdown, Buffalo had one final chance at victory. With only 1:08 remaining, Ferguson went to work: a 10-yard pass to Braxton (accompanied by a 15-yard roughing the passer penalty), a 20-yard pass to Rashad and a 10-yard pass to J.D. Hill. Suddenly, the Bills were on the Raiders 13. Ferguson then eluded the Raiders' pass rush, firing a perfect 13-yard strike to Rashad for the winning touchdown with 26 seconds left. Leypoldt's extra point gave the Bills a heart-stopping 21–20 victory. Bills fans in Rich Stadium and across Western New York celebrated the improbable upset and awaited the next week's showdown with the two-time defending Super Bowl champion Dolphins.

In front of another wild, sellout crowd, the Bills led Miami 3–0 when Buffalo linebacker Jim Cheyunski forced Mercury Morris to fumble on the Bills 6-yard line, thwarting a Dolphins scoring threat, but Simpson fumbled the ball back to Miami on the next play and the Dolphins immediately scored from the Bills 1. Buffalo would continue to make mistakes, again handing a victory to Miami. Late in the first half, Rashad dropped a sure touchdown pass, and then Leypoldt missed a 27-yard field goal that would have cut Miami's 7–3 lead.

At the start of the second half, Braxton fumbled at the Bills 9, giving the Dolphins their second easy touchdown of the game. After Buffalo scored on a 22-yard Simpson run, Leypoldt inexplicably missed the extra point to leave the score at 14–9. Another Bills mistake set up Miami's third touchdown as Bills cornerback Dwight Harrison interfered with Dolphins receiver Paul Warfield, giving Miami a first down at the Bills 20-yard line. Morris scooted around the end for a 17-yard touchdown run and a 21–9 Miami lead.

Harrison later had another costly personal foul penalty, helping to set up Yepremian's clinching field goal with the Bills trailing 21–16 and fighting to regain possession of the ball. Leypoldt's missed extra point proved especially detrimental because Buffalo was down by 8, and at that time the NFL did not have a 2-point conversion rule after scoring a touchdown.

The Bills won six games in a row after the loss to Miami and were tied with the Dolphins at 7–2 entering the teams' rematch on Nov. 17 in Florida.

Buffalo thought it scored first as Tony Greene intercepted Bob Griese in the end zone and raced 105 yards for a touchdown. But All-Pro cornerback Robert James was called for holding Dolphins receiver Howard Twilley, thus nullifying the interception and the touchdown. The officials gave Miami the ball with a first down at the Bills 2-yard line. On the next play, Csonka plowed in for the touchdown and a 7–0 Dolphins lead. A crushing turn of events for the Bills.

Late in the first half, Griese fired a 49-yard touchdown pass to All-Pro wide receiver Warfield, and Miami went to the intermission leading 14–0. The teams traded touchdowns in the third quarter. Buffalo faced an uphill struggle entering the final 15 minutes, trailing 21–7, and it had lost Ferguson to a badly bruised knee. He was replaced by rookie Gary Marangi.

One minute into the fourth quarter, Morris fumbled and Bills linebacker Dave Washington scooped up the loose ball and ran 42 yards for a touchdown, cutting the Miami lead to 21–14. On the Dolphins' next possession, they fumbled and Washington recovered again. Marangi promptly fired a 44-yard touchdown pass to Hill to tie the game at 21. It was Marangi's first career touchdown pass, and the Dolphins were stunned!

Miami promptly drove 81 yards with the help of a James pass interference penalty on Nat Moore, with the drive ending on an 11-yard touchdown run by Don Nottingham. As seemed to happen in many games throughout the mid-1970s, a questionable official's call had a big impact on the outcome of a Dolphins/Bills game.

Marangi, in his most gutsy performance as a pro, directed the Bills on a 71-yard drive that included five completions for 51 yards and three scrambles for 20 more yards. The thrilling drive was capped off by a 5-yard strike to wide receiver Bob Chandler with 56 seconds left, tying the game at 28.

The Bills defense, however, could not hold the Miami offense in the final minute. Griese led the Dolphins on an 81-yard drive in only four plays for the winning score with 19 seconds left. Nottingham broke through the defense at the 23-yard line and sprinted to the end zone for the game-winning touchdown. It was a heartbreaking loss for the Bills as they played with the grittiness and toughness of a playoff team, only to come up short against the two-time defending champions.

Despite the tough loss to Miami, the Bills bounced back to win their next two games and qualify for the playoffs for the first time since 1966. They traveled to Pittsburgh for the playoffs and were beaten by a legendary Steelers team 32–14. The Steelers went on to win Super Bowl 9 that season and would win four NFL titles over the next six years.

The 1975 Bills had the top-rated offense in professional football. They mixed a potent running game, with Simpson posting one of the best single-season rushing marks of all-time with 1,817 yards, and a solid passing offense behind Ferguson's 25 touchdown passes. Buffalo started the season strong with four consecutive victories before losing to the New York Giants in a 17–14 "Monday Night" heartbreaker. Their 4–1 record again set up a first-place showdown with the 4–1 Dolphins on Oct. 26 at Rich Stadium.

A sellout crowd of 79,141 watched Buffalo start the game with a flourish as Bills safety Steve Freeman intercepted Griese's first pass of the game and returned it 30 yards for a touchdown. Simpson sprinted 26 yards for the Bills' second score and a 13–0 lead. Leypoldt missed the extra point. The game went back and forth, but after a 5-yard Ferguson-to-Chandler touchdown pass midway through the fourth quarter, the Bills seemed in control, leading by 9 points. However, the Dolphins quickly responded and scored with 3:18 remaining in the game on a 5-yard touchdown pass from Griese to tight end Jim Mandich, cutting the Bills' lead to 30–28.

The Bills started the next drive from their own 12-yard line after a penalty on the kickoff. Saban decided to be aggressive and had Ferguson pass on first down. The Bills quarterback misread the defensive coverage and his pass was intercepted by Jake Scott at the Bills 22-yard line. The Dolphins pounded the Buffalo defense for one first down, and then Nottingham rammed in from the 1 to put Miami ahead 35–30.

Buffalo got the ball back with 1:25 left but could not muster a drive as Ferguson was sacked and fumbled. This was the fourth time in three seasons that the Dolphins and Bills had battled for first place in the AFC East, and each time Buffalo finished on the short end of the scoreboard. In each of the four losses, the Bills beat themselves, either by committing turnovers at critical junctures in the game or by being penalized in key situations to propel Miami to the victories. After the game, the Bills' 11th consecutive loss to the Dolphins, Saban lamented in an interview with Peter Pascarelli of the Democrat and Chronicle, "How can I explain how I feel? Our men played hard, but we just made costly errors. It's absolutely brutal to play this hard, and still we haven't beaten them." The Curse seemed to be alive and well in helping Miami win these four critical games.

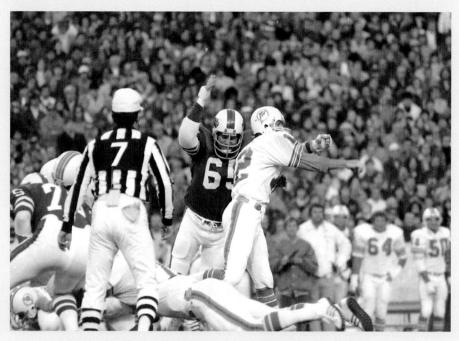

Photo 12. Bob Griese (12) rallies the Dolphins to a 35–30 victory over the Buffalo Bills on Oct. 26, 1975, at Rich Stadium in Buffalo. Griese's career record against the Bills was 18–2–1.

(Photo by Robert L. Smith, Orchard Park, New York)

The Bills played the rematch of 1975 on Dec. 7. Buffalo was still in the race for the AFC East title with a 7–4 record, one game behind the Dolphins. Miami roared to a 21–0 halftime lead driven by third-string quarterback Don Strock, making his first NFL start. Buffalo fought back in the second half with Simpson sprinting 14 yards for the first touchdown while breaking an NFL record by scoring a rushing touchdown for the 12th consecutive game. After a Miami field goal, the Bills scored two consecutive touchdowns. Hill caught a 31-yard pass for a score late in the third quarter, and Simpson took a screen pass from Ferguson and sprinted 62 yards for a touchdown to cut Miami's lead to 24–21 with 9:23 left.

The Bills forced a fumble on the Dolphins' next possession with Buffalo linebacker John Skorupan recovering at Miami's 28-yard line. However, referee Gene Barth ruled it was not a fumble. The Bills sideline went berserk with the no-fumble call. Defensive end Pat Toomay bumped an official in the ensuing argument, and Buffalo was subsequently penalized 15 yards. In the postgame locker room, Bills owner Ralph C. Wilson Jr. said, "The official who made that call should be barred from football. Anyone that incompetent shouldn't be allowed to officiate." Toomay added, "I saw the fumble, and I ran over there, and pushed the official out of the way to get at the ball. It was an unbelievable call."

On the very next play, Nottingham broke a 56-yard run to the Bills 1-yard line. Dolphins running back Norm Bulaich then scored, ensuring a 31–21 Buffalo defeat. The loss eliminated the Bills from the playoff race. It was a devastating defeat for the team, and it would help send Buffalo spiraling into poor seasons in 1976 and 1977.

Buffalo opened the 1976 season at home versus the Dolphins on "Monday Night Football." The Bills had a tumultuous training camp as Simpson held out in a contract dispute until the day before the opening game, and Buffalo came into the game distracted by the turmoil.

The Bills' run of bad luck against Miami needed no time to resume. Saban had built his offense around Braxton when it seemed likely that Simpson would not be playing, but the burly fullback was lost for the season to an injury on the season's first offensive play. Even so, the Bills battled the Dolphins as Ferguson passed for 282 yards and three touchdowns. But Buffalo blew any opportunity it had of winning the game when Leypoldt missed three field-goal attempts. The Bills lost the game by 9 points. "No question about it, the three missed field goals did it," Saban said during his post-game press conference. "Our special teams killed us. The loss of Braxton killed us. The whole offense was built around him in the preseason, and when you lose a man like that, you lose a lot. It was an upsetting game, it's a tough way to coach, not really worth it." Those were prophetic words, as Saban's frustrations led to his resignation two days before the Bills' sixth game of the season.

There had been a lot of speculation for over a year that Saban was unhappy with not having more control over decision making within the organization. The Bills lost several key players during the previous two off-seasons (Earl Edwards, Ahmad Rashad, Pat Toomay, Dave Washington, etc.) and the handling and ultimate signing of Simpson the day before the opening game, none of which sat well with Saban. The Bills got off to a rough start in 1976, losing three of five games, and that certainly took its toll on him.

Wilson was somewhat surprised and certainly disappointed by Saban's decision and especially the timing of it, being the Friday before a game and in the middle of the season. Also, Saban had five more years to run on his 10-year contract. Wilson felt betrayed by Saban because this was the second time Saban had walked out on him, or at least that is how Wilson saw it. And Wilson thought loyalty was a most important trait.

Despite Saban being the second-most successful coach in Bills history (70–47–2 .595 and 2 AFL championships), he was not put on the Bills Wall of Fame until the fall of 2015, more than a year after Wilson's death and 6 ½ years after Saban's passing.

Offensive line coach Jim Ringo took over the head coaching duties of the 2–3 team, and the Bills lost nine consecutive games, including a 45–27 loss to the Dolphins, to end the season with a dismal 2–12 record. In the loss to Miami, Simpson rushed for 203 yards, including a 75-yard touchdown run, but it couldn't prevent the Bills' 14th consecutive loss to the Dolphins.

The 1977 season opened in front of a Rich Stadium sellout crowd versus Miami. The Bills began the campaign with a stout defensive effort, but mistakes again sealed their fate. The Bills defense limited the Dolphins to 148 yards of offense, but an interception by Curtis Johnson and a fumble by Bills kick returner Charles Romes led to 10 points in Miami's 13–0 victory. Buffalo outgained the Dolphins by 176 yards but continually committed errors, including two missed field goals by kicker Neil O'Donoghue.

This game was Simpson's last against Miami as a Buffalo Bill. He was injured later in the season and was traded to the San Francisco 49ers at the end of the year. His career record in games against Miami was 1–16. Only a 28–3 victory in his rookie season of 1969 kept him from being winless in this jinxed matchup.

Buffalo ended the 1977 season, and Ringo's head coaching career, with a 31–14 loss to Miami. The Bills were never in the game as the Dolphins sprinted to a 21–0 first-half lead behind two Griese touchdown passes. Buffalo amassed 434 yards of offense, but three Ferguson interceptions and a fumble stymied the Bills until the game was out of reach.

The 1978 season brought new optimism as highly regarded and successful head coach Chuck Knox left the Los Angeles Rams and came east to lead the Bills. Knox won five consecutive NFC West titles for the Rams from 1973–1977 with a stellar 54–15–1 regular-season record. He had been named Associated Press NFC Coach of the Year in 1973, but his failings in the playoffs with only a 3–5 record and never making it to the Super Bowl led to his exit from Los Angeles. Knox had a lot of work to do to rebuild the fledgling Buffalo franchise, but better days were ahead. The Bills opened Knox's first season with two consecutive losses heading into their Week 3 game in Miami. Buffalo was competitive with the Dolphins, trailing only 24–17 early in the fourth quarter. The Bills had the ball with a chance to tie the game, but they could not move it and had to punt. The Dolphins proceeded to march 78 yards for a score, clinching the 31–24 victory. Miami shredded the Bills, rushing for 275 yards.

Knox said in the postgame news conference, "No excuses, no jinxes, no heat, we just got beat. I don't call a bad snap over the punter's head a jinx, or poor tackling and blocking a jinx." The Bills' loss to the Dolphins was the 17th consecutive, tying an NFL record for most consecutive losses to one team.

The Bills' rematch with Miami that season on Nov. 12 was probably the most controversial loss throughout "The Streak." Buffalo, 3–8 at that point, trailed 25–24 with 1:42 left in the game. Buffalo was moving the ball and had a second down and 6 from its 46-yard line. Ferguson fired a beautiful pass to Roland Hooks at the Miami 25-yard line. Hooks caught the ball, but the officials ruled the pass incomplete. If the instant replay rule had been in effect, it is likely the play would have been overturned and ruled a completion. A sack of Ferguson led to the end of the Bills' drive and their hopes for a comeback.

The call on Hooks was one of several controversial decisions by this crew throughout the game. At the start of the contest, ex-Bill Jim Braxton appeared to fumble the ball over to his old team, but officials ruled the play was not a turnover — even though it certainly looked like one on replay. Miami eventually marched 79 yards on the opening drive for a touchdown as Delvin Williams sprinted in from 25 yards.

Miami's third touchdown of the game, which gave them a 22–14 lead, was set up by a 36-yard pass interference penalty against Bills linebacker Randy McClanahan, a questionable call. With Buffalo trailing by 8 and driving for a score, it appeared as if Miami safety Tim Foley interfered with Reuben Gant at the Dolphins 5-yard line. However, the officials did not call the penalty, forcing the Bills to settle for a field goal.

Wilson was again incensed after the game, saying, "The officials stole the game from us." Bills offensive lineman Joe DeLamielleure said, "Football is a great game. Why don't they let us play?" The loss by Buffalo, its 18th consecutive to a single team, broke the NFL record.

In preparing for the 1979 season, the Bills had one of the best drafts in team history, even though they didn't sign their No. 1 selection, linebacker Tom Cousineau from Ohio State. Cousineau signed with the Canadian Football League's Montreal Alouettes, who provided him a contract that was twice what Buffalo had offered. The Bills added several talented players including wide receiver Jerry Butler, nose tackle Fred Smerlas, linebacker Jim Haslett, offensive tackle Jon Borchardt and safeties Jeff Nixon and Rod Kush. All of these players started for the Bills during the Chuck Knox era.

Buffalo opened the season at home against the arch-rival Dolphins. The disdain for Miami continued to grow for Bills fans, as the losing streak mounted. Bills publicist Budd Thalman said before the game, "I have been around for 12 of them, but that's plenty. It's been very frustrating, and very emotional, with a lot of games that could have gone either way. I guess I've learned to hate them."

The Bills jumped to a 7-point lead when Sherman White blocked a field-goal attempt by Dolphins kicker Uwe von Schamann, and Charles Romes dashed 76 yards with the loose ball for the touchdown. Miami scored in the third quarter to cut the Bills lead to 7–3. Later in the quarter, the stadium was hit with monsoon-like rain, soaking the field and creating extremely difficult conditions for the players, even on artificial turf. Despite the terrible conditions and the continuing rain, Miami put together a 77-yard, 14-play drive. It was capped off by a 1-yard plunge for a touchdown by Csonka.

Von Schamann missed the extra point, and the Dolphins had a precarious 9–7 lead.

With 1:47 left in the game, Keith Moody returned a Miami punt 28 yards to the Dolphins 35-yard line. The Bills moved the ball to the 18-yard line with three running plays and a nifty 11-yard pass to Gant. This set up a game-winning field-goal attempt of 34 yards by Tom Dempsey with four seconds left. The drenched Buffalo crowd was excited, anticipating the end to the miserable 18-game losing streak against Miami. Dempsey, who had a club foot resulting from a birth defect, had been able to overcome that to have a solid NFL career. For many years he held the NFL record for the longest field goal in history, a 63-yard game-winner while he was with the New Orleans Saints.

After a Miami timeout, the Dolphins' attempt to freeze the kicker, the ball was snapped, Dempsey approached the ball, swung his leg back and struck the ball solidly. Buffalo fans gasped in pain as the kick sailed wide left. "The Streak" had reached 19 consecutive losses.

Buffalo lost its 20th consecutive game to Miami on Oct. 17 by a 17–7 score. The Bills were dominated by the Dolphins, only scoring on a 3-yard run by Hooks. The 1970s came to an end and Buffalo was 0–20 against Miami. The Bills fans' hatred of the Dolphins had grown to monumental proportions.

With Knox's third season in 1980, Buffalo fans were hopeful for their first playoff team since 1974 as he had added more talent in the offseason to his young but maturing team. The Bills' 1980 draft landed future stars including guard Jim Ritcher and running back Joe Cribbs, as well as future starters in tight end Mark Brammer, guard Ervin Parker and punter Greg Cater. In addition, Knox added veteran stalwarts in guard Conrad Dobler, linebacker Phil Villapiano, fullback Roosevelt Leaks and wide receiver Ron Jessie.

The Bills opened the 1980 season on Sept. 7 in front of 79,598 eager fans on a gorgeous sunny day against the despised Dolphins. The Bills scored first on a 40-yard field goal by Nick Mike-Mayer late in the second quarter that was set up by a Jeff Nixon interception, his first of three for the game. The contest was a bruising defensive battle. It was also turnover-filled, as Buffalo committed seven, including five Ferguson interceptions, and Miami lost six. The Dolphins finally broke through early in the third quarter on a Tony Nathan 4-yard pass reception for a touchdown.

Miami held the 7–3 lead late into the fourth quarter. With the game seemingly drifting away and another loss staring them in the face, the Bills began a drive from their 32-yard line with 6:44 remaining. This battle was eerily like so many other Buffalo-Miami games, in which the Bills saw their chances of winning end through a mistake or a controversial officiating call. This time, a key 29-yard pass set the Bills up at the Miami 11-yard line. Two more plays pushed Buffalo to the Miami 4, but a field goal would still have left them behind by a point. On third and goal, Ferguson under heavy pressure lofted a pass to fullback Leaks who gathered it in for a touchdown with 3:42 remaining. The crowd erupted into a frenzy, smelling an end to "The Streak" with the Bills now leading 10–7.

On the ensuing Miami drive, Don Strock replaced Griese, who'd had an unproductive day against the Bills' new 3–4 defensive alignment. Strock fired a pass from the Miami 33 that Bills linebacker Isiah Robertson intercepted at the 50-yard line and returned to the Miami 11. Now the crowd was going crazy. The fans really could anticipate an upset victory over Miami and an end to "The Streak," but there was an uneasiness in the stands.

As each play unfolded, the nervousness and anxiety in the crowd heightened. On third down from the Dolphins 6-yard line, Frank Lewis caught a 5-yard pass and was wrestled to the ground just short of the goal line with 2:05 left. The officials came onto the field to measure for the first down. The crowd gasped as the officials ruled the Bills inches short of the first down. Knox immediately decided to go for fourth down at the Miami 1, clinging to a 3-point lead. He knew that if the Bills could get the first down, and ultimately a touchdown, they would clinch the victory. Knox also figured that if the Bills failed, the Dolphins would start their drive to win or tie the game from the Bills 1 — 99 yards away from victory. Buffalo lined up for the fourth-down play, as nervous tension reverberated throughout the stadium. The ball was snapped, and Ferguson spun and handed the ball to Cribbs, who leaped over the pile of linemen into the end zone for a touchdown.

The Rich Stadium crowd went crazy. Twenty years of frustration were released on that touchdown. The stands were shaking as fans celebrated, screamed, cheered and carried on as they had never done before. As the game clock expired, fans rushed the field as if the team had won the Super Bowl. Both goal posts were torn down. Wilson called it "the biggest win in franchise history." Knox said, "It was a great game by a bunch of guys who weren't going to be denied." Robertson said, "I am happy for the Bills, but

I'm more happy for the fans. These fans have such enthusiasm." The victory helped set the stage for the Bills 11–5 season and an AFC East title.

After the end of "The Streak," the rivalry between Miami and Buffalo continued to be one of the most intense in the NFL through the rest of the 20th century. The Bills somewhat avenged that run of losses by dominating the Dolphins during the Jim Kelly era. From 1987 to 1995, the Bills and Dolphins continually battled for supremacy in the AFC East. The teams played 11 times after Nov. 1 during those years, with the Bills winning every time. These victories included several contests that ultimately decided the AFC East, along with two playoff tilts and an AFC championship game. With all the accolades thrust on Dan Marino throughout his illustrious career, he never beat the Bills in a meaningful game. He was 4–5 in contests during those years played between the two clubs in September and October but was 0–11 in games played after Nov. 1, when the stakes were at their highest.

Despite avenging some of the Curse of the 1970s with the dominance over Marino-led teams, the losing streak of the 1970s was costly to the Buffalo franchise. Bills teams in 1973, '74 and '75 were particularly good and could have been contenders for the Super Bowl … but they never could overcome the Dolphins, who were always in the way. The Curse continued to hang over the franchise, and over Buffalo's professional sports teams. The Miami jinx for the entire decade of the 1970s will forever live in Bills history, and the Dolphins will always be a hated rival for those who remember that era.

Chapter 8
THE SABRES LOSE THE CUP

After several years of trying to gain a National Hockey League franchise, Buffalo finally was awarded a team when brothers Seymour H. Knox III and Northrup Knox, attorney Robert O. Swados and other investors were granted ownership on Dec. 2, 1969. Vancouver was also added to the NHL, making it a 14-team league. The Knox brothers' grandfather, Seymour H. Knox I, made his fortune in five-and-dime stores and combined his 100 stores with Frank and Charles Woolworth's in 1912 to form the F.W. Woolworth Co., one of the most successful five-and-dime businesses in the country, propelling the family to great wealth. The Knox brothers had success in their own right as Seymour Knox III was a vice president at Dominick & Dominick, a diversified financial services institution, and Northrup was chairman of Marine Midland Bank. Swados was a partner in the Cohen and Swados law practice and served as secretary to the NHL's board of governors and as the league's general counsel.

The franchise became the first major league hockey club in Buffalo history. The owners paid $6 million for the right to bring the sport's best players to Western New York. A superstitious person might wonder why Buffalo and Vancouver, either of which could be considered the league's 13th franchise, have not won a Stanley Cup in their 50-plus years in existence?

The Knox brothers went to work immediately. They pursued and signed Toronto Maple Leafs legend George "Punch" Imlach as their general manager and coach on Jan. 16, 1970. Imlach had led the Leafs to four Stanley Cup championships in the 1960s.

In April, the franchise selected the Sabres name, after a wildly popular name-the-team contest with more than 13,000 entries and 1,047 different names. Some of the more creative names included: Mugwumps, Flying

Zeppelins, Border Riders, Eager Beavers and Buzzing Bees. A news release from the team announcing the new nickname said, "A sabre is renowned as a clean, sharp, decisive, and penetrating weapon on offense, as well as a strong parrying weapon on defense." Seymour Knox III said they chose the name because "a Sabre is a weapon carried by a leader and could be used effectively on both offense and defense." The name also was distinct among all the other professional sports teams in Buffalo's history.

The Buffalo ownership group conceded one important condition to receive the franchise: enlarging Memorial Auditorium to a seating capacity of 15,360 from 10,449. The roof was raised 24 feet, adding an $8.7 million upper level that was completed in 1971.

It was agreed as part of the expansion process that Buffalo and Vancouver would receive the top two picks in the 1970 NHL amateur draft. It was also determined that they would each get one of the top two choices in the league's intra-league draft and that there would be a special expansion draft.

The NHL held the player selection meeting on June 9 at the Queen Elizabeth Hotel in Montreal to determine the top picks in each of the three drafts. The first pick in each procedure was decided by games of chance, lending a somewhat surreal sense to the occasion. A table was set up for Buffalo and Vancouver for their array of team personnel, including the general manager, coaches, scouts and executives. Behind the teams were media tables and additional chairs. Every seat was filled by reporters and curious fans. The opening "lottery," which featured a coin flip by NHL President Clarence Campbell, determined which expansion team would have the first crack at players who had been waived by other clubs. The Sabres won the coin flip. That was helpful, because Vancouver owned the rights to 40 players entering the draft while Buffalo had none. (Vancouver had a team in the Western Hockey League the prior season, and those players were under contract to the club.) The result enabled Buffalo to claim goaltender Joe Daley, who had been with the Pittsburgh Penguins, and thus he became the first player on the Sabres roster.

A cheap-looking roulette wheel was brought to the center of the room for what would determine the first choice in the expansion and amateur drafts. The wheel had 13 numbers, with Imlach choosing the high numbers for the Sabres beginning with eight and Vancouver receiving the numbers from one to six. Seven was a neutral number.

Campbell spun the wheel for the first pick in the expansion draft. When the wheel stopped, it was on eight. The Sabres won again. When the expansion draft was conducted the next day, the Sabres with the first pick selected right wing Tom Webster from the Boston Bruins. Interestingly, the Bruins had tried to work out a deal with the Sabres not to take Webster (by giving them left wing Garnet Bailey and other considerations) so that they could deal Webster to Detroit for goalie Roger Crozier. Imlach heard about it, scrapped the tentative transaction with Boston and then shipped Webster to the Red Wings for Crozier. The expansion pool helped fill out the team's roster with the selection of 20 players, most notably Phil Goyette, Gerry Meehan, Don Marshall and Tracy Pratt.

For the all-important amateur draft's first choice and the right to select Gilbert Perreault, the order was determined in the same fashion with a spin of the wheel. Perreault was considered the top pick in the draft and a generational talent who had stardom written all over him. He had led the Montreal Junior Canadiens to back-to-back Memorial Cup championships and was the Ontario Hockey Association Player of the Year in 1969–70 after compiling 122 points with 51 goals and 71 assists. Campbell spun the wheel again. While every Sabres employee and fan held their breath, the wheel stopped on 11. Campbell misread the number as one and declared the Canucks the winners, but Buffalo representatives pointed out the correct number. "Gentlemen, there has been a mistake," Campbell sheepishly announced. Sabres management and fans were jubilant with the victory that featured No. 11 — the same number Perreault wore in junior hockey and would wear throughout his Sabres career. After the three drafts and at the end of a hectic and eventful week in Sabres history, Imlach said, "The Buffalo Sabres will be the first expansion team to win the Stanley Cup." The Sabres were off to an excellent start.

Buffalo opened its inaugural season on the road in Pittsburgh versus the Penguins on Oct. 10, 1970. To almost everyone's surprise, the Sabres stunned the Penguins, winning 2–1, with defenseman Jim Watson scoring the first goal in Sabres history. Perreault netted the game-winner and Crozier backstopped the victory with superb goaltending.

Buffalo hosted its first NHL game at Memorial Auditorium, affectionately referred to as the Aud, on Oct. 15 against the defending Stanley Cup champion Montreal Canadiens. It was an electric atmosphere with an overflow crowd of 10,331, including some fans sitting in temporary folding chairs and others in standing room areas. Singer Joe Byron got the crowd wound up with his rendition of both the Canadian and American national anthems. A tradition began that night with the Sabres having both countries' anthems sung before each game, and it has continued to this day. Seymour Knox III walked to center ice, dropped the ceremonial first puck between the Sabres' Floyd Smith and Montreal's Jean Béliveau, and Buffalo's own NHL team was finally a reality in the Queen City. The Sabres lost 3–0, but the fans were hooked. Since that opening night, their passion for hockey and the Sabres has continued to grow and has been among the league's best until 2021–22 when the consistent losing over the past decade has finally taken its toll.

Another memorable night during the first season was Nov. 18 — the Sabres' first game against the Toronto Maple Leafs. Imlach wanted to win the game badly, having been let go by Maple Leafs owner Stafford Smythe in 1969. After spotting Toronto a 1–0 lead, Buffalo drubbed the Maple Leafs 7–2 in a spanking that would not be forgotten by Leafs players or fans. An intense rivalry was born that night. Buffalo finished its first season with a 24–39–15 record — respectable for an expansion team. Perreault did not disappoint, leading the team with a rookie-record 38 goals and 72 points. At the end of the season, he was awarded the Calder Memorial Trophy, which honors the league's top rookie.

The Sabres' second season did not go as the team had hoped. Their record in year two dipped to 16–43–19, third-worst in the league. However, they were laying the foundation for a team that would eventually get to the play-offs in 1973 and the Stanley Cup Final in 1975.

Buffalo selected left wing Rick Martin in the first round of the 1971 amateur draft while also securing left wing Craig Ramsay and defenseman Bill Hajt. These three players all played major roles for the Sabres throughout the next decade. In addition, Buffalo solidified its roster with two excellent trades. The Sabres acquired right wing René Robert from Pittsburgh in exchange for Eddie Shack and sent goalie Joe Daley to Detroit for forward Don Luce and defenseman Mike Robitaille. The Robert trade filled out a line with Perreault and Martin that Buffalo News reporter Lee Coppola named the French Connection.

The Sabres showed major improvement in 1972–73, with a 37–27–14 record, and qualified for the playoffs for the first time. Joe Crozier had taken over as head coach in 1972 with Imlach retaining his general manager post.

Buffalo added defensemen Jim Schoenfeld and Larry Carriere in the amateur draft and defenseman Tim Horton via trade. The Sabres defense showed marked improvement throughout the season, but the year is mostly remembered for the way the French Connection line came together. They scored 95 goals among them and captured the imagination of the hockey world. They were the Sabres' top three scorers, with Perreault collecting 88 points, Robert 83 and Martin 73.

The Sabres' first playoff series was against the Montreal Canadiens, boasting the league's best regular-season record at 52–10–16. The young Sabres were expected to be an easy opponent for the powerful Canadiens. The bright-eyed Sabres played the first two games of the series in the famed Montreal Forum. Behind a Ramsay goal, Buffalo led into the second period when Canadiens center Jacques Lemaire scored to tie the game. Montreal's Yvan Cournoyer scored a power-play goal in the third period to give the Canadiens a hard-fought 2–1 victory over Buffalo. In the second game, the Sabres jumped to a surprising 2–0 first-period lead behind goals by Perreault and Martin. However, the Canadiens completely overwhelmed Buffalo in the second and third periods, scoring five consecutive goals on the way to a 7–3 victory.

The Sabres came home to a raucous crowd for the first-ever NHL playoff game at Memorial Auditorium. Buffalo fans went home disappointed as the Canadiens scored two goals 16 seconds apart in the second period to break open a 1–1 game and went on to take a 5–2 victory and a 3–0 series lead. Perreault led the Sabres' onslaught with two goals in their 5–1 domination of the Canadiens in Game 4, and Buffalo peppered Montreal goalie Ken Dryden with 50 shots on goal en route to the team's first playoff victory.

Game 5 back at the Montreal Forum was expected to be easy for the Canadiens as the Sabres had yet to win a game in the Forum in the team's three-year history. Buffalo played a solid game, getting goals from Martin and Robert and outstanding goaltending from Crozier, but the score was tied at 2 at the end of regulation. The Sabres shocked the Canadiens as Robert scored the game-winning goal with 9:18 gone in overtime, sending the series back to Buffalo. It was the moment when the Sabres showed they could play with anyone in the league, at least for a game.

Still, the Canadiens were the best team in the NHL in 1973, and they showed the Sabres their proficiency in Game 6, scoring four goals in the first period on the way to a series-clinching 4–2 victory. Buffalo fans displayed their appreciation to their team by chanting "Thank You, Sabres" as the final seconds ticked down at the end of the game. Coach Joe Crozier said in the postgame locker room, "It was the most unbelievable feeling I've ever had. You can't find better fans than the ones in Buffalo." Despite the Sabres' loss in the series, they had acquitted themselves well. The Canadiens went on to win the Stanley Cup, defeating the Chicago Black Hawks, four games to two, in the finals.

Buffalo took a step back in 1973–74, finishing the season with a 32–34–12 record, and was out of the playoffs. However, Imlach made two key acquisitions, obtaining defenseman Jerry Korab and left winger Brian Spencer in separate deals. Korab helped to further solidify the defense, especially after the horrific loss of Horton who was killed in a car crash. Spencer brought a toughness that the team sorely lacked.

The highlight of the season was Martin's pursuit of 50 goals. Going into the final game of the season he needed one goal for 50. He electrified the home crowd, scoring a hat trick against the St. Louis Blues with Nos. 50, 51 and 52. Martin became the 10th player in NHL history to score 50 goals in a single season, and he set an NHL record with 133 goals in his first three seasons in the league.

Before the start of the 1974–75 season, Imlach replaced Joe Crozier as head coach with Floyd Smith. The Sabres added right wing Danny Gare in the second round of the amateur draft. Buffalo started the season slowly at 3–3–1. However, the Sabres emerged as a dominant team, going unbeaten in 10 consecutive games, losing one and then reeling off an 11-game unbeaten streak for a stellar 21–4–4 record after 29 games. The Sabres continued their strong play despite having to play rookie goalie Gary Bromley for most of the games because of Crozier's health issues. Late in the season, Imlach acquired goaltender Gerry Desjardins from the New York Islanders solidifying the position.

Buffalo won its first of three Adams Division titles on March 23, 1975, with a 9–4 victory over the California Golden Seals. The Adams Division was formed in 1974 as part of the Prince of Wales Conference and existed until 1993. It was the forerunner of the Northeast Division, which became the Atlantic Division. The Sabres finished the regular season with a 49–16–15 record, tying Montreal and Philadelphia with 113 points for the most in the league. Robert was the first Sabre to score 100 points, garnering 40 goals and

60 assists. He was followed closely by his linemates with Perreault scoring 96 points and Martin 95.

The Sabres played Chicago in the 1974–75 quarterfinals of the NHL playoffs, seeking their first playoff series victory. Buffalo won Game 1, 4–1, behind key contributions from three former Black Hawks. The Sabres jumped to a 3–0 first-period lead highlighted by an early goal from Gare and punctuated by the third goal from former Black Hawk Fred Stanfield. Desjardins, who played parts of three seasons in Chicago, made 18 saves in backstopping the victory, with excellent defensive play from Korab, the third ex-Chicago player.

Desjardins was outstanding in Game 2 with 27 saves while allowing only a single goal to Stan Mikita in the second period. The Sabres responded to Mikita's goal with three goals, first from Gare and two from Rick Dudley, giving the Sabres a 3–1 lead. Buffalo hung on in the third period behind Desjardins, winning the game 3–1 to take a 2–0 series lead.

The Sabres lost a highly entertaining third game in Chicago on a Mikita goal 2:31 into overtime, 5–4. Game 4 in Chicago was a hard-fought, tight-checking game through the first two periods with the contest deadlocked at one goal each. The Sabres blew the game open in the third period. Jim Lorentz scored 17 seconds in, followed by goals from each member of the French Connection. The Sabres eventually netted five goals in the third period, turning the close game into a 6–2 rout and a commanding 3–1 series lead.

Buffalo came home to Memorial Auditorium for Game 5 and did not disappoint the home crowd, skating to a 3–1 series-clinching victory. Robert scored the go-ahead goal 1:16 into the third period, giving the Sabres a 2–1 lead. Lorentz sealed the game and the series by scoring his second playoff goal with 4:06 remaining.

The Sabres moved on to face the powerful Canadiens in the semifinals. Montreal was led by 53-goal scorer Guy Lafleur, center Peter Mahovlich, center Lemaire, right winger Cournoyer and goalie Dryden. Montreal had won four Stanley Cup titles in the previous seven seasons.

The young Sabres were confident they could play against and beat Montreal, despite their loss to them in the playoffs two years before. The two teams had the same regular-season point total, with Buffalo awarded home-ice advantage in the series because the Sabres had 49 regular-season wins against Montreal's 47.

Buffalo battled the Canadiens in Game 1 and led 5–4 in the final minute. However, Montreal kept the puck in the Sabres' end, putting pressure on Crozier. Late in the game with the clock ticking down, Lemaire fired the puck from behind the net and it struck Gare's stick, ricocheting into the net above Crozier's shoulder for the game-tying goal with only 24 seconds remaining. The game went to overtime and Gare made up for his earlier mistake, taking a cross-ice pass from Craig Ramsay and firing a 15-foot slap shot past Dryden for the game-winner 4:42 into the extra period. The Sabres also won Game 2, 4–2, thanks to their checking line. (The trio of Luce, Ramsay and Gare was a combined plus-151 during the regular season, an amazing number.) The French Connection was shut out, but Luce, Ramsay and Gare each scored a goal to spur the victory.

Buffalo went to the Montreal Forum for Games 3 and 4 and was routed 7–0 and 8–2, respectively. The Sabres came home desperately needing a victory and started strong, outshooting Montreal 21–5 in the first period, but only led 3–2. The Canadiens scored a goal in the second period and another early in the third to take a 4–3 lead, but Ramsay netted a goal for the Sabres on the power play with 6:18 left in the game, ultimately sending the game to overtime.

In the extra session, Robert beat Dryden with a 40-foot slap shot with 5:25 gone, following a faceoff win by Perreault. Robert said to the media after the game, "If we had lost this game, it would have been very tough for us to win in Montreal." The Sabres outshot the Canadiens 45–19.

Then came the best moment in the five-year history of the team. Buffalo defeated the Canadiens 4–3 in the Montreal Forum on May 9, sending the Sabres to their first-ever Stanley Cup Final. Ramsay scored a short-handed goal 2:05 into the game, Martin scored at 8:51 and Peter McNab followed at 17:53 of the first period, staking the Sabres to a 3–1 lead. Lorentz made it 4–1 for Buffalo entering the third period.

The Sabres and goalie Desjardins held off a spirited rally by Montreal as the Canadiens scored twice to cut the Sabres' lead to 4–3, but they could not score the equalizer. More than 5,000 Sabres fans greeted the team at the Niagara Falls airport at 2 a.m., welcoming them home. Sabres defenseman Carriere said several years later, "I get goose bumps thinking about it now. It was one of the most inspiring things I've ever been a part of." Robitaille, a Sabres defenseman and later a television broadcaster for the team, said, "I would have to think that the most amazing thing I've seen in the game of hockey is how Punch Imlach took a team from scratch and in five years had them in the finals. It was one of the most astonishing things I've ever seen." More than 40 years later, the members of the Sabres still talk about what a wonderful night — and early morning — that was.

The defending Stanley Cup champion Philadelphia Flyers, also known as the Broad Street Bullies, were the Sabres' opponent in the Stanley Cup Final. The Flyers' reputation was one of toughness, nastiness and intimidation. Opposing players always knew that a trip to Philadelphia would be a long night — and the Flyers had the home-ice advantage for the series. Philadelphia's approach was matched with highly skilled players and the league's best goalie. It was a daunting challenge for the maturing Sabres squad.

Flyers goalie Bernie Parent was dominant in Game 1. Despite the Sabres outshooting the Flyers 22–8 in the first two periods, the game was scoreless entering the third stanza. Philadelphia displayed its skill in scoring four goals in the third period to pull away for a 4–1 victory.

In Game 2, a repeat of Parent's terrific goaltending and a very tight-checking game by the Flyers were too much for the Sabres to overcome. Buffalo trailed 1–0 early in the third period but got the equalizing goal from Korab at 2:18. However, that was the Sabres' final shot on goal of the night. Flyers superstar Bobby Clarke scored the go-ahead goal at 6:43, and from that point on the Flyers clamped down, winning the game 2–1. Buffalo still had yet to win at the Spectrum in Philadelphia or beat Parent.

Game 3 was one of the strangest in Sabres history. It has become known as the Fog Game. Buffalonians were basking in a beautiful spring day with 80-degree temperatures. However, without air conditioning, the sweltering conditions inside the Aud produced fog coming from the ice. The game was halted several times to try to dissipate the fog. Despite the conditions, the contest was very entertaining from start to finish.

Buffalo repeatedly battled back from deficits throughout the game. The Flyers led 2–0 when one of the strangest things ever at a Sabres game occurred. During the early part of the game, a bat had been flying above the ice and would periodically swoop down. After a normal stoppage of play, Lorentz was preparing to take a faceoff when he noticed the bat flying down toward the ice. He swung his stick and made contact, killing the bat instantly. It is the only known animal killed during an NHL game.

Photo 13. Buffalo Sabres star Jim Schoenfeld (6) attempts to score on Flyers goalie Bernie Parent during Game 3 of the 1975 Stanley Cup Final at Memorial Auditorium in Buffalo.

(Getty Images, Bruce Bennett Studios)

Shortly after the bat incident, the Sabres were given new life as Gare and Martin scored goals 17 seconds apart, tying the game at 2. However, Rick MacLeish scored for the Flyers a little more than two minutes later, giving them the 3–2 lead after the first period. Luce scored 29 seconds into the second period, but Reggie Leach took the lead back for the Flyers with a goal at 14:30. Rookie defenseman Hajt scored his first career playoff goal, pouncing on a rebound of a Martin shot, squeezing it past Parent and tying the game at 9:56 of the third period. Regulation time ended with the score knotted 4–4. The stifling heat and foggy conditions continued to have an impact on the game, but the teams played on.

Both squads had chances to end the game in overtime. However, the Sabres cashed in as Robert took a carom off the boards to the left of Parent and fired a 20-foot shot through the fog and into the net to win the game at 18:29. Between the overtime and the conditions, it became one of the most memorable goals in Sabres' history. Korab said afterward, "It was like playing in a graveyard." Parent said, "It got so bad that I couldn't see the puck when it was 10 feet inside the blue line." Maybe the Sabres found the way to beat Parent was not to let him see the puck by flooding the arena with fog. The result ended Buffalo's 15-game winless streak against the Flyers.

Trailing the series two games to one, the Sabres put together their best game, beating the Flyers 4–2. Buffalo spotted the Flyers a 1–0 lead, but the Sabres exploded for three goals against Parent as Korab, Perreault and Lorentz all scored second-period goals to give Buffalo a 3–2 lead. The Sabres tightly checked the Flyers in the third period until Gare scored into an empty net with 32 seconds remaining, clinching the game for Buffalo and evening the series at two wins apiece.

Philadelphia returned home to the friendly confines of the Spectrum and jumped on the Sabres in the first period. The Flyers scored three goals before the Sabres knew what hit them. From there, the Flyers left the game in Parent's hands, and he was up to the task, shutting down the Sabres while only allowing a late goal to Luce in the 5–1 victory.

For Game 6, the Sabres were happy to be back at the Aud. Smith decided to switch goalies and went with Crozier. The veteran matched Parent save for save throughout the first two periods and the game was tied at zero through 40 minutes.

Flyers left winger Bob Kelly scored the game's first goal 11 seconds into the third period. Parent was as brilliant as ever, making several terrific saves to keep the Sabres off the scoreboard. Bill Clement ended the Sabres' Cup hopes, scoring a goal with only 2:47 left. Parent finished the series in style with a shutout. Following the game, he was voted the playoffs' most outstanding player, receiving the Conn Smythe Trophy. He was clearly the difference in the series.

Lorentz said about Parent, "He was just on another planet." Robert added that Parent was probably the best goalie he had ever played against. The Flyers star was incredible in his four wins, allowing only three goals in 240 minutes while making 100 saves — several of them of the stand-on-your-head variety. Though the Sabres lost, they knew they had been defeated by an outstanding team, and they expected to be back in the Stanley Cup Final again soon. The future of the team appeared incredibly bright with an out-standing nucleus of players.

Surprisingly, that group never reached another Stanley Cup Final. The Curse enters the conversation concerning the fact that the Sabres ran into two of the greatest dynasties in NHL history. The Canadiens, with much the same team that Buffalo defeated in 1975, won the next four consecutive Stanley Cup titles from 1976 through 1979. They were followed by the New York Islanders, also winners of four consecutive titles, from 1980 through 1983.

The Sabres finished the 1975–76 regular season with 105 points and placed second in the Adams Division to the Boston Bruins. They won their first-round playoff series, defeating the St. Louis Blues two games to one in a short three-game series. However, Buffalo was fortunate to win the series as both victories came in overtime. Next up were the Islanders, and the Sabres won the first two games of the series. Buffalo dominated Game 1 in a 5–3 win, behind the French Connection with two goals by Robert and one each by Martin and Perreault. The Sabres won Game 2 in overtime on Gare's game-winner. Buffalo led the series two games to none but lost the next two in Nassau Coliseum. The Sabres still had plenty of confidence, as the team was accustomed to playoff success by this point and figured it would continue.

This is where the Buffalo Sports Curse, or at least The Curse of Bert Marshall, comes into play. In Game 5, the teams were tied 3–3 as the final seconds of regulation time wound down. Marshall, a defenseman who had scored only three playoff goals in his career, took a harmless shot from the blue line with 17 seconds left. It shockingly went in. The Islanders won that game 4–3 and captured Game 6 and the series with a 3–2 triumph as Clark Gilles scored the game-winner with 14 minutes left. It took until 1980 for the Sabres to regain any postseason confidence.

Buffalo had another solid regular season in 1976–77 with 104 points, finishing only 2 points behind the Bruins in the Adams Division. The playoffs were almost a repeat of 1976. The Sabres defeated Minnesota in the short three-game series, two games to none. Their second-round series foe was the Islanders again, and this time New York swept Buffalo out of the playoffs. It was a very disappointing end to the Sabres' season. The pattern continued in 1977–78: second place in the division, win the first round (against the New York Rangers), lose the second (to Philadelphia).

The Sabres took a further step back in 1978–79. It was a tumultuous season that saw the team fire Imlach as general manager and Marcel Pronovost as coach. Buffalo recovered from a terrible start and seemed to be playing good hockey as the playoffs approached. However, they lost their first-round series to the Penguins. In the decisive third game, played in Memorial Auditorium, the Sabres lost on a goal by Pittsburgh's George Ferguson only 47 seconds into overtime. Buffalo players took the loss hard, as several players were in tears in the locker room after the game.

It was the end of the era of the French Connection. Before the start of the 1979–80 season, Robert was traded to Colorado, and the trio would never play another game together. It had been an amazing run for all concerned. Perreault is still considered by many to be the greatest player in Sabres history, and Martin and Robert are not far behind. Even without Robert, the Sabres ended the 1979–80 season with a 47–17–16 record (110 points) and finished first in the Adams Division, but lost to the Islanders in the playoffs. Many fans consider the 1970s the golden era of Sabres hockey.

The Buffalo Sports Curse refused to allow the Sabres to get that elusive Stanley Cup during this golden era, and it would be a long 24 years before the team would return to the Final.

Legendary coach Scotty Bowman was introduced to the fray in 1979. Bowman never had a losing season in his 30 years as head coach, won nine Stanley Cups and holds the NHL record for all-time coaching wins with 1,244. But, even Bowman, who had led the Canadiens to their four consecutive Stanley Cup victories just before making the move to the Sabres, was not immune to the Curse and could not manage to bring the Cup to Buffalo.

Coincidentally, the next team he coached, the Pittsburgh Penguins, won the Stanley Cup the first season he was there, 1991–92.

So here's a guy who OWNS the Cup four straight years, comes to Buffalo and can't make it happen, then goes to the Flightless Waterfowl and wins the Cup again. Go figure! From the summer of 1980 to the spring of 1996, Buffalo won exactly one seven-game playoff series: a stunning 1993 sweep of the Bruins. It was a long stretch of very mediocre hockey — never good enough to truly contend and yet rarely bad enough to secure top talent in the draft. A cursed franchise, maybe; an underachieving one, without a doubt.

Chapter 9
THE SHORT BUT SWEET TALE
OF THE BRAVES

While Buffalo had actively sought an NHL team for several years, the city's pursuit of an NBA team was a much shorter effort — but was successful nonetheless. Shortly after Buffalo landed a hockey franchise, the Buffalo Braves were born. On Jan. 20, 1970, the NBA awarded an expansion team to Buffalo, along with Cleveland, Portland and Houston (the latter eventually dropping out). The franchise was awarded to Neuberger-Loeb, a New York investment firm; a syndicate of investors, headed by Philip Ryan and Peter Crotty, paid a $3.7 million fee to the NBA for the Buffalo franchise.

The team called Memorial Auditorium its home arena. Former New York Knicks and St. Bonaventure head coach Eddie Donovan and former Syracuse Nats star Dolph Schayes were hired as Buffalo's general manager and head coach, respectively. In the spring of 1970, the franchise was nicknamed the Braves after a contest attracted 14,138 entrants with more than 1,000 names suggested. The team's original colors were blue, red and gold.

It soon became apparent that the newly formed syndicate did not have the deep pockets needed to run an NBA team. As the Braves' initial season drew closer, the league was desperate to find an owner for the franchise. Paul Snyder was fresh off selling Freezer Queen, a pioneering company in the frozen food industry with the introduction of the TV dinner that at its peak employed more than 1,000 people in Buffalo. He was approached by the NBA and asked to purchase the club. After Snyder and his son attended a preseason game in Niagara Falls that ended with an exciting 1-point victory by the Braves, Snyder agreed to buy the team.

The Braves opened their inaugural season on Oct. 14, 1970 with a stirring 107–92 win over the equally new Cleveland Cavaliers in front of 7,129 at Memorial Auditorium. Don May led all scorers with 24 points, and Dick Garrett scored the first basket in Braves history.

Led by little-known players like May, Garrett, Emmette Bryant, Mike Davis, John Hummer and Bob Kauffman, the Braves struggled throughout their first season and finished 22–60. Buffalo's performance was good for a seventh-place finish in the Eastern Conference, only ahead of the Cavaliers. With mostly the same cast of players, along with draft choices Elmore Smith, Fred Hilton and Randy Smith, the Braves finished an identical 22–60 the following season.

Snyder was being pressured by the NBA to secure weekend dates for the Braves to play home games at the Aud. The Sabres owned Sunday nights (as well as Thursdays), and Canisius College basketball had the rights to Saturdays for its home games. The Braves could only secure Tuesday and Friday nights for games, with Fridays competing with local high school games. Snyder believed that affected the Braves' ability to draw good crowds.

Snyder tried negotiating with Canisius College President James M. Demske, S.J., to secure Saturday game dates, but the two parties were unable to find a compromise. Demske was protecting Little Three basketball (Canisius, Niagara and St. Bonaventure) and thought if he gave up Saturdays to the Braves, it would destroy college basketball in Western New York. In retrospect, it seems that the two should have been able to find a compromise, especially considering that the college basketball season was much shorter than the NBA's. Also, it is surprising that Snyder did not pursue scheduling more afternoon games on the weekends; they took place in other cities and may have proven popular under the circumstances. In the end, the cruel irony is that the birth of college basketball's Big East Conference in 1979 without the inclusion of the Little Three colleges meant the sport began losing relevance in Western New York — a situation that has continued to this day. Canisius eventually stopped playing almost all home games at the Aud. But Buffalo had already lost its NBA team by then.

After the dismal results of the first two seasons, Snyder hired Jack Ramsay, the former Philadelphia 76ers coach, to become the Braves' new head coach to start the 1972–73 season. Though the team's record was 21–61 in Ramsay's first season, he and Donovan began to put the pieces in place to make Buffalo a playoff team in future years.

The Braves drafted and signed Bob McAdoo, who joined Kauffman and Elmore Smith up front, and significantly increased the playing time of Randy Smith. McAdoo led North Carolina to the Final Four in his junior year, averaging 19.5 points and 10.1 rebounds per game. After his junior season, he was granted hardship status for the NBA draft and skipped his senior year. The Braves selected him with the second overall pick in the 1972 NBA draft. It was a team with some interesting pieces, but they didn't quite fit together.

Before the start of the 1973–74 season, the construction job continued as the Braves drafted guard Ernie DiGregorio from Providence College with the team's first pick. They also acquired power forward Garfield Heard and center Kevin Kunnert from the Chicago Bulls and swapped Elmore Smith for small forward Jim McMillian from the Los Angeles Lakers.

The Braves also changed their team colors, featuring a light blue, orange and black. The new-look franchise showed immediate improvement on the court as they flirted with a .500 record throughout the season. In early February, Ramsay pulled one more good-sized trade, acquiring veteran forward Jack Marin and guard Matt Guokas from the Houston Rockets, solidifying the team's depth and experience.

Buffalo came together as a team during the season, improving from 15–21 on Dec. 26 to finish with a 42–40 record. That was good for third place in the Atlantic Division and a playoff spot. McAdoo — somewhat miscast as a small forward the season before — became a dominant player as he utilized his athleticism like few before him. At 6 feet, 9 inches tall, he played as a big man, but he also could move to the perimeter and shoot like a guard. He led the league in scoring, averaging 30.6 points per game with a .547 shooting percentage — a matchup nightmare for every team. DiGregorio led the league in assists (8.2 per game) and in free-throw percentage (.902). The Braves led the NBA in scoring at 111.6 points per game. They were a very entertaining team and saw a big increase in announced attendance, drawing 427,270 for their 41 home games to rank fourth in the league. In addition to drawing well in Buffalo, the Braves played several home games in Toronto during the regular season, trying to expand their fan base into Canada.

Buffalo was an exciting young team that nobody wanted to meet in the playoffs. The Braves drew the top seed in the East, the Boston Celtics (56–26), for the first round. The Celtics were led by top players John Havlicek, Jo Jo White and Dave Cowens. But the upstart Braves had beaten Boston in the

Photo 14. Buffalo Braves forward Bob McAdoo (11)
shoots around Paul Silas (35) of the Boston Celtics
in Buffalo's 98–93 playoff victory on April 26, 1976,
at Buffalo's Memorial Auditorium.
(Photo by Robert L. Smith, Orchard Park, New York)

final two meetings of the regular season, and they were confident they could compete with the Celtics and possibly pull off the upset.

The Braves played very well in their first playoff game at Boston Garden. Buffalo held a 17-point lead midway through the third quarter and still led 81–69 entering the final period. But the Celtics exploded in the fourth quarter, as Cowens poured in 20 points, leading Boston to a 107–97 victory. It was a missed opportunity for the young Braves, since they didn't expect to have many good chances to win on the road.

Buffalo bounced back in Game 2 at Memorial Auditorium in front of 17,507. McAdoo led the way with 17 second-half points in his 23-point, 20-rebound performance, helping the Braves to a 115–105 victory. The Braves lost Game 3 back in Boston, 120–107, despite 38 points from McAdoo.

Game 4 was an absolute classic — a physical, tightly contested game that was close throughout. McAdoo was unstoppable, firing up 40 shots and scoring 44 points. A record-breaking crowd of 18,119 at the Aud witnessed an exciting finish. Havlicek fired in a bank shot with nine seconds remaining, tying the game at 102. After a Braves timeout, DiGregorio hurriedly dribbled the ball up the court and fired a pass to McAdoo. McAdoo quickly took a shot, but it bounced off the rim. With perfect timing, Braves forward McMillian tapped the rebound into the basket just before the buzzer sounded. The Buffalo crowd erupted in joy as the Braves won the game 104–102, tying the series at two games apiece.

The Braves had a great chance to put a dagger in the heart of the Celtics, leading Game 5 93–89 with 3:13 remaining. However, McAdoo had his worst shooting game of the series (5 for 20), and the Celtics defense clamped down on the versatile superstar. Boston outscored the Braves 11–4 in the final three minutes, defeating Buffalo 100–97. McAdoo had a chance to tie the game with 28 seconds remaining but missed a corner jump shot, and the Celtics rebounded the miss, effectively closing out the game. The Braves had excellent chances to win two of the three games in Boston but could not execute in the final minutes to pull out a victory. A win in either game would have put the Braves in the driver's seat for a major upset in the series.

Game 6 was back at Memorial Auditorium in front of another sellout crowd that witnessed one of the best games in Braves history. McAdoo poured in 40 points, with Heard and DiGregorio each pitching in 20. Buffalo trailed 97–88 late in the fourth quarter but went on a spirited rally to cut the deficit to 104–100. Marin then stole the Celtics' inbounds pass and fed

McAdoo for a dunk, cutting the lead to two. Then McAdoo stole another Boston pass and his layup tied the score at 104 with only seven seconds remaining. After a time out, the Celtics took the ball out at half court. White inbounded the ball to Havlicek, and his attempted shot was blocked by McAdoo. White picked up the errant rebound and wildly fired an off-target shot toward the basket as the buzzer sounded. This outstanding game was headed to overtime.

Not so fast. Referee Darell Garretson called a foul on McAdoo for bumping White on the shot. Braves coach Ramsay was incensed at the call. He argued that there was absolutely no foul on the play, and if there was, then at least one second should be put back on the clock. Garretson disagreed with both points and gave White the foul shots with no time left. White made two of the three free throws, clinching the victory and the series for the Celtics. The Braves' season was suddenly over.

Bob Matthews of the Democrat and Chronicle reported, that after the game, Ramsay said, "It's a lousy way to end a playoff series. It was a borderline call, and they didn't even know how much time, if any, was left. They wouldn't even check with the timer. They just walked off the court in that pompous, official way of theirs." Braves owner Snyder went to the officials' dressing room after the game and challenged head official Mendy Rudolph's view that there was no time left when the foul was called. Rudolph stuck to his opinion and slammed the door in Snyder's face.

It was a terrible way for this extremely competitive series to end, especially when it was becoming apparent the Braves were every bit as good as the Celtics. The Braves were haunted — and probably felt a bit cursed — by the two games they led late in Boston and let slip away. And this game felt like it had been stolen from them. Buffalo filed a protest with the league the next day, as video replay clearly showed there was one second left on the clock, and thus the Braves should have had one more chance. The NBA quickly denied the protest, and the Braves' season was officially over. It was a huge missed opportunity for Buffalo. The Celtics went on to win the NBA championship, defeating the Milwaukee Bucks four games to three, while the Braves went home wondering what might have been.

The Braves returned pretty much intact for the 1974–75 NBA season with the addition of guard Bob Weiss. From the outset, the Braves were contenders as they displayed on opening night in the Boston Garden. Buffalo defeated the defending league champion Celtics 126–119 as DiGregorio played one of his best games as a pro with 33 points, nine assists and five steals. Buffalo started the season 4–1 and soon had the best record in the NBA after compiling an 11-game win streak. DiGregorio suffered a serious knee injury in a game at Golden State in the middle of that streak in late October. The injury cost him 51 games and when he returned late in the season, he was not the same.

Despite the loss of DiGregorio, the Braves posted the finest record in team history, going 49–33 while finishing with the third-best record in the league. McAdoo again led the NBA in scoring, averaging 34.5 points per game while also pulling down 14 rebounds per game. He was the league's most outstanding player. Randy Smith, a former Buffalo State star, blossomed with DiGregorio out, becoming the team's second-leading scorer, averaging 17.8 points per game and leading the club in assists with 6.5 per contest.

The Eastern Conference had the three best teams in the NBA by record during the regular season. It meant the third-place Braves had to play the second-best Washington Bullets (60–22) in the first round. The Bullets were a solid club led by forward Elvin Hayes, center Wes Unseld and guard Phil Chenier.

The series opened in Washington, and McAdoo poured in 35 points leading the Braves' upset over the favored Bullets 113–102. Heard and Smith each chipped in with 24 points in the Braves' surprising victory. Buffalo's fast break overwhelmed the Bullets. Ramsay said afterward that the Braves were "the best team I ever coached, and the one with the best chance of going all the way." However, Washington returned the favor two nights later, taking back home-court advantage by defeating the Braves 120–106 in Buffalo. The Bullets were led by Hayes' 34 points and Chenier's 23, more than offsetting McAdoo's 36 points.

The teams split Games 3 and 4, each winning on its home court. Washington took a 111–96 decision but Buffalo answered with a 108–102 win. In Game 4, McAdoo poured in 50 points, displaying a tremendous array of offensive prowess. Before the game, he was presented the NBA MVP award. As teammate Ken Charles said after the game, "If he isn't the best there is, let me find the guy that's better, and let me pinch him to see if he's human. When Mr. McAdoo wants to get hot, nobody's going to stop him."

Game 5 was back in Washington. If the Braves could win, they could clinch the series back in Memorial Auditorium. In a defensive tussle. Buffalo trailed Washington 94–89 in the final minute, but Braves forward McMillian

Photo 15. Buffalo Braves guard Ernie DiGregorio scores on a
layup in a playoff victory over the Boston Celtics on
April 26, 1976, at Buffalo's Memorial Auditorium.
(Photo by Robert L. Smith, Orchard Park, New York)

drove to the basket on back-to-back possessions, scoring buckets on each and cutting the Bullets' lead to 94–93 with 18 seconds remaining. However, Washington center Unseld snared an offensive rebound off a Hayes missed shot and converted the follow, clinching the game for the Bullets. They won, 97–93. Hayes played a terrific game, nearly matching McAdoo's output from the previous game by pouring in 46 points.

Game 6 in Buffalo was the best of the series as both teams battled back and forth, but the Braves would not be denied. McAdoo scored 37 points and was helped by teammates McMillian, who pitched in with 20 points, and Smith, who had 16. With the score knotted at 87 in the fourth quarter, McAdoo scored 9 of the Braves' next 11 points as Buffalo pulled away, taking a 98–90 lead on their way to the 102–96 victory to force a deciding Game 7.

Game 7 was anticlimactic as the Bullets jumped to a 29–13 first-quarter lead, were in command 57–38 at halftime and coasted home with a 115–96 victory. The Braves were eliminated for the second consecutive season in their first series. "Things look particularly good for this team for the future. Tonight, we just played one of the worst games we played all year," Ramsay said.

The Braves again showed they had the ability to play with the best teams in the NBA but could not win a close game that would have turned the series in their favor. The Bullets reached the NBA Finals, losing to Golden State.

Led again by the incomparable McAdoo, the Braves were back in the NBA playoffs in 1976. Buffalo added 6-foot-11 Tom McMillen and 6-foot-9 John Shumate to its already strong team. Buffalo finished the regular season in second place in the Atlantic Division behind the Celtics with a 46–36 record. McAdoo led the league in scoring for the third consecutive season, averaging 31.1 points per game. Smith had another solid season, averaging 21.8 points per game and leading the team in assists. The Braves qualified as the fifth seed; a new playoff format matched them against No. 4 Philadelphia in the first round in a best-of-three series.

The matchup opened in Philadelphia on April 15. Buffalo played a complete game, with McAdoo leading the team with 37 points and 21 rebounds in its 95–89 victory. Jim McMillian contributed 23 points and Shumate added 16 along with stellar defense on 76ers star George McGinnis, holding him to 20 points. The Braves came home to host Game 2 and played the worst playoff game in their brief history, getting blown out by the 76ers 131–106.

If Buffalo were to win its first playoff series, it would have to win the deciding game at the Spectrum in Philadelphia. The 76ers started Game 3 strong and led 72–59 in the third quarter. But the Braves battled back, pulling within 2 points at 89–87 entering the final period. The fourth quarter was back and forth. Shumate, who had suffered a concussion in Game 2 and was not considered likely to play in Game 3, suited up and played a pivotal role down the stretch for the Braves.

In the waning seconds of regulation time, the Braves trailed 111–109 and Buffalo put the ball in McAdoo's hands. He drove the lane, missed a tough shot but was fouled by the 76ers with only one tick left. McAdoo calmly sank both free throws, even with the Spectrum crowd's shouting literally shaking the basket, in the most pressure-packed moment in franchise history. That sent it to overtime.

The lead traded hands in the extra session until Shumate scored two critical baskets for the Braves, giving them the lead in the final seconds. Then, Charles was fouled and sank both free throws, clinching the 124–123 victory for Buffalo. Shumate scored 23 points on 10 of 12 shooting, grabbed 10 rebounds and helped 76ers star McGinnis foul out midway through the fourth quarter. McAdoo pitched in his normal dominating game with 34 points and 22 rebounds as the Braves won their first playoff series.

A rematch with the Celtics in the conference semifinals awaited the Braves, who were eager to avenge the heartbreaking series loss from two years earlier.

With the new playoff format, the first two games of the best-of-seven series would be played in Boston and the next two in Buffalo. Boston took advantage of the Braves' fatigue in the first contest, as the Celtics received a bye into this round. Boston won Game 1 107–98, as Cowens scored 30 points. The Braves played tougher in Game 2 but still fell short. Buffalo cut the Celtics' lead to only 3 points late in the game, but Don Nelson sank multiple free throws to keep the Braves at bay in Boston's 101–96 victory and a 2–0 series lead.

DiGregorio sparked the Braves in Game 3, coming off the bench to lead the fast break attack. Smith powered the Braves with 29 points and McAdoo chipped in with 24 as Buffalo defeated the Celtics 98–93. The Braves evened the series with a spine-tingling 124–122 victory at the Aud. Smith sank a 22-foot jump shot over White with three seconds left, winning the game for the Braves. Smith (29 points) and White (28) had battled each other throughout the contest, but Smith earned the last laugh. McAdoo contributed 30 points to the winning effort but fouled out with 1:11 to play, so Smith stepped up and delivered.

The Braves could still not find a way to win in Boston, with the Celtics playing solid in winning Game 5, 99–88. DiGregorio moved into the starting lineup for that game, as Ramsay hoped he could continue to supply a spark to the Buffalo offense. Game 6 was a must-win for the Braves if they wanted to force a decisive final contest in the best-of-seven series. Buffalo battled Boston throughout, but Charlie Scott of the Celtics played a terrific game, scoring 31 points along with eight assists and two steals. However, despite Scott's heroics, the Braves still had a chance late when Smith sank a jumper with 40 seconds left, cutting the Celtics' lead to 104–100. Buffalo regained possession soon after that. Smith took the ensuing inbounds pass and drove to the basket to score on a nifty reverse layup, cutting the Boston lead to only 2.

But wait … there was another whistle. Official Darell Garretson, whose name was still familiar to Braves fans from the 1974 playoffs, made another controversial call. He ruled that Smith was out of bounds when he initially caught the ball on the inbounds pass. Basket nullified, game over, season over for the Braves. It was another difficult and disappointing end to an intense series with the Celtics. Buffalo twice had played toe-to-toe with Boston in a playoff series only to fall painfully short each time.

After the season, the downward spiral of the Braves and the dismantling of the franchise began. Snyder was still unable to find a compromise to secure weekend game dates as the pressure from the NBA intensified. Ramsay and Snyder, who had some conflict during the season, realized that the relationship had run its course and Ramsay was let go the day after the Braves' loss to the Celtics. He went on to coach in Portland, where the Trail Blazers won the NBA championship in 1977.

Tates Locke, an excellent college coach but with only one year of professional experience, was hired to replace Ramsay. It was a tumultuous offseason in Buffalo beyond the coaching change. In June, Snyder threatened to move the club to Florida if he could not sell 5,000 season tickets. He set an initial deadline, but Buffalo fans responded by purchasing tickets, and Snyder extended the time.

While the ticket drive was happening, the City of Buffalo successfully obtained a restraining order against the proposed move of the team. NBA commissioner Larry O'Brien delayed any action on Snyder's request, once notified of the order.

In the meantime, the American Basketball Association had been absorbed into the NBA. Snyder had discussions with John Y. Brown, owner of the ABA Kentucky Colonels. Rather than paying his way into the NBA with his ABA franchise, Brown worked a deal with Snyder to become part owner of the Braves. As soon as the deal was consummated, it was clear Brown was going to play an active and dominant role in the day-to-day running of the Braves.

Buffalo selected Notre Dame star Adrian Dantley, a Brown favorite, in the 1976 NBA draft. Brown then spearheaded the sale of Jim McMillian to the Knicks for $500,000, opening up a starting job for Dantley. In addition to dealing McMillian, Brown also traded or released Charles, Guokas, Heard and Marin. Rumors were circling that Brown was trying to cut costs, and they appeared to be true.

Buffalo acquired ABA refugee Moses Malone from the Portland Trail Blazers in exchange for its 1978 first-round draft pick. The Braves had a solid frontcourt with McAdoo, Shumate and Dantley. However, McAdoo's contract was set to expire at the end of the year, and the Braves thought Malone represented some insurance against a possible McAdoo departure. Even so, there weren't enough minutes to go around in the Braves' frontcourt.

An opening-night crowd of 16,121 packed Memorial Auditorium as Buffalo won 108–105 over the 76ers and Julius Erving. It was Dr. J's first game as a 76er following the ABA/NBA merger. Shumate and DiGregorio led the team with 21 points each in the victory, as McAdoo missed the game with a sore back.

Malone did not last long with the Braves. He demanded more playing time, so Buffalo traded him to the Houston Rockets after the team's second game of the season. He went to the Rockets in exchange for Houston's first draft pick in both 1977 and 1978 and $100,000 in cash. In Malone's two games with Buffalo, he played a total of six minutes and scored zero points. After leaving Buffalo, Malone became a Hall of Fame player. He won the NBA MVP award three times, was a 12-time All-Star and led Philadelphia to the NBA championship in 1983. He was elected to the Naismith Memorial Basketball Hall of Fame in 2001. It was the worst trade in Braves history, at least for a few weeks.

Buffalo defeated the Celtics 118–107 on Nov. 13, putting them in a tie for first place with the 76ers. It was the last time the franchise would ever be in first place. The Braves lost six games in a row and eight of the next nine. In a Dec. 3 win over the New York Knicks, McAdoo and Dantley each scored 30 points, and it looked as if the team was pointed back in the right direction.

However, on Dec. 6, in the most stunning move in Braves history, McAdoo and Tom McMillen were traded to the Knicks for center John Gianelli and $3 million in cash. It is considered one of the biggest trades in Buffalo sports history. It also ranks right up there with the most one-sided swaps in the history of the NBA. If Brown's other moves had not signaled a beginning of the end for the Braves franchise, this certainly did. Brown had succeeded in completely tearing apart a very good Braves team. In a matter of six weeks, he had essentially given away two of the Top 75 NBA players of all time, Malone and McAdoo.

After the trade, Buffalo won only 20 of 60 games for the remainder of the season, finishing 30–52 and well out of the playoffs. Attendance also took a nosedive as the team was having trouble drawing more than 6,000 a game; only 3,534 showed up to watch as the season ended with a loss at home to Chicago. Locke was fired along the way, with general manager Bob MacKinnon taking over for seven games. Buffalo then turned to Joe Mullaney, who was head coach at Providence College when DiGregorio played there, and he finished the season.

On March 25, Snyder announced he was selling his remaining ownership share in the Braves to Brown, who in turn committed to keeping the team in Buffalo. He said, "I think Buffalo is a good market for basketball. I think we have a healthy franchise." He immediately named Norm Sonju, in his first stint with an NBA team, as president. Sonju later hired Cotton Fitzsimmons as head coach. Fitzsimmons had coached at Phoenix and Atlanta before coming to Buffalo.

Brown and Sonju continued to make moves, trading Dantley and ridding the team of almost anyone who had been in Buffalo during the Snyder years, with only Randy Smith and Shumate remaining from the playoff team of 1975–76. And the moves they made did not work as the Braves finished the 1977–78 season with a 27–55 record, the second-worst in the league. Buffalo did acquire a pair of talented players in Nate Archibald and Billy Knight, but both suffered season-ending injuries. That essentially ruined any chance that the club had of playing competitive basketball. The only highlight of the season was Smith, as he continued to play at an All-Star level. He was named MVP of the All-Star Game, after scoring 27 points in 29 minutes.

The Braves' final game in the NBA came on April 9, 1978 in the Boston Garden. Both the Celtics and Braves had no playoff hopes, but the game turned memorable for other reasons. Celtics legend John Havlicek played in his final game in the NBA, scoring 29 points in a 131–114 win. It also was the final game ever played by two veteran guards: the great Dave Bing and — fittingly — DiGregorio, who, if not for his 1974 knee injury, might have changed the course of pro basketball in Buffalo. They were both reserves on the Celtics at that point. Swen Nater scored the final basket for Buffalo.

With the dismantling of the team complete and the apathy of Buffalo fans reaching new heights, the Braves' attendance plummeted. Brown informed the city on May 8, 1978, that the Braves were opting out of the lease for Memorial Auditorium because the team had fallen below the threshold of 4,500 season tickets. At the press conference announcing the decision, Sonju said, "Everyone will naturally assume this decision means the club is leaving Buffalo. But the decision has not been made. The owners need more time to talk to other cities, go over other possibilities. And it enables more time for thoughts on how to keep the team in Buffalo."

Nobody believed the rhetoric, as people assumed Brown was looking to move the franchise. At first, everyone thought it would be to his hometown of Louisville or Birmingham, Alabama, which committed to selling 8,000 season tickets. Then Sonju announced on May 31 that the team was moving to Dallas, but that hit several snags and fell through. For a short time, it seemed as if inertia might keep the Braves in Buffalo because there were no plausible destinations.

No one guessed what the outcome of the story would be, which resulted in the end of NBA basketball in Buffalo. Brown announced that he was trading franchises with Irving Levin, owner of the storied Boston Celtics. The NBA had been in a pickle as Levin wanted a team on the West Coast, closer to his home. But the league could not have its most storied franchise, with its 13 championships, move from Boston to San Diego. NBA attorney and future commissioner David Stern orchestrated the swap and the movement of the Braves to San Diego. It was a complicated deal as some Braves players went to Boston while others went to San Diego. Brown became owner of the Celtics and Levin was the owner of the former Buffalo franchise, to be called the San Diego Clippers.

It was a sad ending to the NBA in Buffalo, and the city was done a real disservice by the league. As Fitzsimmons said after the deal was announced, "I think Buffalo got a raw deal as far as the NBA." All basketball fans of Western New York felt the same way. Even Brown years later said to The Buffalo News, "We didn't understand the potential for pro basketball (in Buffalo)."

The Braves in 1976 were fairly close to having a team that could win an NBA championship. The team came close to beating the Celtics in the playoffs in 1974 and 1976, and Boston went on to win the title both times. But once Ramsay was let go as coach, the franchise began a downhill spiral that made a departure feel inevitable.

The Curse reigned over the franchise throughout its eight-year existence. From the original owners lacking the money to run the team, to Father Demske and Snyder unable to reach a compromise on the use of Memorial Auditorium, to Darell Garretson making two critical calls in the Celtics' favor, to Ramsay's departure, to the trades of Malone and McAdoo, and the ownership of John Y. Brown, Buffalo always seemed to be fighting an uphill battle during its eight years of play. The fans of Buffalo could have celebrated an NBA championship with Hall of Famers Bob McAdoo and Moses Malone — but for that darn Curse!

Since the Braves left town in 1978, Buffalo has not had an NBA franchise, and it would be a surprise if the NBA located a team in the city in the future.

Chapter 10
FERGUSON'S PLAYOFF RUNS SLIP AWAY

The victory over Miami on Sept. 7, 1980 that ended the Miami jinx and "The Streak" propelled the Buffalo Bills to five straight wins to start the season. Included in the Bills' 5–0 start was a dominant 24–7 victory over the Oakland Raiders and a thrilling 26–24 win at San Diego. Both Oakland and San Diego were considered serious playoff contenders and potential Super Bowl participants.

Buffalo trailed the New England Patriots by one game going into Week 8 when the teams met in a key AFC game. The Bills dominated the contest as the defense shut down New England's offense, holding the Pats to a mere 148 yards. Bills rookie running back Joe Cribbs ran for 118 yards, his first 100-yard rushing game as a pro. Cribbs also scored two touchdowns in leading Buffalo to a 31–13 victory and a tie for the AFC East lead with a 6–2 record.

In early November, the Bills led the Jets at New York 17–0, but New York battled back to tie the game at 24 in the fourth quarter. Late in the game, Cribbs returned a Jets punt 15 yards to set up a drive on New York's 48-yard line. Quarterback Joe Ferguson fired a 17-yard pass to tight end Mark Brammer to the Jets 31. The Bills called their last timeout with only 12 seconds remaining. Everyone was anticipating that Buffalo would try a short sideline pass to get better field position for an attempt at a winning field goal. Ferguson crossed the Jets up as he went for broke. Wide receiver Frank Lewis ran a deep inside route toward the goal line. Ferguson dropped back and fired a strike to Lewis, streaking past the surprised Jets defenders to score the winning touchdown. It was a key win for Buffalo as it kept them tied for first place in the division with New England.

In Week 12, the Bills had a showdown with the defending Super Bowl champion Pittsburgh Steelers. In front of the third-largest crowd in Rich Stadium history, the Bills spotted Pittsburgh an early 7–0 lead on a 2-yard run by Franco Harris. Buffalo responded with two Ferguson-to-Jerry-Butler touchdown passes, 29 and 10 yards, respectively. Buffalo led at intermission 14–10.

The second half was dominated by the Bills, holding Pittsburgh to a late field goal, while the Buffalo offense continued to move the football against the vaunted Steelers defense. Buffalo manufactured two second-half touchdown drives of 86 and 70 yards as it physically pounded the Steelers. Bills safety Bill Simpson — talked out of retirement to come to Buffalo after Jeff Nixon suffered a season-ending injury — said after the Bills' 28–13 victory, "From now on, nobody is going to bully us around." Ferguson said in the locker room, "This is the most satisfying win I've ever had."

Buffalo's next home game on Dec. 7 was one of the more memorable in team history. The Bills, 9–4, entered the game in first place in the AFC East as they faced Chuck Knox's former team, the Los Angeles Rams, who were in second place in the NFC West with their 9–4 record.

The game with the Rams was a physical defensive contest as both teams struggled to move the football. The first score did not come until late in the third quarter when Bills safety Steve Freeman intercepted a Pat Haden pass and ran 47 yards for the score. After the touchdown, the Bills offense came to life after a defensive stop, marching to the Rams 1-yard line. On fourth down and inches, Knox went for it, but Roosevelt Leaks fumbled into the end zone and the Rams recovered. Knox's gamble kept Los Angeles within a single touchdown of tying the game.

The Rams promptly marched 80 yards in 14 plays, capped by a Mike Guman 3-yard touchdown run tying the game at 7–7. In the fourth quarter, the Bills had two more chances to take the lead but were again stopped on a fourth and 1, this time at the Rams 8-yard line. And on their final possession, Buffalo fumbled at the Rams 11-yard line, sending the game to overtime.

The Bills forced Los Angeles to punt early in the extra session. Ferguson methodically moved the Bills downfield, converting two key third downs and completing a 30-yard pass to Lewis to the Rams 12. Bills kicker Nick Mike-Mayer, who had earlier in the game missed two field-goal attempts, nailed a 30-yarder to win the game for Buffalo 10–7.

The Bills players and fans celebrated the big victory. Many of those in the crowd did not leave the stadium immediately. As Ken Gurnick, a Valley News reporter, described, "The emotion, and intensity on the AstroTurf field was only barely exceeded by the insane crowd of 77,133, a mob so captivated by their beloved Bills they demanded, and received, an unprecedented curtain call 10 minutes after the game was over, with nearly the entire roster reappearing on the field to take their bows." Several Bills players, led by nose tackle Fred Smerlas and linebacker Jim Haslett, gathered in a line with several Buffalo Jills cheerleaders, à la the Radio City Rockettes, dancing and kicking to the Bills fight song, "We're Talking Proud," celebrating the victory.

This win was special because it put the Bills on the verge of the AFC East title, something they had never won since joining the NFL in 1970. In addition, many of the coaches and some key players were former Rams. As Knox said in his postgame press conference, "They battled, they scratched. This was about as much intensity as I've seen on a football field. These guys wanted to win so damn bad it almost brought tears to my eyes. It was very satisfying because it was the Rams. A game like today, it was what football's all about." Bills defensive end Ben Williams said, "Coach Knox deserves the game ball. They didn't want him in Los Angeles, but we want him in Buffalo because he is a great man."

The Bills' next game was a showdown with the Patriots in Foxborough, Massachusetts. Buffalo needed a win to clinch the AFC East. However, it was not to be as the Patriots were a fired-up football team, and the Bills — coming off the emotional win over the Rams — were lethargic. Then the Curse reared its ugly head, as Ferguson went down early in the game with a severely sprained ankle. With backup quarterbacks Dan Manucci and David Humm subbing for Ferguson, the Bills did not score any offensive points and lost by the uncommon score of 24–2. The loss to New England set up a huge game for Buffalo in San Francisco on Dec. 21. Win the game and they would be AFC East champions, lose and they would miss the playoffs.

The game was played in fog and a steady rain, with a field that slowly turned into a swamp. Though the 49ers came into the game with a 6–9 record, they were making rapid progress and building a dynasty under coach Bill Walsh and second-year quarterback Joe Montana. Ferguson wrapped his ankle tightly and played the entire game despite the injury.

The Bills and 49ers traded touchdowns and each missed an extra point, so the game was tied 13–13 in the third quarter. Buffalo went ahead 16–13 on a 25-yard Mike-Mayer field goal. On the Niners' next possession, the Bills forced a punt, and the center snap flew over the head of punter Jim Miller, who was tackled for a safety, giving Buffalo an 18–13 lead. The Bills flirted with danger in the fourth quarter as they clung to the 5-point lead. San Francisco drove to the Bills 8-yard line, but Bills linebacker Lucius Sanford pummeled 49ers running back Earl Cooper to force a fumble that cornerback Mario Clark recovered.

The 49ers had one more chance, driving into Bills territory in the final seconds. Montana attempted two Hail Mary passes for the winning touchdown. Bills fans across Western New York, watching on television, had some anxious moments as they realized all that the Bills had accomplished throughout the 1980 season could be lost in the fog and rain of San Francisco. When Montana's final pass fell incomplete, all of Bills Nation breathed a huge sigh of relief as Buffalo had hung on for a hard-fought victory and its first AFC East title.

However, Ferguson's injury was irritated, and the Bills lost middle linebacker Shane Nelson with a broken wrist. Still, they looked forward to the team's first playoff game since 1974: a date in San Diego with the 11–5 Chargers, the AFC West champions.

The Bills received the opening kickoff, but on the game's fifth play Ferguson re-injured his ankle while attempting to pass and had to leave the game. Manucci subbed for Ferguson and drove the team into field-goal range, but Mike-Mayer's 44-yard kick hit the upright. San Diego responded with a 69-yard drive of its own, resulting in a Rolf Benirschke field goal and a 3–0 lead.

Buffalo, with Ferguson back in the game, marched 72 yards in 12 plays. Leaks capped off the drive with a 1-yard plunge for the touchdown and a 7–3 Bills lead. Near the end of the first half, Charlie Joiner caught a pass from Dan Fouts at the Chargers 35-yard line. Bills cornerback Charles Romes nailed Joiner to force a fumble that safety Bill Simpson recovered at San Diego's 33-yard line. Two passes from Ferguson to Lewis got Buffalo in the end zone, with the touchdown coming on an 11-yarder as only 16 ticks remained on the clock. Buffalo went to the locker room leading 14–3.

The Chargers came out blazing to start the second half. They drove 70 yards in only four plays, highlighted by a 45-yard pass from Fouts to Joiner. Two plays later, Joiner again beat Clark for a 9-yard touchdown. San Diego's next possession ended with a blocked punt by the Bills' Lou Piccone, putting

Photo 16. San Diego Chargers running back Chuck Muncie (46) runs away from Buffalo Bills safeties Steve Freeman (22) and Bill Simpson (45) during an AFC divisional playoff game on Jan. 3, 1981, at Jack Murphy Stadium in San Diego. The Chargers defeated the Bills 20–14.

(Peter Read Miller via AP)

the ball on the San Diego 38. However, Ferguson threw an interception on the Chargers 9-yard line — another key drive without points.

The Bills continued to make critical mistakes as they clung to their 14–10 lead. Ferguson hit Lewis with a 40-yard pass to San Diego's 21-yard line, but the play was called back by a Ken Jones holding penalty. San Diego's ensuing possession ended with another Benirschke field goal, cutting the Bills' lead to a mere 1 point, 14–13.

With less than five minutes remaining, Buffalo forced a big turnover as Scott Hutchinson leveled San Diego punt returner Mike Fuller, and the Bills recovered. Buffalo drove to the Chargers 30-yard line, and on an important third down and a yard to go, Cribbs was stopped short of the first down. Rather than going for fourth and 1, Knox chose a 49-yard field-goal attempt by Mike-Mayer. He promptly shanked the kick. The lead stayed at a precarious 1 point.

After the missed field goal, Fouts marched the Chargers to midfield. On second and 10, he fired a pass intended for wide receiver John Jefferson. Romes stepped in front of the pass and had the ball in his hands, but he dropped it. On third and 10, the Bills blitzed both linebackers trying to pressure Fouts. The future Hall of Famer fired the ball to little-used wide receiver Ron Smith, who caught the ball at the Bills 40-yard line. Simpson came up to make the tackle but slipped. Simpson was in single coverage, and once he fell to the ground, Smith was all alone. He sprinted to the end zone for a touchdown, putting the Chargers ahead 20–14 with 2:08 remaining.

Ferguson tried to rally the Bills on their last possession of the game, passing 18 yards to Lewis to the Bills 48-yard line. On the next play, he threw a long pass intended for Butler, but the pass was underthrown and intercepted by Glen Edwards, ending the Bills' threat and their inspiring season.

Ferguson played the game with terrific heart and guts, with a severely sprained ankle that did not allow him to put much pressure on that leg. He was forced to pass off his back foot and had no mobility from the rush. Ferguson threw three interceptions and was sacked three times while completing just over 50% of his passes. He had been sacked only 20 times in 16 games during the regular season.

The injury clearly affected his performance in this game. Despite that, the Bills still led with 2:15 left. If Simpson hadn't fallen, the Bills still would have had an excellent chance to win the game. The Curse kept the Bills from winning this game. The combination of Simpson's fall and Ferguson's injury were too much for this gutsy team to overcome.

Had the Bills beaten San Diego, they would have hosted the Oakland Raiders in Buffalo for the AFC championship. The Bills had beaten Oakland 24–7 earlier in the season. In the cold and snow of Buffalo, it is hard to imagine the Bills not beating the Raiders and being on their way to their first Super Bowl. Instead, Oakland headed to San Diego, beat the Chargers for the AFC championship, and went on to defeat Philadelphia 27–10 to win Super Bowl 15. The Bills very likely would have won the Super Bowl had they beaten San Diego and had a healthy Ferguson. They were clearly a superior team to the Raiders in 1980.

The 1981 Buffalo Bills had a single purpose: Win the Super Bowl. After their thrilling 1980 season, the Bills were the pick of Sports Illustrated writer Paul "Dr. Z" Zimmerman to win the NFL championship. They began the season as if they were on a mission, winning their first two games over the New York Jets and Baltimore Colts by a combined score of 66–3. Buffalo struggled after its blazing start, losing five of the next nine games, and was 6–5 entering a pivotal game on Nov. 22 versus New England.

Buffalo's performance in the critical game against New England was poor, especially considering that the Patriots had come into the game with a 2–9 record. New England played a hard-fought game and scored a touchdown with 1:56 to play, taking a 17–13 lead, and it looked bleak for the Bills.

It got worse, as Buffalo went three-and-out following the kickoff. However, the Bills defense stopped the Patriots in three plays. Buffalo took over the ball at its own 27-yard line after the New England punt. The Bills had no timeouts remaining, as they had used them to try to get the ball back, and were 73 yards from paydirt with only 35 seconds remaining. Most of the fans had left the stadium, sensing the Bills had little chance to come back.

On first down, Buffalo running back Roland Hooks made a spectacular catch at the Patriots 36-yard line, for a 37-yard gain. The clock continued to run as the Bills sprinted to the line of scrimmage to get another play off. Ferguson fired the ball out of bounds with 12 seconds left. Knox sent in the "Big Ben" play, the idea being that Lewis, Butler and Hooks would line up on the same side of the field and sprint to the end zone, and Ferguson would throw the ball into a crowd — hoping one of them could get it. Such plays, it should be noted, rarely work.

Ferguson dropped back to pass and lofted the ball high downfield. Patriots linebacker Mike Hawkins tipped the ball, and Hooks snatched it out of the air for a most amazing Buffalo victory. The few fans remaining in the stadium were delirious. The miracle victory kept the Bills in the race for the playoffs. A loss would have been damaging to their chances.

Buffalo used the momentum to reel off four wins in a row. The Bills defeated the Redskins 21–14 the next week, captured a thrilling 28–27 win over San Diego and took a repeat victory over the Patriots (no miracles needed this time) 19–10.

Buffalo's 10–5 record set up an AFC East title showdown with the Dolphins. A victory in Miami, and the Bills would win their second consecutive division championship. It was not meant to be, as the Bills lost their 13th consecutive game at the Orange Bowl. Miami played a terrific defensive game in beating Buffalo 16–6. The loss to the Dolphins dropped the Bills to third in the AFC East behind Miami and the Jets, but Buffalo's 10–6 record was still good enough for a playoff berth. The Bills and Jets were the combatants in the AFC wild-card game on Dec. 27 at Shea Stadium in New York. The Bills would have to win three games on the road to qualify for the Super Bowl, since they were the lowest-seeded team in the AFC playoffs.

The Jets hosted Buffalo on a dreary, damp and cold day. New York won the toss and elected to receive the football, a decision they would regret. On the opening kickoff, the Jets' Bruce Harper returned the ball and was hit by Bills linebacker Ervin Parker, forcing a fumble. The pigskin bounced into the hands of Romes, who promptly raced 26 yards for a touchdown. Just 16 seconds into the game, Buffalo had a 7–0 lead.

The Bills raced to a 24–0 lead on two touchdown passes of 50 yards and 26 yards from Ferguson to Lewis and a Mike-Mayer 29-yard field goal. The Jets finally got on the scoreboard on a Richard-Todd-to-Mickey-Shuler 30-yard touchdown in the second quarter. Early in the fourth quarter with Buffalo leading 24–13, Cribbs cut through a hole in the Jets defense and sprinted 45 yards for a decisive touchdown — or at least so Bills fans thought. The extra point by Mike-Mayer put the Bills ahead 31–13 with 10:16 remaining in the game.

But the Jets, playing in front of a friendly sellout crowd of 57,050, were not done yet. Todd responded with an eight-play, 80-yard drive culminating with a 30-yard touchdown pass to Bobby Jones and a seven-play, 58-yard drive, with Kevin Long muscling the final yard for a touchdown. The Bills lead was cut to a precarious 31–27 with 3:44 left.

After the Jets' score, New York's defense again shut down the Buffalo offense, forcing a three-and-out. After the Bills punt, Todd confidently trotted onto the field with a drive starting at the Jets 20-yard line, with 2:36 to play and two timeouts remaining. The Jets began their march down the field — a 29-yard Todd pass to Shuler, then a 26-yard strike to Derrick Gaffney. The Bills defense finally tightened and on third and 12 from the Bills 27, Freeman intercepted a Todd pass. For a moment, a Buffalo victory seemed assured. But no — the striped shirts called a penalty against the Bills. Clark's holding call nullified the interception, giving the Jets an automatic first down. It was a very questionable call, and Knox was beside himself.

New York recorded another first down to the Bills 11. On the next play, Todd's pass intended for Shuler in the end zone was incomplete, stopping the clock with 10 seconds left. On second down, Todd faded to pass and spotted Gaffney open 4 yards deep in the end zone. His pass was on target but — seemingly out of nowhere — Bills safety Bill Simpson cut in front of Gaffney to intercept it. He ran for a few yards and then intentionally fell to the ground. Knox and all Bills fans immediately looked for a penalty flag, but to everyone's surprise there was none. Buffalo had secured its first playoff victory since 1965, holding on to the heart-pounding 31–27 win in a true wild-card game.

The Bills were able to overcome four Ferguson interceptions and some key penalties that overturned a couple of big plays. This Buffalo team continued to display great courage and heart, overcoming much adversity to prevail. With the big victory, the Bills moved into the AFC divisional playoff round, traveling to Cincinnati the next week for a rematch of an early-season overtime loss to the Bengals.

On Jan. 3, 1982 before 55,420 at Riverfront Stadium in Cincinnati, the Bengals began the game by racing to a 14–0 first-quarter lead. Both touchdown drives started in Bills territory. The first started at the Buffalo 41-yard line after a 27-yard Mike Fuller punt return. Charles Alexander toted the ball the final 4 yards.

The Bengals' second touchdown was set up when Ken Riley intercepted a Ferguson pass, giving Cincinnati the ball at the Buffalo 48-yard line. Eight plays later, Pete Johnson plunged the final yard for a 14–0 Bengals lead. It looked like Cincinnati would blow the game wide open as it moved the ball

Photo 17. Charles Alexander runs for one of his two touchdowns in the Cincinnati
Bengals' 28–21 victory over the Buffalo Bills in an AFC divisional playoff game
on Jan. 3, 1982, at Riverfront Stadium in Cincinnati.

(Photo by Robert L. Smith, Orchard Park, New York)

on its next possession to the Bills 9-yard line, but the drive stalled, and Robb Riddick blocked the Bengals' field-goal attempt.

Buffalo got back into the game just before the end of the first half. With time running down, Ferguson fired a 54-yard strike to Butler, who carried the ball to the Bengals 10-yard line. Ferguson fed the ball to Cribbs, who crashed into the end zone from the 1-yard line with only 10 seconds left. Buffalo now only trailed 14–7 at intermission.

Buffalo appeared ready to take control of the game in the second half. On the Bills' first possession, they moved the ball to the Cincinnati 44-yard line. Cribbs took the handoff on a cutback sweep, ran around the left end, bolted through the Bengals defensive line and raced for the tying touchdown. The good feelings didn't last long. On the Bengals' ensuing possession, a very questionable 18-yard pass interference call on Clark kept the Cincinnati drive alive. A few plays later, Alexander cut through a hole in the Bills defense and raced 20 yards for the go-ahead touchdown.

The Bills answered with a 79-yard, 14-play drive that consumed the final 6:46 of the third quarter. Ferguson fired a 21-yard touchdown pass to Butler on the first play of the fourth period, tying the game at 21. However, the Bills lost Cribbs with a bruised knee on the drive, and he did not return to the game. Buffalo also lost Leaks to an injury.

The Bengals again answered, driving 78 yards in nine plays capped off by a 16-yard touchdown strike from Anderson to Cris Collinsworth, giving Cincinnati a 28–21 lead.

Late in the game, Buffalo began a drive at its own 30-yard line. Butler caught a pivotal 17-yard pass for a first down, and a late hit by the Bengals tacked on 15 more yards. Key passes to Hooks, Cribbs' replacement, and Mark Brammer put the Bills at the Cincinnati 20. After a Ferguson incompletion, the Bills faced a fourth and 3 with 2:58 remaining. Failure to convert on this fourth down would likely end Buffalo's season. The Bills called a time-out to discuss the situation. A little confusion on the sideline preceded the play, but Buffalo quickly got to the line of scrimmage and snapped the ball. Ferguson executed the play perfectly, lofting a 5-yard pass to Lou Piccone for a big first down. However, there was a flag on the play and the Bills were called for delay of game. What a stunning penalty! A delay-of-game call following a timeout is extremely rare in professional football. Knox vehemently argued the call, but to no avail.

The Bills now had fourth down and 8 from the 25-yard line. Ferguson tried to fire a pass into the end zone for Hooks, but the pass was incomplete. The Bengals took over and ran the clock down. Buffalo got the ball back with 25 seconds left and attempted the Big Ben play — the one that had propelled them to their miraculous victory over New England earlier in the season. However, this time it did not work, as the game's final pass was incomplete, and the Bills' season came to a crushing end. The victory was the Bengals' first postseason win. They would win again the next week, capturing the AFC championship and a berth in the Super Bowl.

The Curse played a big role in this game as the Bills lost two key players on the same drive in the third quarter and had two game-changing penalties. Clark's pass interference led to a key Bengals touchdown, and the inexplicable delay-of-game penalty cost them a chance to tie the game. It was another very disappointing defeat, just like the one in 1980. Neither team was able to overcome the Curse to bring a championship to Buffalo.

There was reason for optimism as the Bills started their 1982 season with two victories — but the beginning of the NFL season was overshadowed by a threatened player strike. Therefore, no one associated with the team — players, coaches or fans — was happy when the players decided to strike on Sept. 21. The walkout lingered for 57 days before an agreement was finally reached on Nov. 16. Even worse, the Bills roster was said to be split over the issues raised by the labor action. The long strike forced the NFL to go to a nine-game season and a 16-team postseason tournament. Buffalo only needed to go 3–4 in the remaining seven games to have a winning record, but its team cohesiveness and momentum were long gone.

The Bills' first game after the strike was Nov. 21 against the Dolphins at Rich Stadium. The Bills had seven turnovers — the big one was a Cribbs halfback option pass that was intercepted in the end zone, costing Buffalo the game. Miami won 9–7 on three field goals. The Bills lost five of the seven games after the strike and missed the expanded playoff format by one game. Knox quit at the end of the strike-marred season in a disagreement over decision-making authority within the Bills organization.

Without Knox at the helm and with the loss of several key players over the next few seasons from retirements, injuries and not re-signing, the Bills struggled. The players lost included Brammer, Clark, Cribbs, Ferguson, Leaks, Lewis, Mike-Mayer, guard Reggie McKenzie, linebacker Isiah Robertson, Simpson and defensive end Sherman White. The Bills also drafted poorly and when they did draft well, the team could not sign the player, losing Jim Kelly to the USFL. He signed with Houston on June 9, 1983 and began play for the Gamblers in the spring of 1984. The Bills' difficulties resulted in some of their worst seasons ever during the next seven seasons, twice going 2–14. A curse wasn't needed to keep the Bills at the bottom of the league then; they earned that distinction on their own. It took the hiring of Bill Polian as general manager and Marv Levy as coach a few years later to turn the team around and set it on a bittersweet ride that would really test the Curse.

Chapter 11
THE BILLS' SNAKEBIT SUPER BOWL RUN

Bill Polian put his stamp on the franchise very quickly, making several moves that paid huge dividends for the Bills.

With the demise of the USFL, in August 1986 he signed Jim Kelly to a 5-year, $8 million contract, the richest contract in NFL history to that point. In addition, he inked center Kent Hull, linebacker Ray Bentley, safety Dwight Drane and kicker Scott Norwood from the bankrupt league. He added tackle Will Wolford, running back Ronnie Harmon and defensive tackle Mark Pike in the 1986 draft, and in 1987 he selected linebacker Shane Conlan, defensive end Leon Seals, cornerback Nate Odomes and fullback Jamie Mueller.

On Halloween in 1987, Polian pulled off a blockbuster three-team trade to acquire linebacker Cornelius Bennett, and he also adroitly snared Thurman Thomas in the second round of the 1988 draft. Polian hired Marv Levy to be head coach on Nov. 3, 1986.

The results were almost immediate. The Bills improved to 7–8 in 1987 and surprised the NFL by winning the AFC East in 1988 with a 12–4 record. The Bills went all the way to the AFC championship game but lost to Cincinnati 21–10, falling one game short of the Super Bowl.

The Bills had high expectations heading into the 1989 season, but Kelly suffered a knee injury in Week 5 and was lost to the team for three games. After the game, he pointed fingers at certain teammates, blaming them for his poor play — and the "Bickering Bills" were born. Later in the season, two Bills coaches, Nick Nicolau and Tom Bresnahan, traded punches during a film session, and Kelly and Thomas had a public feud followed by a staged apology. Meanwhile, the Bills struggled to a 9–7 finish but still won the AFC

East title. Buffalo met the Cleveland Browns in the AFC divisional playoffs and lost a heartbreaker 34–30, after Ronnie Harmon dropped the potential winning touchdown pass with 9 seconds remaining.

The Bills players sat disappointed and dejected in the dingy locker room of Cleveland Municipal Stadium on Jan. 6, 1990, after the loss to the Browns. But their second-half performance with a no-huddle attack, which placed them within a dropped pass of victory, was a harbinger of things to come.

That offseason, offensive coordinator Ted Marchibroda lobbied head coach Levy to institute the no-huddle offense as the Bills' primary approach for the 1990 season. Buffalo began that year with a vengeance, running off nine victories in its first 10 games, including two of the most amazing wins in team history.

The Bills stunned the Denver Broncos on Sept. 30, scoring 20 points in 77 seconds in the fourth quarter to come from a 21–9 deficit to earn an improbable 29–28 victory. The comeback was sparked by Bennett's 80-yard blocked punt return for a touchdown with 10:27 remaining in the game. Two plays later, Leonard Smith intercepted a John Elway pass and returned it 39 yards for another score, putting the Bills ahead for the first time 22–21. On the next play from scrimmage, Elway fumbled the snap and Bennett recovered at the Broncos 2-yard line. Running back Kenneth Davis ran in for the touchdown on the next play, securing the Bills' remarkable comeback victory. The next week, the Bills trailed the Los Angeles Raiders 24–14 in the fourth quarter. Then J.D. Williams scored on a 38-yard blocked punt return and Odomes "stole" the ball from Raiders receiver Willie Gault and sprinted 49 yards for another touchdown. They helped the Bills score 24 unanswered points on the way to a shocking victory.

After a 27–24 loss to Houston in late November, the Bills fully revved up the no-huddle attack. They opened the Dec. 2 game versus Philadelphia in full no-huddle mode, outscoring the Eagles 24–0 in the first quarter before the Eagles knew what hit them. The Bills held on to win 30–23, and their new fast-paced offense was the talk of the league.

The 11–2 Bills met the 11–2 New York Giants at the Meadowlands on Dec. 15 in what would turn out to be a Super Bowl 25 preview. The Giants scored on the opening drive on an O.J. Anderson 1-yard run, capping a 71-yard drive in 11 plays. The Bills immediately responded, using only 1:28 of the clock to move 74 yards in six plays, with Jim Kelly finding Andre Reed in the end zone for a 6-yard touchdown pass.

Buffalo took the lead for good on a 78-yard, 11-play drive finished by a 2-yard touchdown run by Thurman Thomas. The no-huddle offense looked unstoppable. In their first two possessions against the league's best defense, the Bills ran 17 plays for 152 yards and two touchdowns. The Giants responded with a field-goal drive to cut the Buffalo lead to 14–10. On the Bills' next drive, both Kelly and Pro Bowl tackle Will Wolford were hurt on the same play. Wolford suffered a sprained right knee and then fell on the back of Kelly's left leg, with Kelly suffering a sprained left knee a split second later. The Buffalo defense rose to the occasion, holding the Giants to a single field goal in the second half for a big 17–13 win over New York. The catch was that the Giants had seen and played against the Bills' no-huddle attack. It would prove immensely helpful when they prepared for the Super Bowl six weeks later.

The next week, behind an excellent performance from backup quarterback Frank Reich, Buffalo played a spirited game as the defense cooped up Dolphin quarterback Dan Marino in the Bills' division-clinching 24–14 victory over Miami. Buffalo dominated the line of scrimmage as the team rushed for 206 yards on 47 attempts, led by Thomas's 154 yards. In addition, Reich completed 15 of 21 passes for 234 yards. After the game, Levy said about the team's offensive line, "They played superbly. They pass-protected well and blocked effectively for the run." Regarding Reich, he said, "Outstanding. He did a great job, very poised, he threw the ball well, made good decisions, and ran our offense very well." The victory also meant Buffalo had clinched home-field advantage throughout the AFC playoffs.

The 13–3 Bills entered the playoffs on a roll and, with Kelly returning to the lineup, dominated the 1990 AFC playoffs as no team had done in history. Buffalo scored 44 points to beat the Dolphins in the divisional round, although the 44–34 final score did not convey the closeness of the game. The Bills jumped to a 13–3 first-quarter lead on a Kelly-to-Reed 40-yard touchdown pass to open the scoring, followed by two short Scott Norwood field goals. Buffalo stretched the lead to 20–3 with a Thomas 5-yard touchdown run early in the second quarter. The Dolphins responded with a 64-yard touchdown pass from Marino to Mark Duper and a Marino 2-yard touchdown run. In between, James Lofton caught a 13-yard touchdown pass from Kelly, so the Bills' halftime lead was 27–17.

The teams traded field goals in the third quarter, but when the Dolphins scored on a Roy Foster 2-yard pass from Marino early in the fourth quarter, the Bills' lead was down to 30–27. The Buffalo fans were starting to squirm in their seats, fearing a comeback win by Miami. Instead, it was as if the Bills were toying with their opponent. As soon as the Dolphins got close, Buffalo put together two consecutive touchdown drives: a Thomas 5-yard run capped off the first drive, and a 26-yard Kelly-to-Reed pass completed the second. The Bills had a safe 44–27 lead, even when it shrank on a garbage-time touchdown by the Dolphins late in the game.

Buffalo's offense was dominant, as Kelly was 19 of 29 for 339 yards with three touchdowns, and the Bills run game produced 154 yards on 37 attempts for a total offense of 493 yards. The headline in the Democrat and Chronicle the next day said it all: "Completely Buffaloed."

The Bills moved onto the AFC championship. Waiting were the Los Angeles Raiders, who did some talking leading up to the game. The "Just Win, Baby" Raiders were giving the Buffalo no-huddle offense no respect. Buffalo News sports editor Larry Felser reported that the Raiders were full of confidence on Sunday morning. "We're going to win," confided a Raider football man. "We're going to do everything: Run against them; pass against them."

Then the game started. The Bills received the opening kickoff and immediately went to their fast-paced attack. Buffalo's first five plays were a 12-yard run, a 14-yard pass, a 15-yard pass, a 5-yard run and a 9-yard pass. Less than three minutes into the game, Raiders defensive end Howie Long was gassed and requested a timeout. It was more like a basketball timeout when a team is tired after giving up too many fast breaks. The respite did not help. Three plays later, Kelly fired a 13-yard touchdown pass to Lofton to give the Bills a quick 7–0 lead. The Raiders responded, driving 57 yards in six plays and settling for a 41-yard Jeff Jaeger field goal.

The next 23 minutes of the game brought a Buffalo onslaught that had not been seen in a championship game in the NFL since the Chicago Bears defeated the Washington Redskins 73–0 in 1940. The Bills scored 34 unanswered points on five touchdowns: a 12-yard Thomas run, a 27-yard interception return by Darryl Talley, two Kenneth Davis touchdown runs of 1 and 3 yards and a Lofton 8-yard touchdown reception. By the time the carnage was finished, the Bills led 41–3 at halftime. Buffalo played more conservatively in the second half but still padded the lead a bit to beat the demoralized Raiders 51–3. The Bills set an NFL record for the largest margin of victory in an AFC championship game. Hall of Fame coach Sid Gillman said after the game, "Buffalo is the best team I have seen in years. It was like a seven-on-seven drill in midweek. The Bills just went straight through them." In the two playoff games, Buffalo outscored their opponents 95–37 while amassing 995 yards of total offense.

The Bills qualified for their first Super Bowl in franchise history with the victory over Los Angeles. However, the United States was at war with Iraq, and there was serious consideration of postponing the Super Bowl. That did not happen, but the game was played under the tightest security of any sports event in U.S. history up to that time. It took fans several hours to get through the multiple levels of security at the gates, and no cameras or binoculars were allowed. There were even snipers on the roof at Tampa Stadium. Super Bowl 25 was one of the most closely contested Super Bowls ever played. It began with a stirring rendition of the national anthem by Whitney Houston and a spine-tingling flyover by the U.S. Air Force. The game took over from there.

The Giants scored first on a time-consuming 11-play, 58-yard drive that took 6:15 off the clock and ended with a Matt Bahr 28-yard field goal. Buffalo responded with a six-play, 66-yard drive with a 23-yard Norwood field goal. The first quarter ended in a 3–3 tie, but the Giants had possessed the ball for more than 10 minutes. The Bills put together their most effective drive of the game, spanning the end of the first quarter and the beginning of the second. Kelly drove the club 80 yards in 12 plays as Don Smith leaped over the pile from the 1-yard line for the touchdown, putting the Bills ahead 10–3.

On the Bills' next drive, they moved the ball to midfield but were unable to crack into Giants territory. Rick Tuten's punt pinned New York deep in their own end at the 7-yard line. With the Giants facing a second and 10, Bills defensive end Bruce Smith exploded off the edge, sacking quarterback Jeff Hostetler in the end zone while simultaneously trying to strip the ball from him. Hostetler, with just his right hand clutching the football, somehow was able to hang onto the ball while falling to the ground, fully absorbing the ferocious hit from Smith. It was a huge play because the Bills settled for a safety instead of what could have been a touchdown. Also, Smith was penalized for excessive celebration following the play, and that cost Buffalo some yardage on the ensuing punt.

The Bills were unable to add to their lead on their next two possessions. Their first drive after the safety was a quick three-and-out. The second was stymied by a 5-yard penalty against Wolford that turned a third and 2 into a third and 7, and the Bills came up 2 yards shy of the first down.

The Giants took advantage of the situation. In one of the key drives of the game (87 yards, 10 plays), New York killed off all but the final 20 seconds of the half in scoring a touchdown. The Giants scored on a third and 10 from the 14-yard line on a pass from Hostetler to Stephen Baker, and the lead was cut to 12–10. "What I really felt like is we had some opportunities in the first half, and we didn't take great advantage of them," Lofton said later.

In another huge drive, New York opened the second half by marching 75 yards in 14 plays, taking 9:29 off the clock. Anderson finished the march with a 1-yard plunge, and the Giants were now in the lead 17–12. The Bills will forever be haunted by a key play on that drive. With the Giants facing a third and 13 from the Bills 32, Hostetler threw a short pass to Mark Ingram, who proceeded to break multiple Buffalo tackles as he lunged and dove the final yard for a huge first down. New York scored the go-ahead touchdown five plays later.

Buffalo finally got going on its last drive of the third quarter, moving the ball from its 37-yard line to the Giants 31 on three consecutive Kelly passes. On the first play of the fourth quarter, Kelly crossed up the New York defense, running a draw play to Thomas, who sprinted around the right end for a 31-yard touchdown. The touchdown put the Bills back in the lead 19–17.

The Bills defense again allowed a long, time-consuming drive. The Giants moved from their 23 to the Bills 3-yard line in 14 plays, using another 7:32 off the clock. Buffalo stopped New York on third and goal as Bennett batted down Hostetler's pass. Bahr came on and made the 21-yard field goal, giving the Giants back the lead 20–19.

The teams traded punts, and the Bills had one final chance. They started a drive at their own 10-yard line with 2:16 remaining and only one timeout. In one of Kelly's gutsiest moments of his career, he drove the Bills 61 yards in eight plays, setting up a field-goal attempt with eight seconds left. On the drive, Kelly scrambled three times for 18 yards and completed two passes for 10 more, and Thomas had two key runs for 33 yards.

As Norwood prepared for the 47-yard field-goal attempt that would decide the outcome, the atmosphere in the stadium was electric. Jim O'Brien had booted a game-winning field goal in the waning seconds of Super Bowl 5 to lift the Baltimore Colts to a 16–13 win over the Dallas Cowboys — the only Super Bowl to that point in which a last-second kick had won a game. Now, Norwood had the chance to do the same. The problem for Buffalo was that Norwood had never made a field goal of that length on grass in his professional career. It was a lot to ask of Norwood, to set a personal best under this set of circumstances. The snap by Adam Lingner was good, the hold by Reich was excellent and Norwood struck the ball well. As the kick left his right foot, it appeared to be long enough and would curve in as all his kicks did, but this one did not, as it sailed "Wide Right." The Bills lost Super Bowl 25 by a single point. The defeat was devastating to the team and its fan base.

The Buffalo Sports Curse was at play in this game without a doubt. The key plays that decided the outcome all went against the Bills. The sack and safety by Smith, and how Hostetler held onto the ball, were simply incredible. The Ingram catch-and-run for a crucial first down, breaking at least six Bills tackles, followed. Then at the end came the "Wide Right" kick. "We had the opportunity to make plays, and we didn't do it," Buffalo center Kent Hull said. "We did everything today opposite of what got us there. That means great execution, and sound defense."

Also, the Giants were helped by the fact they had seen the no-huddle offense at the end of the regular season. New York defensive coordinator Bill Belichick devised a defense it had never run before, a 2–4–5 scheme that dared Buffalo to run the football. With the time of possession dominated by the Giants, the Bills were not patient enough to run the ball more.

Buffalo was the best team in football in 1990 but did not fulfill expectations with a win in Tampa. Today, the kick is one of the most-remembered plays in Super Bowl history. Many believe this was the Bills' finest team, and this game was their best chance to win a Super Bowl. But the Curse did not let an NFL championship come to Buffalo. Even Bills running back Kenneth Davis thought there was something sinister at play when he said on the ESPN documentary "Four Falls of Buffalo" that the reason Norwood's kick did not curve in as they usually did was because the military helicopters flying overhead affected the flight of the ball. Maybe true, maybe not, but either way, the Curse kept the Bills from winning their first Super Bowl.

The next season, Kelly and the Bills were determined to return to the big game and avenge their Super Bowl 25 loss. Despite Bruce Smith missing 11 regular-season games, the Bills dominated the AFC. Buffalo raced to a 5–0 start, lost to the Chiefs in a Monday night rout and then reeled off five more consecutive wins to stand at 10–1. The Bills lost on a field goal to New England and then won three more in a row to clinch their fourth consecutive AFC East title and home-field advantage throughout the AFC playoffs.

Photo 18. Buffalo Bills kicker Scott Norwood (11) misses a last-second 47-yard field goal in Super Bowl 25 on Jan. 27, 1991, in Tampa, Florida. The New York Giants edged the Bills 20–19 before 73,813 fans at Tampa Stadium.

(AP Photo/Al Messerschmidt)

Buffalo finished the regular season with another 13–3 record. The Bills offense was the top-ranked unit in the NFL, averaging more than 390 yards per game, and was second in the league in scoring, averaging 28.6 points.

Buffalo opened the postseason with a payback rout of Kansas City. The Chiefs had dominated the Bills during the regular season in Kansas City, winning 33–6. This time, the Bills were in control from the beginning as they built a 17–0 halftime lead behind two long touchdown passes from Kelly to Reed. Buffalo continued pouring it on in the second half, building up a 37–7 lead and cruising to a 37–14 victory.

The AFC championship game between the Bills and Denver Broncos was billed as Kelly vs. John Elway, two future Hall of Famers. However, the game did not play out that way, as it turned into a monumental defensive struggle. There was no scoring in the first half. The first touchdown of the game was scored by the defense, as Bills nose tackle Jeff Wright tipped an Elway pass that was intercepted by Carlton Bailey at the 11-yard line. Bailey secured the ball and rumbled for a touchdown and a 7–0 Buffalo lead.

The Bills tacked on a Norwood 44-yard field goal, extending their lead to 10–0 with only 4:18 remaining. It seemed like an almost insurmountable lead, as backup quarterback Gary Kubiak had replaced Elway earlier in the fourth quarter. Elway left the game with a deep thigh bruise from a third-quarter hit by Leon Seals. However, it appeared as if the Bills defense relaxed as Kubiak capped an eight-play, 85-yard drive with a 3-yard keeper for the touchdown. Trailing 10–7 with only 1:43 left in the game, the Broncos attempted an onside kick. To the shock of the 80,272 in attendance, Denver recovered the ball. The Broncos were in business to tie or win the game with a drive starting at their 49-yard line.

On the first play after the recovery, Kubiak fired a 7-yard pass to Steve Sewell, and Bills defensive back Kirby Jackson stripped the ball and recovered it. Buffalo ran out the clock and escaped with the hard-fought 10–7 win. The Bills were on their way to Super Bowl 26 in Minneapolis to play Washington. The 14–2 Redskins had won the NFC championship with a 24–7 defeat of the Atlanta Falcons in the divisional round and a 41–10 shellacking of the Detroit Lions in the championship game. The Redskins, led by their offensive line, nicknamed "The Hogs," and quarterback Mark Rypien, were the highest-scoring team during the regular season, amassing 485 points. Rypien had an impressive group of receivers, including Hall of Famer Art Monk, Gary Clark and Ricky Sanders, and a stout running game with backs Earnest Byner, Ricky Ervins and Gerald Riggs. They also had an aggressive defense, finishing third in the league in turnovers and second in points allowed.

Buffalo's second straight NFL championship game started badly and went downhill from there. Thomas, the 1991 NFL MVP, misplaced his helmet before the opening kickoff, causing him to miss the Bills' first two offensive plays of the game. On the Bills' second offensive play, Davis ran the wrong way, and Kelly had to scramble for a 4-yard gain. However, it was a play the Bills had practiced all week with Thomas, expecting that he might be wide open for a big gain. The hole had opened up just as the Bills had planned, and had Thomas been in the game, the play might have gone for a big gain. Instead, Kelly took a sack on third down, and Buffalo punted.

Neither team scored in the first quarter as both quarterbacks, Kelly and Rypien, traded interceptions. The officials were allowing the defensive backs to play very aggressively and were not calling penalties on the combative play. This was a big disadvantage to the Bills and their quick-strike passing offense. The Redskins defenders became more and more aggressive as the game evolved.

Washington broke the scoring drought early in the second quarter on a 64-yard march to a field goal, as Chip Lohmiller booted it from 34 yards out. The Bills went three-and-out on their next possession, and the Redskins — aided by a roughing the passer penalty against Bennett — drove for their first touchdown. Rypien hit Byner on a 10-yard pass for a 10–0 Redskins lead. On the second play of the Bills' next possession, Kelly was hurried and fired a pass intended for Lofton that was intercepted by Darrell Green at the Washington 45-yard line. Less than three minutes later, the Redskins were in the end zone, again aided by a Bills penalty, on a 1-yard run by Riggs. The touchdown gave Washington a 17–0 lead.

The Bills had one final chance before the half to get on the scoreboard. Starting with great field position at the Redskins 41, Kelly completed a 21-yard pass to Keith McKeller. Two plays later on third and 18, Kelly fired a pass intended for Reed at the Washington 8-yard line. Reed was manhandled by Redskins defender Brad Edwards while attempting to catch the pass. Everyone in the building was expecting a flag for pass interference, but none was thrown. Reed went ballistic at the non-call, taking his helmet off and throwing it to the ground in disgust. Reed had been dealing with an aggressive defense for the entire half, but he thought this play was so blatantly illegal that it ignited his anger. Instead of awarding the Bills a first down on a pass interference penalty, the officials gave Reed an unsportsmanlike conduct penalty. Buffalo was pushed out of field-goal range, and the Redskins finished the half up by 17 points.

The first play of the second half pretty much sealed the Bills' fate, as Kelly fired an interception to linebacker Kurt Gouveia, who returned it to the Buffalo 2-yard line. On the next play, Riggs crashed over for the touchdown and a commanding 24–0 lead for Washington. Buffalo fought back and scored a field goal and touchdown on its next two possessions, cutting the lead to 24–10. But the Redskins drove 79 yards in 11 plays on their next series and delivered the dagger on a beautifully lofted 30-yard touchdown pass from Rypien to Gary Clark, who beat J.D. Williams, as the 'Skins extended their lead to 31–10.

The fourth quarter was anticlimactic, although the Bills scored two touchdowns. Washington tacked on two field goals in a 37–24 victory. Buffalo played its most error-prone game of the season, committing five turnovers and allowing five sacks. The Bills were unable to create any running attack, rushing for only 43 yards, and Kelly was under constant duress.

A few key plays turned the game against the Bills, and they were never able to recover. Buffalo committed key penalties or made critical mistakes at critical junctures in the game, especially in the first half when the contest was still in doubt. The Redskins' first three touchdown drives were set up or aided by Bills penalties and/or turnovers. And Thomas' lost helmet cost the Bills an opportunity to take an early lead and was a big missed opportunity. Who knows what would have happened had Buffalo jumped in front early? The Curse hung over this game like the fog over ships in a harbor. The Bills could not shake their doldrums to play like the team they were.

"I can't remember a game I coached and lost that was more hurtful," Levy said. "The harder you work, the harder it is to surrender." Kelly, who had suffered a concussion in the fourth quarter but missed only one play, said, "Sometimes I had an open man, and didn't hit him, sometimes there were balls we didn't catch, and sometimes blocks slipped away."

Buffalo was not going to let two Super Bowl losses deter it. The Bills had a great start to the 1992 season, winning nine of their first 11 games, but they struggled down the stretch in losing three of five. They absorbed critical losses: to Indianapolis 16–13 in overtime; a 24–17 loss to the lowly Jets, on a Kelly interception returned for the winning touchdown; and a 27–3 drubbing

Photo 19. Buffalo Bills wide receiver Andre Reed throws down his helmet in disgust after he thought he had been interfered with by Washington defenders, but no call was made by the officials. The play occurred during second-quarter action in Super Bowl 26 on Jan. 26, 1991, at the Metrodome in Minneapolis.

(AP Photo/Ed Reinke)

by Houston on the last day of the season. The loss to the Oilers cost Buffalo the AFC East crown for a fifth consecutive season.

Making matters worse, Kelly suffered a knee injury in the Houston game and would miss at least the Bills' first playoff game. Buffalo qualified as a wild-card participant but would have to win three games to get back to the Super Bowl, a tall task.

The Bills played the Oilers the week after getting drubbed, but this time the game was at Rich Stadium on Jan. 3. Nobody could have predicted how this game would play out. Houston was a well-oiled machine in the first half, building a 28–3 lead as quarterback Warren Moon was unstoppable. He completed 19 of 22 passes for 218 yards and three touchdowns, as the Bills had no answers for him.

On the fourth play of the second half, if matters could get worse for the Bills, they did. Oilers safety Bubba McDowell intercepted a Reich pass that bounced off the hands of tight end McKeller, and McDowell raced 58 yards for another Houston touchdown and an incredible 35–3 lead. At that point, many disgusted Bills fans began leaving the stadium, thinking the Bills' season was over.

Reich, though, had other ideas. He had led the greatest comeback in college football history in 1984, a 42–40 Maryland victory over Miami (Florida) after trailing 31–0. He told his teammates just to take it one play at a time. The Bills scored on their ensuing possession, a 50-yard drive in 10 plays capped off by a Kenneth Davis 1-yard run. Trailing 35–10, the Bills tried an onside kick, surprising Houston with Buffalo kicker Steve Christie recovering his own kick at the Bills 48-yard line. Four plays later, Reich found Don Beebe down the left sideline, wide open for a 38-yard touchdown.

Buffalo held the Oilers on their next possession, and Reich had the Bills on the move again. He was now carving up the Houston secondary. An 18-yard pass to Lofton started the drive. After a short running play and a penalty, he threw a 19-yard pass to Davis and then a 26-yard strike to Reed for the touchdown. Suddenly, the Bills only trailed 35–24 with more than 19 minutes left in the game.

On the Oilers' next possession, Moon threw a first-down pass intended for Webster Slaughter that was intercepted by Henry Jones and returned to the Houston 23. Three plays later, the Bills faced a fourth and 5 from the Oilers 18. Levy decided to go for it. Reich made the decision look brilliant as he fired a perfect strike to Reed, sliding across the end zone for the touchdown. As Bills broadcaster Van Miller said on the air with the score 35–31 and more than a quarter left, "The Bills are back in it, big time."

Early in the fourth quarter, Moon engineered a 13-play, 76-yard drive to the Bills 14, setting up an Al Del Greco field-goal attempt and a 7-point lead for the Oilers. However, the snap was errant and the holder, Greg Montgomery, dropped the ball as the Bills swarmed on Del Greco. Buffalo took advantage of the Oilers' misfortune as Reich marched the Bills 74 yards, finishing the drive off with a 17-yard beauty to Reed. Buffalo was in the lead with about three minutes left. Miller could not contain himself, and after the touchdown, he came up with one of the signature descriptions of his long career: "It is pandemonium, it is fandemonium, it is fantastic."

The Oilers did not quit. They came back and drove 63 yards to kick the tying field goal. If not for a shoestring tackle by Bills defensive end Phil Hansen on Houston's Lorenzo White, the Oilers might have won the game in regulation on a long touchdown run. This incredible game went to overtime.

On the third play of the extra session, Bills cornerback Odomes intercepted Moon's pass intended for Haywood Jeffires. Two plays later, Christie booted the winning field goal, and the Bills had completed the greatest comeback in NFL history, winning 41–38. Buffalo News columnist Larry Felser's story was headlined, "One play at a time, Reich wrote a fairy tale." The only talk of a curse after that game was by the Oilers, who never did play in a Super Bowl during their time in Houston.

The Bills stormed into Pittsburgh the following week for the divisional playoff game, with tremendous momentum but without Kelly, as he was still nursing his injury. The Buffalo defense played a terrific game, and Reich put forth a workmanlike effort in a 24–3 defeat of the Steelers. The Bills rushed for 169 yards, and Reich was 16 of 23 for 160 yards and two touchdowns in the victory. The Buffalo defense held the Steelers to only 240 yards of total offense while also forcing two turnovers.

Buffalo was back for its third consecutive AFC championship on Jan. 17, traveling to Miami. Kelly returned to the lineup to face the Dolphins, but again the Bills swarming defense was the star of this game. Buffalo forced five Dolphins turnovers, completely shut down Miami's running game (33 yards) and kept Dan Marino in check. The Dolphins scored only a single touchdown midway through the fourth quarter, with the Bills comfortably ahead 26–3. Christie kicked five field goals, and Thomas and Davis contributed touchdowns in the Bills' convincing 29–10 win for their third consecutive AFC championship. The Bills became only the third team to qualify for three consecutive Super Bowls and would face their third different NFC East opponent, the Dallas Cowboys, in the fabled Rose Bowl in Pasadena, California.

The Bills started Super Bowl 27 strong, blocking a Dallas punt on their first possession of the game and recovering on the Cowboys 16-yard line. Four plays later, Thomas ran in from the 2-yard line and the Bills were up 7–0. On Buffalo's next possession, Kelly fired a pass intended for Beebe that was intercepted by James Washington and returned to the Bills 47-yard line. The Cowboys soon scored a tying touchdown on a nifty pass from Troy Aikman to tight end Jay Novacek.

The Bills' next drive started at their own 10-yard line. The first play changed the game for good. Kelly was sacked by Charles Haley for an 8-yard loss but also coughed up the football to James Jones of Dallas, who fell into the end zone for the go-ahead touchdown. Kelly sprained his right knee on the play and was lost for the remainder of the game.

From that point forward, the Bills could do nothing right. Buffalo turned the ball over four more times in the second quarter — two interceptions and two fumbles — as Dallas built a 28–10 halftime lead. Buffalo cut the Cowboys' margin in the third quarter to 31–17. But in the fourth quarter, the Bills turned the ball over three more times, propelling the Cowboys to a 52–17 victory.

The most memorable play for the Bills from this game was Beebe racing the length of the field to catch Cowboy defensive end Leon Lett, who was showboating with a fumble recovery and was about to score a touchdown. Beebe incredibly caught him from behind and knocked the ball away just before Lett crossed the goal line. It did not matter to the outcome of the game but showed that the Bills never would give up. Beebe will be associated with that play forever.

Nothing but a Curse could explain the complete unraveling of the Bills after Kelly's fumble and injury. Buffalo set a Super Bowl record with nine turnovers, never giving itself a chance to compete with Dallas. The Bills became the first team to lose three consecutive Super Bowls. Lofton said in the Bills' somber postgame locker room, "Say what you want, but only an earthquake in Santa Monica could have stopped the Dallas Cowboys tonight." Kelly added, "You always wonder why, why us? We turned the ball over nine times, and you can't beat a college team doing that."

Photo 20. Buffalo Bills receiver Don Beebe strips the ball away from an
unsuspecting Leon Lett of the Dallas Cowboys at the goal line
in the fourth quarter of Super Bowl 27 at the Rose Bowl in Pasadena,
California, on Jan. 31, 1993. Beebe's hustle prevented a touchdown after
Lett had recovered a fumble and began celebrating too early.
(AP Photo/Chris O'Meara)

The Bills were still determined to go back to the Super Bowl again and finally get that elusive title. To get to Super Bowl 28, the Bills would have to play all four teams in the NFC East, which included the Giants, Redskins and Cowboys, during the regular season. It became the payback tour.

After routing the Patriots on opening day 38–14, the Bills traveled to Dallas to face the Cowboys. The Bills defeated Dallas 13–10 in a hard-fought defensive struggle; victory finally was secured when Matt Darby intercepted Aikman at the Bills 1-yard line with 12 seconds remaining. The key to the victory was the Bills forcing four Cowboys turnovers. In Week 5, the Bills defeated the New York Giants 17–14 at Rich Stadium before a national television audience. Henry Jones returned an interception 85 yards for a touchdown in the first quarter, and Pete Metzelaars caught an 8-yard touchdown pass from Kelly with 2:27 remaining to win it for the Bills. The final leg of the revenge tour came on Nov. 1 in a Monday night game with the Redskins. The Bills stunned Washington on a 65-yard touchdown pass from Kelly to Reed in the first quarter, and the Buffalo running game dominated the Redskins as Thomas rushed for 129 yards and a touchdown in the Bills' sweet 24–10 victory. The Bills upped their record to 6–1 with the win.

Buffalo hit a bumpy road after that, losing three of five to drop to 8–4. However, the team reeled off four wins to finish the season. Down the stretch, the Bills edged the Eagles 10–7 to secure a sweep of the NFC East. Buffalo beat the Dolphins the next week in a critical AFC East showdown, 47–34. With a 12–4 record, Buffalo won its fifth AFC East title in six years and secured home-field throughout the conference playoffs.

In the coldest game in terms of temperature in Bills history (zero degrees) and the third-coldest wind-chill game in NFL history (minus 32), Buffalo slipped past the Raiders 29–23 in the divisional round. Despite the harsh conditions, Kelly completed 27 of 37 passes for 287 yards and two touchdown passes to Billy Brooks, including the game-winning 22-yarder.

The AFC championship was set to be a duel between Kelly and Joe Montana of the Chiefs, one of the greatest quarterbacks in NFL history. But this was Thurman Thomas' signature day. The Hall of Fame running back rushed for 186 yards on 33 carries and three touchdowns in the Bills' 30–13 beatdown of the Chiefs. Bruce Smith made sure that Montana would not be around for any fourth-quarter heroics, knocking him out of the game on a hit in the third quarter. With the victory, the Bills became the first team in

NFL history to make four straight Super Bowl appearances. It was a tremendous achievement, one that may never be duplicated.

The Bills were back in the Super Bowl again and almost nobody except Buffalo fans wanted them. But they were there and had another chance to win it all. The Bills played an outstanding first half in Super Bowl 28 against the defending champion Cowboys at the Georgia Dome in Atlanta. The teams traded field goals on the first two possessions, and Christie set a Super Bowl record for the longest field goal with his 54-yarder.

On the Bills' second possession, Kelly threw a 7-yard flare pass to Thomas, but he fumbled while struggling for extra yardage, and Darren Woodson recovered at midfield for the Cowboys. Dallas took advantage of the good field position and moved to the Bills 7, where Buffalo stopped them, forcing a 24-yard field goal by Eddie Murray. The Cowboys had a 6–3 lead.

The Bills responded with their best drive not only of the game but of the season, in terms of number of plays. Buffalo ran 17 plays in a methodical 80-yard march. Thomas finished it off on a 4-yard run for the touchdown. The Bills mixed their plays very well, with eight passes and nine runs.

With Buffalo leading 10–6, Dallas drove into Bills territory late in the first half when Odomes came up with a huge play. He intercepted Aikman at the 12-yard line and raced 41 yards to the Dallas 47. The Bills took over with 1:03 left in the half, and quickly Kelly had them on the move. He completed a 12-yard pass to Thomas, a 22-yard pass to Reed and a 3-yard pass to Thomas, moving Buffalo inside the Dallas 10. But then Kelly overthrew McKeller, and an ill-advised shovel pass to Thomas went nowhere. It was a huge stop for the Cowboys as they held the Bills to a field goal and only a one-touchdown deficit at the half, 13–6. Buffalo outplayed Dallas in the first 30 minutes as they ran 12 more plays, had 216 yards in total offense to the Cowboys' 170 and had a 15–10 edge in first downs.

The Bills started the second half from their 28-yard line, and immediately they were on the move. They quickly moved the ball to the Buffalo 43. The next play completely changed the game. Thomas took the handoff from Kelly and knifed through the line for what looked like another good gain. That's when Lett slapped the ball loose, with Washington taking the ball for Dallas. Washington weaved his way through the Bills offense, breaking a couple of tackles on his way to a 46-yard fumble return for a touchdown. The Cowboys tied the game, demoralizing the Bills. After three straight losses in

Photo 21. Buffalo Bills running back Thurman Thomas (34) fumbles the ball during the third quarter of Super Bowl 28 against the Dallas Cowboys on Jan. 30, 1994, at the Georgia Dome in Atlanta.

(AP Photo/Susan Ragan)

Super Bowls — all with a Curse hanging over them — Buffalo's fragile level of confidence received a shattering blow.

From that point on, the Cowboys dominated the game behind the running of Emmitt Smith. On the next Dallas possession, Smith ran the football on seven of the eight plays, amassing 61 yards, and finished the drive with a 15-yard jaunt into the end zone. Kelly threw an interception on the first play of the fourth quarter with Dallas leading 20–13, and the Cowboys quickly turned that into a Smith 1-yard touchdown run. Dallas added a Murray field goal later in the quarter and the Bills went down to defeat, 30–13.

This game hinged on two vital plays, or the Bills would have walked out of the Georgia Dome with the first championship in Buffalo history. The good ol' Curse again played a significant role.

The two big plays of the game both involved Thomas. The first was the terrible play call to run a shovel pass into the middle of the Dallas defense late in the first half. A touchdown would have given the Bills a 17–6 lead, and the Cowboys might have been forced to change their approach in the second half. Besides, Kelly had been picking apart the Dallas secondary. He was 19 of 26 in the first half for 176 yards. A pass play to either Brooks or Reed might have worked for a touchdown.

The other huge play was Thomas' fumble early in the second half. The Bills were moving the ball and had some momentum. A touchdown would have put Dallas behind by two scores and gotten away from Smith and its powerful running game. Instead, the fumble return tied the game, the Bills lost their composure and Dallas walked off with the victory.

"If I don't fumble, it's a different football game," Thomas said after the game. "It's the downfall of my career. … You have one of the best games of your career a week ago, and then play horrible. … Why did I pick this time to have one of my worst games ever?"

The Bills became the only team to appear in four consecutive Super Bowls, and the only team to lose four in a row. As Bryan Burwell reported in USA Today, "The Bills — a good team with the terrible misfortune of coming along in the midst of a prolonged NFC storm — surely could sense (after the fumble) the Cowboys had regained control of the proceedings."

To get to four straight Super Bowls was an incredible accomplishment — one that has been recognized as the years have gone by. However, the Curse led the Bills to never play at their best when it mattered the most. In three of the four Super Bowls, mistakes killed them against exceptionally good teams. And in the other, strange things happened on Norwood's kick!

As of this writing, Buffalo has not been back to the Super Bowl since walking off the turf at the Georgia Dome on Jan. 30, 1994 — more than a quarter-century ago. The glass slipper still awaits.

Chapter 12
MLB BID STRIKES OUT

Since Buffalo lost its Federal League baseball franchise in 1915 when the league folded, the city was relegated to minor league baseball. The sport was still popular, but many local fans yearned for a major league baseball team for Buffalo to call its own.

The birth of the Continental League in 1959 brought Buffalo a chance to secure a Major League Baseball franchise. William Shea, a New York City attorney, came up with the idea of the Continental Baseball League in 1958. It was proposed to be a third major league, but unlike the Federal League, it wanted to be part of Organized Baseball and sought acceptance within Major League Baseball. Shea's motivation for the new circuit was to bring a second MLB team to New York City, following the loss of the New York Giants and Brooklyn Dodgers to the West Coast in 1957.

The new league's creation was formally announced on July 27, 1959, with an expectation of an eight-team circuit. Teams in five cities were named: Denver, Houston, Minneapolis, New York and Toronto. The league was scheduled to begin play in 1961, and three additional teams would be added by that time. Branch Rickey, former Brooklyn Dodgers president, was named the president of the Continental League on Aug. 18, 1959. The three additional teams were Atlanta (added on Dec. 8), Dallas-Fort Worth (on Dec. 22) and Buffalo (on Jan. 29, 1960).

Buffalo tax attorney Robert O. Swados was leading the effort for Buffalo. The chief financier behind the franchise was Reginald B. Taylor, his client, who at one time had been a New York State probation commissioner. He was heavy into horses and had the money to make the franchise a reality. Swados also was able to secure support from John Stiglmeier, an important local politician with a baseball passion; Louis M. Jacobs, head of Sportservice (today known as Delaware North); Buffalo mayor Frank Sedita; and Buffalo Bills owner Ralph C. Wilson Jr.

Rickey bought into the concept of the Continental League and became president because "he believed that there were many growing markets in the United States which could support big-league teams and that they were being ignored," as Rickey's grandson Branch B. Rickey related. He brought credibility, knew his way around the majors and had many key relationships to help make the league a reality. Rickey and Shea also backed Taylor and the Buffalo bid as the eighth franchise. They knew Taylor had the financial wherewithal, and Buffalo's Bisons had the best attendance record in minor league baseball. They also needed eight franchises for the proposal to have a chance at success.

The Continental League plan was to begin playing in 1961 with seven of the eight cities new to the major leagues. The new league would take advantage of the changing demographics of the country and would help to exponentially grow the game. It would not play against the current major league clubs for four to five years while building its own star players and becoming competitive at the highest level of the sport. Rickey also boldly proposed that each team would share the money received from the television networks to help ensure competitive balance and financial success for all the teams.

Buffalo's biggest challenge to meet the requirements of the new league was securing a ballpark of appropriate size. Though Offermann Stadium, where the Bisons played, was a beautiful minor league ballpark, its seating capacity did not meet the needs of the new league. The Buffalo Bills of the new American Football League had agreed to sign a lease for the use of Civic Stadium if $3 million in improvements were made to the ballpark. That facility, built in 1937, had a seating capacity in excess of 40,000. Mayor Sedita was reluctant to make a significant investment in the old stadium for a new football team that would only play about nine games a year in it. However, if he could get the Bisons to move or the new Continental League franchise to play there, an upgrade could be justified.

The challenge the Continental League team and Sedita faced was that Sportservice owned Offermann Stadium and retained all the concessions revenue from the park. Jacobs also was the majority shareholder of the Bisons. He was against moving the team, predicting it would suffer financial losses because Civic Stadium's layout was not conducive to baseball. Fans would be much farther from the action than they were at Offermann, and the outfield fence dimensions were skewed because of the physical layout of the park. However, after the continued insistence of Taylor, Rickey and Shea, and a politically motivated attempt by Swados at a shareholder vote of the Bisons, Jacobs relented.

Buffalo was now positioned to become a franchise in a third major league that would begin play in 1961. However, though Major League Baseball played along with Shea and Rickey for a while, they were making their own plans behind the scenes. The response came in the summer of 1960 when the American and National leagues announced they would expand by two teams each. Priority would be given to markets that did not have major league baseball.

The American League relocated the Washington Senators franchise to Minneapolis (a proposed Continental League city) and replaced the Senators with an expansion team. They added the Los Angeles Angels as the second expansion team and the A.L.'s first West Coast team. The National League added the Houston Colt .45s (a second Continental League city), and the owners of the New York Continental League team were given the 10th franchise, which became the Mets.

Shea had met his primary objective of securing a National League team for New York. Once that occurred, the demise of the Continental League was imminent. Essentially, the majors had successfully divided and conquered the Continental's potential owners by offering some of them expansion teams. On Aug. 2, 1960 the Continental League formally disbanded.

The excitement around a major league baseball team that had gripped the city since the Jan. 29 announcement came to a crashing end. The Curse seemed to lurk over the proceedings as again the city was denied.

A postscript to the story: The Bisons did indeed move to War Memorial Stadium in 1961 and swept the Junior World Series (International League champion vs. American Association champion) over the Louisville Colonels that season. As for Offermann Stadium, it was demolished soon after the Bisons' departure and replaced by a school. The cozy baseball-only structure is still missed by the few old enough to have watched games there.

Triple-A baseball in War Memorial Stadium suffered a slow decline through the 1960s, partly because of the ballpark and of the perceptions of the neighborhood around it. Eventually, the team moved to Winnipeg in 1970. The city was without a team of any kind until 1979, when Mayor James D. Griffin led an effort to place a Double-A Eastern League team in Buffalo.

Bob Rich Jr., chairman and majority owner of Rich Products Corp., purchased the minor league Buffalo Bisons baseball franchise in 1983 with the intention of bringing major league baseball to Buffalo. After purchasing the team, he quickly upgraded it from Double-A to a Triple-A American Association team in 1985 by acquiring the Wichita Aeros for $1 million. Rich also pursued the building of a new downtown stadium, which opened in 1988 as Pilot Field. The 19,500-seat stadium was expandable to 40,000, with an eye toward accommodating a major league team.

Major League Baseball positioned itself for further expansion in the National League on Aug. 7, 1985, with the signing of a new collective bargaining agreement with the players that stipulated the National League could expand by two teams.

National League President Bill White formed an expansion committee in 1989 that comprised Houston Astros owner John McMullen, New York Mets President Fred Wilpon and Pittsburgh Pirates board chairman Doug Danforth, who chaired the committee. With the announcement, White also said that nothing would happen with expansion until a new CBA with the players was completed.

The owners and players signed a new CBA on March 19, 1990, and the owners began to move ahead quickly with plans to add two expansion teams in the National League. Initially, 10 cities/regions were competing for the franchises: Buffalo, Charlotte, Denver, Miami, Nashville, Orlando, Phoenix, Sacramento, Tampa-St. Petersburg and Washington, DC.

The National League criteria for the expansion cities' rankings were:
1. Strong local ownership
2. An open-air, baseball-only stadium
3. Government backing
4. Fan support

Once the National League turned serious about expansion after the CBA negotiation, Rich and the Bisons immediately entered the fray with their application. Buffalo had a lot to show the expansion committee, as not only did the city have a new state-of-the-art expandable downtown stadium, but the Bisons had set a minor league attendance record in 1988, selling 1,061,319 tickets. The Bisons would continue to exceed 1 million fans in attendance for six consecutive seasons. Before that run, only one minor league team in history had drawn a million fans in one season (Louisville, in 1983).

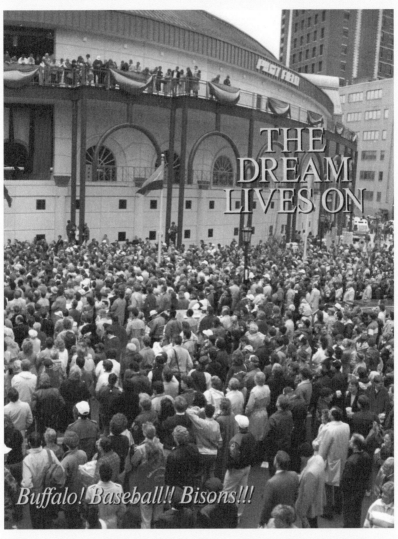

THE
DREAM
LIVES ON

Buffalo! Baseball!! Bisons!!!

Photo 22. Buffalo Bisons yearbook featuring opening-day crowd at
Pilot Field in Buffalo, New York, on April 14, 1988.
(Author's collection)

The Rich family also had plenty of money. At the time, Forbes pegged their net worth to be between $350 and $500 million. In addition, the city had sold $26.1 million in bonds that would be utilized for the expansion of Pilot Field. As the process got underway, based on the specified criteria, it appeared that Buffalo had a strong case to secure one of the two franchises.

The National League Expansion Committee met on Dec. 18, 1990, and reduced the number of finalists to six. Three were from Florida — Miami, Tampa-St. Petersburg and Orlando — with the understanding that only one of the three could get a franchise. The other three finalists, effectively competing for one franchise, were Buffalo, Denver and Washington, DC.

Danforth said at the time that the finalists were "the most qualified in terms of financial stability, significant community identification, and long-term commitment to a baseball club and their community."

Buffalo was extremely excited to be among the finalists, and many fans believed the city had a legitimate chance to land one of the expansion teams. When the finalists were announced, Bob Rich Jr. sent a letter to The Buffalo News, raising concerns about the viability of a major league team in Buffalo. His points centered around the high franchise fee of $95 million, the escalating salaries of the players and the decision by existing franchises not to share television revenues with new teams in their first year of operation. In addition, investments would need to be made in a farm system and in expanding Pilot Field by about 20,000 seats and adding other necessary elements to the facility.

But his letter did say, "We are committed to bringing Major League Baseball to Western New York, and we're committed to bringing affordable family fun to the fans of this area." And at a news conference on Dec. 18, Rich also said, "Buffalo deserves this more than any of the four cities that were not on the list, and any of the cities that were on the list with us. Buffalo and Western New York have proven themselves to be great baseball fans."

In the spring of 1991, the National League Expansion Committee met with each of the six finalists at their sites. The committee came to Buffalo on March 25 to talk to the leaders of Buffalo's expansion group, including Bob Rich Jr. and his wife, Mindy, as well as to tour Buffalo and Pilot Field. Before meeting with the expansion committee, Bob Rich said, "We're very much in the hunt. We're excited about bringing Major League Baseball to Buffalo if it's affordable for the fans."

BUFFALO
Bisons

September 20, 1990

Mr. Haywood C. Sullivan
General Partner
BOSTON RED SOX
Fenway Park
4 Yawkey Way
Boston, MA 02215

Dear Haywood:

  Tuesday we had the opportunity to present our case for
Major League Baseball in Buffalo to the National League
Expansion Committee. Today, we would like to share an element
of that presentation with you by sending you the enclosed video
and leave-behind.

  It was an exciting and much-anticipated moment for us, and
we feel that the enclosed materials capture the essence of why
we're so positive about the prospect of Major League Baseball
in Buffalo. We hope you'll agree.

         Best regards,

         Bob and Mindy Rich

/pjs
Enclosures

Every Game's An Event!

Administrative Offices (716) 846-2000 / Fax # (716) 846-2258 / Hot Line (716) 852-4700
Bison Baseball, Inc. / P.O. Box 450 /Buffalo, New York 14205-0450
Bison Baseball, Inc. / Pilot Field / 275 Washington Street / Buffalo, New York 14203

**Photo 23. Letter from Buffalo Bisons owners Bob and Mindy Rich to Boston Red Sox
general partner Haywood Sullivan dated Sept. 20, 1990, regarding Buffalo's
presentation to Major League Baseball for an expansion franchise.**

(Author's collection)

Mindy Rich and Mayor Griffin, both big supporters of bringing a major league baseball team to Buffalo, expressed concerns about the financial situation and the exorbitant MLB franchise fee of $95 million. Mindy Rich said, "We're asking them, if we're going to be a partner with Major League Baseball, what is Major League Baseball's long-range plan?"

The following day, it was reported that the meeting with the committee went well. Although the Buffalo group raised issues about the significant cost of MLB salaries and the cost of expansion, Buffalo was still under serious consideration.

Danforth said he saw two positives about Buffalo's bid: solid ownership and a state-of-the-art stadium. He also identified two negatives: market size and available parking. He commented about the Buffalo ownership, "The thing that impresses me the most … is the Riches know what they are doing. They run a very good club, probably the best-run Triple-A franchise that I know of." The committee was also impressed with Pilot Field.

The official decision was expected to come from MLB by the middle of June. As league owners, along with the expansion committee, were attempting to reach the final selection, Danforth raised an issue shared by other MLB owners: They wanted Western New York to have 1 million more people.

Sportswriter Tom Verducci, in assessing each of the finalists' chances, wrote this about Buffalo's candidacy in the Los Angeles Times on June 10, 1991: "Buffalo is the choice of traditionalists. It has a ballpark, Pilot Field, with an old-fashioned feel, and modern conveniences. It has a local owner with deep pockets, Bob Rich Jr., whose family owns the largest privately held frozen foods company in the country, and it has loyal sports fans." He also pointed out that the Bisons had drawn more than 1.1 million fans three years running. In addition, the Bills set NFL attendance records for two consecutive seasons, and the Sabres were playing to almost 100% capacity at the time.

The NL Expansion Committee delayed its announcement until July 6, but word leaked out on June 11 that Denver and Miami would be the cities selected.

Miami was selected for several reasons. Wayne Huizenga Sr. was the owner of Blockbuster Video, which at the time was the nation's largest video retailer. He also was a part-owner of the Dolphins and Joe Robbie Stadium. In addition, Miami was a large television market, in the top 20 in the United States. Additionally, Huizenga was close friends with Pittsburgh Pirates President Carl Barger, who happened to be on Blockbuster's board; Barger's boss, Pirates chairman Danforth, was on the expansion committee. The franchise became the Florida Marlins, now known as the Miami Marlins.

Denver was also a top 20 television market, and baseball had no presence in the Mountain time zone, while both leagues were oversaturated in the Eastern and Central time zones with 22 of 28 clubs. The team became the Colorado Rockies.

Bob Rich and the Buffalo baseball group felt misled by the committee. Buffalo met the four criteria as outlined as well or better than any of the other finalists. Rich said, "When you look at the four criteria that were mentioned, we hit them right on the numbers." He went on to say, "You can tell by the cities that were chosen that the criteria took a back seat to things like television market, and virgin territories." Despite Buffalo having the first "classic retro" ballpark , the best proven track record of fan attendance and loyalty, an ownership group that was clearly committed and had the money, and strong government support, Buffalo was not chosen.

Buffalo's runner-up status could be attributed to a number of factors. First and foremost, Buffalo was the 38th largest television market in the nation at the time, and MLB was looking at expanded revenue sources, with television seen as a critical avenue. The economics of baseball were clearly changing, with significantly increasing player salaries, and it would become harder for smaller market teams to compete. In addition, the commissioner saw the need to enter new markets for baseball, especially in Florida and Colorado, as extremely important. And there was some inside baseball with relationships that helped deliver teams to those two cities. And of course, hanging over all of this was the Buffalo Sports Curse.

The two expansion teams joined the National League for the 1993 season. As of 2022, neither team had won a division title, although the Marlins did win the World Series in 1997 and 2003 as wild-card teams. In the early 2020s, the Marlins had the fewest winning seasons of any MLB franchise, with only seven, and were struggling to consistently draw solid attendance, with only 642,617 fans in 2021. Colorado, though with limited on-field success, had drawn well and was consistently among the top 10 in attendance.

Baseball expanded again in 1998, adding Tampa Bay and Arizona. The expansion process began in 1994, and Buffalo applied by the June deadline but was not selected as a finalist on March 9, 1995. The expansion fee had grown to $130 million, and it was becoming apparent that the economics of baseball had dramatically changed and would not work in Buffalo. In 2005 the Montreal Expos moved to Washington to become the Nationals. So, Buffalo is the only city among the six finalists from 1991 not to have gotten a major league team as of 2022. In addition, Buffalo is also the only one of the Continental League's eight original cities not to have a major league baseball club.

The economics of baseball has been significantly altered since 1991 as Rich predicted it would. The 1990s progressed with free agency, luxury suites and television rights fees, making the cost of running a major league team exorbitant for a city the size and demographic makeup of Buffalo.

You could say again that Buffalo is cursed. The timing killed Buffalo's bid. Had expansion occurred even one year sooner, the city may very well have been awarded a team. But with the changing landscape of the sport's economics, Buffalo was again denied a big-league club.

Major League Baseball is now a league of haves and have-nots. The power and the money are in the control of the large market teams, which consistently spend more than $200 million in payroll while the middle- and small-market clubs can barely compete with payrolls of less than $100 million. In the first two decades of the 21st century only one small-market team has won a World Series: the Kansas City Royals in 2015. Baseball has added a luxury tax and revenue sharing to level the economic playing field slightly, but it's difficult for small-market teams to win consistently.

Buffalo was done a disservice and deserved a franchise based on the published criteria. But it was not meant to be, and with the economics of baseball today, it looks like the Queen City's pursuit of major league baseball is probably forever in the rearview mirror. Damn that Curse.

In 2020, in a most unusual way, Major League Baseball came to Buffalo for the first time in 105 years with the Toronto Blue Jays. During the worldwide Covid-19 pandemic, Buffalo played host to the Blue Jays for 26 "home" games on their 60-game schedule.

With the pandemic raging around the world, the U.S. and Canadian governments closed the border between the two countries and significantly limited travel. As MLB was determining how it would conduct a shortened season, the Canadian government was considering whether it would allow the Blue Jays to play in Toronto and cross the border for their games in U.S. cities. Even though the idea of playing baseball "as usual" in Toronto had the support of the City of Toronto and the provincial government of Ontario, ultimately the Canadian government surprised the Blue Jays with its refusal to allow them to play in Toronto. The decision came down on July 18, only 11 days before the team's scheduled home opener on July 29.

Toronto had to find a facility in the United States — in a hurry — to compete in 2020. The Blue Jays initially looked at Sahlen Field in Buffalo (the former Pilot Field) but were not inclined to play in a minor league facility. The stadium would need several upgrades to make it major league compatible. Toronto considered playing at its spring training facility in Dunedin, Florida. But at that point, Florida had one of the highest Covid-19 infection rates in the country, so Dunedin was not an option. The Blue Jays then considered playing in Pittsburgh's PNC Park or Baltimore's Camden Yards, but Pennsylvania and Maryland officials rejected those ideas.

Toronto was out of options and turned back to Buffalo and Sahlen Field. On July 24, Toronto announced it would play most of its home schedule in Buffalo, after the stadium lighting, training facilities and clubhouses were upgraded. In addition, New York State's permission to stage the games came with the restriction that no fans would attend. With the late decision, there was no time to improve Sahlen Field's facilities for the first scheduled home game. So the Blue Jays were forced to play their opening home games on the road — but batting as the home team.

Toronto played the first 13 games of its season on the road, with two (in Washington) counting as home games, and finished the lengthy road trip with a 5–8 record. The Blue Jays finally opened their home season at Sahlen Field on Aug. 11 against the Miami Marlins. At 6:40 p.m. Toronto pitcher Hyun Jin Ryu threw the first major league pitch in Buffalo in 105 years — dating back to the Federal League. Jonathan Villar fouled the pitch off and four pitches later struck out. Travis Shaw of the Blue Jays got the first hit, singling in the bottom of the first. Brian Anderson of the Marlins hit a home run in the top of the second inning for the first run of the game. Toronto won the game in the bottom of the 10th inning on a walk-off single from Shaw, scoring Anthony Alford with the winning run in a 5–4 victory.

The Blue Jays won only two of their first five games in Buffalo, but soon Toronto turned Sahlen Field into a significant home-field advantage. With 15 former Bisons players on the roster and several of them playing starring roles — including Bo Bichette, Cavan Biggio, Vladimir Guerrero Jr., Lourdes Gurriel Jr., Teoscar Hernández and Rowdy Tellez — the Blue Jays defeated the Yankees in five of seven games, the Mets in two of three, Baltimore in five of seven and completed a doubleheader sweep of the Phillies. Toronto finished its home schedule with a 17–9 record, the second-best home record in the American League in 2020. They also scored the second-most runs at home of any team in baseball. Their success at Sahlen Field spurred the team to a playoff berth, the Blue Jays' first in four seasons. Toronto clinched the berth on Sept. 24 at Sahlen Field with a 4–1 victory over the Yankees.

Buffalo's ballpark provided the team "a clear advantage throughout the 2020 abbreviated season," according to Gregor Chisholm of the Toronto Star. "The Jays' 17–9 record in Buffalo represented the second-highest winning percentage at home in franchise history."

"We made it our home and we played good here. It was a great time here," Blue Jays manager Charlie Montoyo said. The Toronto organization was extremely pleased with how the players and coaches reacted to the venue and made it their advantage.

Buffalo, Sahlen Field and the Bisons received tremendous national attention from media outlets, social media and game broadcasts. It was a great advertisement for Buffalo as a major league city — even without fans. It is a very cruel irony that when Buffalo finally had an MLB team playing within its city limits, no fans could attend the games. Talk about the ultimate tease. The Curse had come up with a unique and unexpected twist.

The good news for Buffalo baseball fans was that the Blue Jays were back at Sahlen Field for part of the 2021 season. The Covid-19 pandemic continued to affect the world, and the Canadian border remained closed. Toronto began the season in Dunedin, Florida, but moved its home games to Buffalo on June 1. With only limited capacity allowed, 5,321 fans saw the Blue Jays beat the Miami Marlins 5–1. In the first major league game played in front of fans in Buffalo in 106 years, Guerrero belted a three-run home run and Gurriel hit a solo shot to lead the Blue Jays to victory.

It was a fun summer romance as Buffalo fans enthusiastically supported the team as they were able to see the New York Yankees, Boston Red Sox and American League East champion Tampa Bay Rays, among others. The Blue Jays played 23 games in Buffalo over an eight-week period in June and July. Toronto did not have quite the same success on the field as 2020, finishing with a 12–11 record at Sahlen Field. The final game was a 7–4 loss to the Boston Red Sox on July 21 in front of 14,607, the largest crowd of the season. The fans fervently supported the team, with the Blue Jays drawing an average of 7,738 per game and outdrawing three other teams: the Tampa Bay Rays (7,405 per game), Oakland Athletics (6,861) and the Miami Marlins (6,464).

The cruel irony is that Buffalo lost out to Miami when the National League expanded in 1991.

Buffalo proved that it could effectively support a major league ballclub, but it is unlikely that a team will permanently come to the city, unless an owner with deep pockets comes along. It was a fun fan experience for a brief fling during the summer of 2021.

Chapter 13
O.J. SIMPSON'S
FALL FROM GRACE

The Buffalo Sports Curse isn't restricted to teams. Sometimes, it can strike someone we might least expect, and it struck one of the most famous and popular athletes to ever wear a Buffalo jersey.

No professional sports athlete in the history of America has fallen further in the eyes of the public than O.J. Simpson. When Simpson was charged with the murder of his ex-wife Nicole Brown Simpson and her friend Ronald Goldman in June 1994, it stunned the sports world. This was as if Tom Brady or Michael Jordan were facing charges for a major crime. Simpson, one of America's most likable celebrities at the time, was still involved in football as an NBC commentator and his popular Hertz commercials still graced our television screens. It was inconceivable that this friendly, dynamic personality could have committed such a hideous crime. It seemed out of character with the public persona Simpson had created.

Simpson was Los Angeles and Hollywood, but he was also Buffalo and your friendly neighbor. He made the city feel major league in every way. He was "The Juice," and he was part of Buffalo's juice. Simpson was a great ambassador for the city of Buffalo and all of Western New York. He was approachable, charismatic and friendly and had an impeccable image. But that all came tumbling down after June 12, 1994.

Simpson's fall from grace was almost immediate, following the double murder charge after the slayings. With all the hype leading up to the criminal trial, many called it the "Trial of the Century," a spectacle that captured the attention of America for 11 months. The trial began with jury selection on Nov. 9, 1994, and opening statements were made on Jan. 24, 1995. It was the lead story just about every day throughout the proceedings. Though Simpson was acquitted on Oct. 3, 1995, the made-for-TV court case exposed Simpson's private behavior before the murders. Much of the evidence presented was very damning.

Despite his acquittal, much of the American public saw the verdict as a miscarriage of justice. When Simpson returned home after the trial, he thought he would resume his celebrity life. Very quickly he realized that was not possible. Simpson was now a pariah and soon found out he was not welcome in many of the communities where he had made his name. The NFL, the Buffalo Bills, the University of Southern California, Hollywood, his corporate endorsement clients — none welcomed him back. Many people who were thought to be close to him deserted him, including close friends, members of his family, some of his defense team and many acquaintances who had ridden his coattails.

His civil trial in 1997, brought by the Goldman family, reinforced the public perception that he was guilty of the murders. Simpson was found liable for the wrongful deaths of his ex-wife and Goldman and was ordered to pay $33.5 million in damages.

Simpson's behavior since the two verdicts has been anything but exemplary. He befriended many less-desirable people, continuing to soil his reputation, and leading him into additional trouble and problems. He was convicted of armed robbery on Oct. 3, 2008, for trying to retrieve some of his lost sports memorabilia. He served nine years in prison in Nevada for the charges. Simpson was granted parole and was released on Oct. 1, 2017. He now lives a quiet life, still not accepted by most of the American public.

Simpson first came into the public conscience as a junior at the University of Southern California. He was a junior college transfer from the City College of San Francisco, where he was a two-time Junior College All-American in football. He scored an incredible 54 touchdowns in his two years at City College. Simpson rushed for 1,161 yards as a freshman and 1,391 yards as a sophomore. He was acclaimed as "the most sensational junior college football player of all-time," as reported in the 1968 USC football guide.

Upon his arrival, Simpson immediately became the featured tailback in USC's vaunted attack. He also helped USC win the 1967 NCAA track championships, placing fifth in the 60-yard dash, sixth in the 100-yard sprint and running the third leg on the Trojans' world record-shattering 4-by-110 relay team.

His first breakout football game at USC came on Sept. 23 against fifth-ranked Texas, when he rushed for 158 yards and one touchdown in the Trojans' 17–13 victory. Simpson's stature continued to grow as he put together games of 190 yards and two touchdowns against Michigan State, 160 yards vs. Washington, 188 yards vs. Oregon State and a 160-yard, three-touchdown effort against fifth-ranked Notre Dame.

Simpson solidified his reputation to the nation on Nov. 18 when No. 4 USC played No. 1 UCLA in a nationally televised game on ABC. The Bruins held Simpson in check in the first half, limiting him to 30 yards. However, with the score knotted at 7–7 in the second quarter, he took a pitchout from quarterback Steve Sogge at the Bruins 13-yard line. He broke a couple of tackles, crashed through a line of Bruins defenders and carried two of them across the goal line for a touchdown and a 14–7 Trojans lead. It was a spectacular run as Simpson displayed his incredible combination of elusiveness and power.

With UCLA leading 20–14 in the fourth quarter, Simpson took a handoff from quarterback Toby Page (who had replaced Sogge) at the Trojans 36-yard line. He faked right, then ran through a hole on the left side of the line, cut sharply back to the right while weaving through half of the UCLA defense and broke into the clear. Simpson sprinted the last 20 yards to the end zone and the go-ahead touchdown. It still is considered one of the greatest runs in college football history. USC held onto the 1-point lead, winning the contest 21–20. After the game, the Trojans were back on top of the college football polls.

The Rose Bowl was somewhat anticlimactic as No. 1-ranked USC beat a 9–1 Indiana team 14–3. Simpson rushed for 128 yards and both Trojan touchdowns. He was named the Player of the Game, and USC was voted the national champions of college football. Simpson concluded his junior season with 1,543 yards rushing, leading the nation, on 291 carries with a 5.3 per carry average and 13 touchdowns. He was a consensus All-American and the runner-up to UCLA quarterback Gary Beban for the Heisman Trophy.

Georgia Tech head coach Bobby Dodd said about Simpson in 1967, "I have never seen a greater football player in college football, and I've seen them all. That 13-yard run on the goal line vs. UCLA is one of the greatest runs I've ever seen." Paul B. Zimmerman who covered football for the the Los Angeles Times from 1931–68 called him "the most exciting collegiate running back I've seen."

In 1968, the defending champion Trojans bolted to a 9–0 record behind Simpson's sensational running. Throughout the season he was an incredible workhorse, carrying the football an average of 35 times per game. Simpson again led the nation in rushing, this time with an NCAA record 1,880 yards, along with 23 touchdowns. In his final regular-season game, played at the Los Angeles Memorial Coliseum against Notre Dame, the Irish held Simpson to the lowest rushing total of his career, 55 yards, as Notre Dame tied the undefeated Trojans 21–21.

The tie did not diminish the matchup for the Rose Bowl, as USC was still ranked second in the country and Ohio State was ranked first. Simpson won the Heisman Trophy in a landslide vote a few weeks before the game. He was also a consensus All-American for the second consecutive year.

The two best teams in college football squared off on New Year's Day 1969. The Trojans jumped to a quick 10–0 lead, propelled by Simpson's 80-yard touchdown run in the second quarter. However, the Ohio State Buckeyes defense adjusted by stacking the line of scrimmage — daring USC to pass. Simpson finished with 171 yards but had only 34 rushing yards after halftime, as Ohio State came back to win 27–16. Simpson's career at USC ended on a down note, but his pro career beckoned.

Southern Cal head coach John McKay summed up his view of Simpson by saying, "If there's a better football player alive than O.J. Simpson, I'd like to see him. He is absolutely fantastic."

In 1969, Simpson was considered the greatest running back to ever come out of college football. At the time, the Buffalo Bills and Philadelphia Eagles were in a battle to see which team was the worst in pro football and would secure the No. 1 pick in the draft for the opportunity to select Simpson. The Eagles were a woeful 0–11 going into a Thanksgiving Day game with the Detroit Lions, and the Bills were 1–10–1 as they prepared to face the Oakland Raiders.

The Eagles defeated the Lions 12–0 in the pouring rain and mud at Tiger Stadium, with veteran Sam Baker kicking four field goals. The surprising Bills trailed the 9–2 Oakland Raiders only 13–10 late in the fourth quarter, with fifth-string quarterback Ed Rutkowski under center. (The four quarterbacks ahead of Rutkowski were all unavailable because of injuries.) Rutkowski led the Bills on a long, sustained drive and faced third and goal at the Raiders 3. Rutkowski took the snap, saw an opening to the left side of the line, darted through the hole and arrived at the goal line simultaneously with

Raiders cornerback George Atkinson. As Rutkowski lunged toward the goal, Atkinson swiped at the ball, knocking it loose, and Oakland's Dave Grayson recovered at the 1-yard line with 3:14 left. Buffalo had one last chance; however, Bruce Alford's 42-yard field goal with 43 seconds left fell harmlessly short, and Oakland held on to the 13–10 victory.

Despite the results of Thanksgiving Day, the Eagles still were in the driver's seat to get the top draft choice. They only had to lose their final two games. However, they beat the expansion New Orleans Saints the following week 29–17, while the Bills' ineptitude returned with a 35–6 pasting at the hands of the Houston Oilers. Buffalo therefore clinched the No. 1 draft pick. Rutkowski would joke many years later that Bills owner Ralph C. Wilson Jr. owed him a bonus check for fumbling at the goal line against the Raiders. On Jan. 28, 1969, with the first pick in the NFL draft, the Bills selected Simpson.

That summer, he reported late to training camp as it took a while for the Bills and Simpson to reach agreement on a four-year, $400,000 contract. He missed the team's first two preseason games, finally making his debut on Aug. 15 at Detroit. Simpson did not get his usual No. 32 jersey, as running back Gary McDermott already had the number and was not about to give it up to the rookie. Simpson wore No. 36 in his professional debut. His first professional football carry came at 14:41 of the fourth quarter when Simpson took a handoff from quarterback James Harris, running for 2 yards. He carried three more times and gained a total of 19 yards rushing. His big play was a 38-yard catch-and-run off a Harris pass, setting up a Bills touchdown. Buffalo lost 24–12, but fans saw enough to be excited about Simpson. It was hard to believe that the best player in college football in at least a generation was playing for the Bills.

Simpson made his regular-season debut wearing his familiar No. 32 jersey (McDermott had been cut) against the New York Jets on Sept. 14. Though the Bills lost 33–19 to the defending Super Bowl champions, Simpson showed flashes of brilliance with a 55-yard catch-and-run off a Harris pass, a terrific 8-yard touchdown run and 68 yards on three kickoff returns.

Simpson's first 100-yard rushing day came against the Denver Broncos on Sept. 28 in a Bills 41–28 victory. He rushed for 110 yards on 24 carries and caught a touchdown pass. However, Bills head coach John Rauch did not want to feed Simpson the ball in the running game, using him primarily as a decoy and pass receiver. Rauch's strategy did not work well, wasting Simpson's immense talents. The Bills struggled to a 4–10 record. Simpson finished his rookie season with 697 yards rushing on 181 carries. He also caught 30 passes for 343 yards and scored five touchdowns.

The 1970 season, the first year of the AFL-NFL merger with teams playing an interlocking schedule, was no better as the Bills finished 3–10–1. Simpson was injured on a kickoff return in a Week 8 game versus the Cincinnati Bengals and was out for the season. He rushed for 488 yards in his injury-shortened season. Rauch and Wilson had a disagreement during the 1971 training camp, and Wilson demanded an apology. Rauch refused and resigned before the start of the 1971 season, putting the organization in complete turmoil. The Bills, under interim coach Harvey Johnson, stumbled through the season and limped home with a 1–13 record, with Simpson rushing for 742 yards.

Many sportswriters and fans were saying that Simpson was a bust. Bob Rubin wrote in his book "All-Stars of the NFL," "As a rookie, the highly touted Simpson was a flop. … His second season (1970) was another disappointment. … Things got even worse in 1971. It was a disastrous season for Simpson, too. In one game, a 43–0 loss to Baltimore, he rushed for minus 10 yards." Chuck Barnes, Simpson's agent, said after his dismal three seasons in Buffalo, "He is a tough sell to ad agencies these days. The agency guys say, 'Simpson, who's he?'" Even Simpson agreed, as he said, "I'd just had three years of nothin." His pro career may have turned out that way had it not been for the hiring of Lou Saban as the Bills' new head coach. Saban had coached Buffalo in the 1960s to two AFL championships. Saban said, "I believe in running the football — basic, hard-nosed football. We have a great runner, a game-breaker who is a big-play athlete. I intend to use him." Saban told Simpson's offensive teammates, "There's your meal ticket. Block for him."

Saban built an offensive line around Simpson that became known as the Electric Company: "They turn on The Juice." The Electric Company included four Bills draft choices: guard Reggie McKenzie, guard Joe DeLamielleure, tackle Donnie Green and tight end Paul Seymour. Saban also traded for center Mike Montler and tackle Dave Foley. He committed to giving the ball to Simpson, and once he did, Simpson's career skyrocketed.

No player has arguably ever put together a better five-year period than Simpson from 1972 to 1976. He rushed for 7,699 yards on 1,513 carries, averaging more than 5 yards per carry. Four times in the five seasons he led the NFL in rushing. Simpson is the only running back in NFL history to rush for over 2,000 yards in 14 games, and his 1975 season with 2,243 total yards from scrimmage and 23 touchdowns, both league records at the time, was considered by many even better than his 2,000-yard-rushing season.

His first 1,000-yard-rushing season was his initial campaign with Saban as head coach in 1972. A rejuvenated Simpson rushed for 1,251 yards on 292 carries. His season was highlighted by a spectacular 94-yard TD run against the Steelers and five 100-yard games.

In two of the next three years, Simpson put together the two greatest individual seasons by a running back in NFL history at that time. He rushed for 2,003 yards on 332 carries, with a 6-yards-per-carry average in 1973. When Simpson broke the 2,000-yard mark on Dec. 16 versus the New York Jets at Shea Stadium, his teammates carried him off the field, recognizing what an incomparable achievement it was. In the postgame locker room, Simpson refused to interview with the media until all his offensive teammates were gathered around him. He made first-team All-Pro and was NFL MVP. It was the greatest single season for a running back in NFL history. He had 11 games with more than 100 yards rushing, and three were more than 200 yards — a first in NFL history.

What made his accomplishments even more amazing was that the Bills only passed the football 213 times for the season. Therefore, everyone in the stadium and on the other team knew Simpson was going to get the football. He out-rushed the second-leading NFL rusher, John Brockington of the Green Bay Packers, by 859 yards, the largest margin in NFL history. At the conclusion of the season, he was named Sports Illustrated's Sportsman of the Year, along with many other individual honors. As of this writing, no running back has rushed for 2,000 yards in 14 games.

In the 1975 season, Simpson rushed for 1,817 yards on 329 carries, averaging 5.5 yards a carry with 16 TDs. In addition, he caught 28 passes for 427 yards and seven more touchdowns. He led the league in yards from scrimmage and broke the NFL record with 23 touchdowns in a single season. He was unstoppable as the Bills led the NFL in offensive production and points in 1975. Simpson out-rushed Pittsburgh's Franco Harris, the league's second-leading rusher, by 571 yards. He continued his phenomenal play in 1976, despite the Bills dropping to 3–11 as a team. Simpson rushed for 1,503 yards, again leading the league in rushing.

The Bills declined in the two seasons after that, and Simpson's numbers suffered as well. Simpson's career as a Bill ended in 1977, as he was injured in a Week 7 game in Seattle and was placed on season-ending injured reserve.

Photo 24. Buffalo Bills running back O.J. Simpson (32) during an NFL game in the late 1970s. "The Juice" set an NFL rushing record (since broken) of 2,003 yards in 1973.

(Mitchell B. Reibel via AP)

He finished the season with 557 yards. Simpson was traded to the San Francisco 49ers in the offseason, where he played for two years, rushing for a total of 1,053 yards. He retired at the conclusion of the 1979 campaign.

Simpson had some of the greatest single games in NFL history. On 35 occasions, he rushed for 100 yards or more in a game and had six 200-yard games.

His greatest games included:

- Oct. 29, 1972 — Simpson scorched the Steelers' rugged defense for 189 yards on 22 carries, including a 94-yard touchdown run, the longest of his career.
- Sept. 16, 1973 — Simpson eclipsed the NFL single-game rushing record as he gained 250 yards against the New England Patriots in the Bills' 31–13 victory in Foxborough. He scored a pair of touchdowns: a scintillating 80-yard run and a 22-yarder.
- Dec. 9, 1973 — Simpson again picked on the Patriots, rushing for 219 yards on 22 carries in the snow at Rich Stadium, averaging almost 10 yards per carry. The Bills won 37–13.
- Dec. 16, 1973 — He broke the NFL single-season rushing record at Shea Stadium with a 200-yard game on 34 carries. It was his third 200-yard game of 1973 and his 11th 100+ yard game, both NFL single-season records.
- Sept. 28, 1975 — In probably his single greatest game, considering the quality of the opponent, Simpson rushed for 228 yards against the defending Super Bowl champion Steelers and their vaunted defense. He had five runs of 10 or more yards, including a tremendous 88-yard touchdown.
- Nov. 17, 1975 — In a shootout on "Monday Night Football" with Cincinnati Bengals quarterback Ken Anderson, Simpson rushed for 197 yards on 17 carries and two touchdowns. His running kept the Bills in the game, but they could not overcome Anderson's 447 yards passing.
- Nov. 25, 1976 — While America was enjoying turkey dinners on Thanksgiving, Simpson was thrashing the Lions defense. He set a single-game rushing record with 273 yards on 29 carries. Despite his performance, the Bills lost 27–14.
- Dec. 5, 1976 — Ten days later, against Miami, Simpson rushed for 203 yards on 24 carries, including a 75-yard touchdown run. It was the last 200-yard rushing game of his career. The Bills lost 45–27.

Simpson was the greatest football player of his generation, both in college and the NFL. As a player he is one of the greatest running backs to ever don a jersey. He is enshrined in both the college and pro football halls of fame.

Until 1994, his off-the-field exploits were as impressive as his on-field performance. Simpson was the first Black athlete to transcend race off the athletic field. As People magazine said in 1975, Simpson was the "first Black athlete to become a bona fide lovable media superstar."

Early in his career, with the help of his agent, Chuck Barnes, Simpson secured several endorsement deals. In the spring of 1969, his first contract was with Chevrolet. The agreement included Simpson appearing at car shows, doing advertisements and lending his name. He also signed his first television contract with ABC and another endorsement deal with Royal Crown Cola. All in all, Simpson made more money through these contracts than he did playing football.

His next big breakthrough came when he signed a deal with Hertz in 1975. Simpson was the first Black man hired for a major national corporate advertising campaign. The campaign was tremendously successful, with Simpson shown running through airports in commercials. It significantly expanded and enhanced his national profile and popularity and was a big winner for Hertz. Many more endorsement offers became available to Simpson as he signed on with TreeSweet orange juice, which was a perfect fit. He also had contracts with Schick razors, Foster Grant sunglasses, Dingo cowboy boots, Wilson Sporting Goods and Spot-Bilt athletic shoes. His natural charisma and almost universal acceptance, along with his spotless image, made him an ideal fit for these brands.

Simpson also began pursuing a movie career while still playing football. Though he had done a few television appearances, his first major movies came in 1974 with appearances in "The Klansman" and "The Towering Inferno." He followed those up with acting roles in "The Cassandra Crossing" in 1976 and "Capricorn One" in 1978. Simpson decided in 1979 to start his own film production company, Orenthal Productions. He appeared in the "Goldie and the Boxer" films, "Cocaine and Blue Eyes" and "Back to the Beach." But what Simpson the actor was known for was his role as Officer Nordberg in the "Naked Gun" trilogy.

He also had a lucrative broadcasting career. Simpson was hired by ABC as a color commentator on "Monday Night Football" in 1983. He appeared on the broadcast alongside play-by-play man Frank Gifford and Howard

Cosell. In 1984, he teamed with Gifford and Don Meredith, and in his final year of 1985 with MNF, Simpson was with Gifford and Joe Namath. He joined NBC in 1989 as part of the "NFL Live" studio show and in 1993, Simpson became a sideline reporter and covered Super Bowl 28 in Atlanta. His broadcast career and his endorsement deals ended after the double murders. Simpson made a huge, groundbreaking impact beyond the football field for Black athletes. He paved the way into corporate America, securing lucrative endorsement contracts and widespread popularity across the American landscape in advertising, movies and broadcasting. Simpson's pioneering work beyond the playing field has helped Black athletes transcend race and become not only popular players but ultra-successful businessmen with boundless opportunity.

But no other athlete in American history has taken a greater fall than Orenthal James Simpson in the most stunning story of the 20th century in American sports.

Simpson was the most popular athlete in Buffalo sports history until 1994. Everybody in Buffalo had a Simpson story to tell. He represented the city on the national stage in an amazing way. The double murders were an incredible tragedy for all the people involved, but it also was a sad period for Buffalo, as it lost one of its biggest national boosters on that fateful day in 1994. Cursed!

Chapter 14
BILLS GIVE UP A
HOME RUN THROWBACK

Jim Kelly led the Bills to four straight Super Bowls in the early 1990s, the only team in NFL history to accomplish such a feat. In addition, Kelly took the Bills to four other playoff appearances — 1988, 1989, 1995 and 1996 — each time falling short of playing in the Super Bowl, usually with some odd extenuating circumstances.

Buffalo surprised the entire league in 1988 by racing to an 11–1 record and clinching the AFC East title earlier than any team up to that time. The Bills defeated the New York Jets on Nov. 20 in the rain and drizzle at Rich Stadium with a Scott Norwood 30-yard field goal in overtime to win the East. Bills broadcaster Van Miller utilized the word Fandemonium in describing fans at the game as he watched thousands storm the field in celebration of the division-clinching win. The ecstatic crowd tore down the goal posts while partying on the field. It was an incredible and exciting scene.

The game was the Bills' first division-clinching win at home since 1966. Buffalo was considered the odds-on favorite to have home-field advantage throughout the playoffs and reach its first Super Bowl. The Bills only needed to win two of their last four regular-season games to clinch that edge.

The following week Buffalo lost in Cincinnati to the 10–3 Bengals, 35–21. The next week the Bills were stunned 10–5 by the inept 3–10 Tampa Bay Buccaneers. Playing at Tampa Stadium, Buffalo's offense bungled its way through most of the game but had one final chance late in the contest. With 3:29 remaining, Kelly drove the Bills to the Bucs 25-yard line in 2:32. Earlier in the game, Norwood had missed a 30-yard field goal, which proved costly as the Bills only would have needed a field goal to win. Instead, the Bills needed a touchdown. However, on the next play Kelly threw an ill-advised pass that was intercepted by safety Eugene Robinson, and the Bucs upset was complete.

The Bills defeated the Raiders at home 37–21 on Dec. 11 and still only had to defeat the Indianapolis Colts in the final week of the season at the RCA Dome to clinch home-field advantage. The Colts were battling for a wild-card playoff berth and needed a win over Buffalo for a chance at the postseason. The Bills jumped to a 14–3 lead and seemed in control when Bruce Smith sacked Colts quarterback Chris Chandler in the third quarter, knocking him out of the game. Indianapolis went to its second-string quarterback, Gary Hogeboom, who had been benched earlier in the season. He led the Colts on two lengthy scoring drives, one of 80 yards in 17 plays and the game-winning drive of 75 yards in eight plays. The winning drive was capped off by a Hogeboom to Albert Bentley 7-yard touchdown pass, resulting in the 17–14 victory.

With the loss, the Bills ended the season having lost three of their final four games. That gave the Bengals home-field advantage throughout the playoffs. Both teams finished with 12–4 records, but Cincinnati won the tiebreaker with its win over Buffalo.

Despite that, the Bills were excited to be making their first playoff appearance since 1981. Buffalo hosted the 11–6 Houston Oilers on Jan. 1 in a divisional playoff game to usher in the New Year. It was the Bills' first home playoff game in exactly 22 years. On a sunny 40-degree day at Rich Stadium, the Bills used a blocked punt, an interception and a blue-collar defensive effort to subdue the Oilers 17–10 and advance to the AFC championship game in Cincinnati.

Buffalo finished its home season with a 9–0 record and lamented the lost opportunity of hosting the AFC championship game because of the late-season losses. Instead, the Bills traveled to Cincinnati for their first appearance in an AFC/AFL championship game since they had lost to the Kansas City Chiefs on Jan. 1, 1967, with the chance to go to Super Bowl 1. The winner of this game would go on to play San Francisco in Super Bowl 23.

The Bengals scored first after Kelly's second interception in the first quarter, driving 19 yards in four plays as Ickey Woods scored from the 1-yard line. The Bills responded with their best drive of the day as Kelly completed four straight passes, the final one to Andre Reed for a 9-yard touchdown early in the second quarter, to tie the game at 7–7.

Photo 25. Ickey Woods (30) of the Cincinnati Bengals runs through the Bills on the way to two rushing touchdowns in the Bengals' 21–10 AFC championship game victory on Jan. 8, 1989, at Riverfront Stadium in Cincinnati.

(Photo by Focus on Sport, Getty Images)

On the Bills' next possession, Kelly moved the team to the Cincinnati 26-yard line, where the drive stalled. Norwood attempted a 43-yard field goal but missed to the left, leaving the game tied. The Bengals seized the momentum, driving 74 yards in 11 plays with Boomer Esiason's 10-yard touchdown pass to James Brooks resulting in a 14–7 lead. Norwood kicked a 39-yard field goal late in the half, cutting the Bengals' lead to 14–10.

In the third quarter Cincinnati drove to the Bills 5-yard line and on second and goal, Bills linebacker Shane Conlan stuffed Woods for a 3-yard loss. However, Buffalo cornerback Derrick Burroughs was flagged for a personal foul penalty and ejected from the game. This was *the* major play of the game, as instead of facing third and 8, the Bengals now had a first and goal from the 4. Woods scored on a 1-yard run two plays later for a 21–10 Bengals lead, and they never looked back. Cincinnati's defense stymied the Bills for the rest of the game. The Bengals intercepted Kelly for a third time with 8:07 remaining, and Buffalo never saw the ball again.

The Bengals finished their home season 10–0, including their two playoff victories. The Bills' loss of home-field advantage turned out to be a deciding factor in the winner of this game and determined the 1988 AFC Super Bowl participant. The next season, Buffalo hosted the Bengals at Rich Stadium in a key regular-season game and soundly won 24–7, exacting some revenge.

Buffalo won its second consecutive AFC East title in 1989 with a 9–7 record. The Bills had to overcome an injury to Kelly that cost him three games and led to some internal dissension. The team became known as the Bickering Bills when Kelly and Thomas had a public feud. In addition, other internal squabbles were going on and two coaches actually came to blows in the Bills locker room. However, when they needed to win the last game of the season to clinch the AFC East, the Bills got everything straight, pummeling the Jets 37–0 at the Meadowlands.

The 9–6–1 AFC Central champion Cleveland Browns hosted the AFC East champion Bills on Jan. 6 in a playoff game at Cleveland Municipal Stadium, otherwise known as The Mistake by the Lake. The Bills had lost three of their final four regular-season games for the second consecutive season, costing them the opportunity to host the Browns.

Buffalo struck first on a 72-yard Kelly to Reed touchdown pass 9:56 into the game for a 7–0 lead. The Browns bounced back with a 45-yard Matt Bahr field goal late in the first quarter and a 52-yard Bernie Kosar to Webster Slaughter touchdown pass early in the second quarter. The big plays continued on the Bills' ensuing drive. James Lofton caught a 19-yard pass from Kelly, and then hauled down a 33-yard scoring strike. The Bills were back in front 14–10.

The back-and-forth game continued as Kosar led the Browns on another scoring drive, capped off by a 3-yard touchdown toss to Ron Middleton. Cleveland's 17–14 lead held up through halftime. The Browns extended their lead in the third quarter to 10 points on Kosar's 44-yard touchdown pass to Slaughter. The teams traded fumble recoveries, and then the Bills took advantage of a short field starting from the Browns 21. Kelly finished the short drive with a touchdown pass of 6 yards to Thomas. On the ensuing kickoff, Browns returner Eric Metcalf dashed 90 yards for a touchdown and Cleveland quickly regained its 10-point lead, 31–21. As of this writing, it remains the only kickoff return touchdown in Browns playoff history.

The Bills, playing with a no-huddle offense, drove 68 yards in 11 plays but had to settle for a Norwood 30-yard field goal. On the Browns' next possession, Cleveland regained its 10-point lead, responding with a field-goal drive of its own as Bahr booted a 47-yarder with 6:50 to go in the game.

Buffalo again moved the ball behind seven completions by Kelly, driving 77 yards, with a 3-yard touchdown pass to Thomas completing the drive. However, Norwood slipped in the icy field conditions and missed the all-important extra point, leaving the Bills trailing 34–30. The Buffalo defense stopped the Browns on three plays, forcing a punt. The Bills took over at their 26-yard line with 2:41 remaining. Kelly again adroitly marched Buffalo down the field, setting the Bills up at the Browns 11-yard line with 14 seconds remaining.

Kelly spotted Ronnie Harmon in the left corner of the end zone. The quarterback lofted a perfect pass that landed right on the fingertips of Harmon, who dropped what surely would have been a touchdown with nine seconds left. On third down, Kelly saw a small window open for a pass to Thomas. As Kelly fired the ball, Browns linebacker Clay Matthews stepped in front of the pass, intercepting it for Cleveland and falling safely to the ground on the 1-yard line. The Bills had lost 34–30 in heartbreaking fashion.

Kelly had his greatest game since coming to Buffalo from the USFL's Houston Gamblers. He completed 28 of 54 passes, despite eight drops by his receivers, for 405 yards and four touchdowns. Harmon's drop of a sure touchdown, and what should have been a victory, lives on in Bills lore as one of the great missed opportunities in team history. The next four seasons, 1990–1993, the Bills went to the Super Bowl.

The Bills entered the 1995 season coming off their first non-playoff year in seven years. Led by a resurgent Kelly and a solid defense, Buffalo won its sixth AFC East title in eight years with a 10–6 record. The Bills clinched the title with a hard-fought 23–20 victory over the arch-rival Miami Dolphins at Rich Stadium on Dec. 17. The Dolphins, despite their loss to the Bills, won the following week, clinching a wild-card playoff berth and a rematch with Buffalo in the first round of the playoffs.

The Don Shula-led Dolphins came to Rich Stadium on Dec. 30 seeking revenge for their loss to the Bills two weeks earlier. However, Buffalo completely dominated Miami in the rematch, jumping to a 27–0 lead and coasting to a 37–22 victory. It was the most prolific rushing game in Bills history as they gained 341 yards on 52 carries. Thomas led the team with 158 yards, Darick Holmes contributed 87 yards, and even little-used Tim Tindale had his career highlight with a 44-yard fourth-quarter touchdown run. Kelly also fired a 37-yard touchdown pass to Steve Tasker in the rout. It was Shula's final game as an NFL head coach, and Bills fans could not have been happier sending him off in such a special way.

The Bills traveled to the AFC Central champion Pittsburgh Steelers for the next round of the playoffs on Jan. 6. The morning of the game began ominously for Buffalo, as star defensive end Bruce Smith woke up with a 103-degree temperature. He had come down with the flu and would be unable to play. The first-team All-Pro and the club's sack leader was the heart and soul of the Bills' highly rated defense. The Buffalo defense was also missing three other starters because of injuries: safety Henry Jones, cornerback Jeff Burris and linebacker Mark Maddox.

Pittsburgh dominated the game in the first half with the help of poor play by Buffalo and with some help from the officials. The Steelers scored touchdowns on their first two possessions, sandwiched by a missed field goal from the Bills' Steve Christie. Pittsburgh's second touchdown was aided by the officials. On a second down and goal from the 10-yard line, Steelers quarterback Neil O'Donnell fired a pass in the end zone to wide receiver Ernie Mills, who caught the pass but with both feet clearly out of bounds. Instead of ruling the pass incomplete, the officials ruled that Mills had been forced out of bounds by defender Kurt Schulz and gave the Steelers the touchdown. It was a bad call.

The Bills' ineptitude on offense continued and, following a punt, the Steelers took over at the Buffalo 43-yard line and drove for a field goal. On Buffalo's next series, the Bills failed to move the ball again. Then center Adam Lingner's snap to punter Chris Mohr was bad, forcing Mohr to run with the ball. He was tackled for a 12-yard loss and the Steelers took over at the Bills 12-yard line. Pittsburgh converted it into another field goal and a 20–0 lead.

On the Bills' next possession, Thomas fumbled on the Steelers 13-yard line after a nice Buffalo drive. Pittsburgh recovered, ending a promising Bills scoring opportunity. The Bills offense finally got moving, scoring a touchdown late in the first half on a 1-yard run by Thomas. However, the Steelers answered with a field goal to end the half with a 23–7 lead.

Another turnover early in the second half led to a fourth Pittsburgh field goal and a 26–7 lead. As if nothing else could possibly go wrong, Kelly was injured and left the game with 5:14 left in the third quarter. But backup quarterback Alex Van Pelt gave Buffalo some life. On his first play, the Bills ran an end-around to Steve Tasker, who broke free for a 40-yard gain. Two plays later, Van Pelt tossed a 2-yard touchdown pass to tight end Tony Cline.

Two series later, Van Pelt had Buffalo on the move again, and the Bills were in business at the Pittsburgh 9-yard line. At that moment, Kelly came out of the locker room and sprinted onto the field, replacing Van Pelt. Kelly's first play resulted in a 9-yard touchdown pass to Thomas, and the Bills were back in the game, trailing only 26–21 with 11:23 left.

The Bills' excitement was short-lived. O'Donnell converted two key third downs on the Steelers' next possession, and running back Bam Morris finished the drive with a 13-yard touchdown run. The Bills tried to respond, as Kelly threw a pass to Bill Brooks. The wide receiver was the victim of pass interference on the play, which resulted in an interception by Jerry Olsavsky of Pittsburgh. But there was no penalty called. Buffalo vehemently argued the call, but the play stood.

Three plays later, Bills backup safety Matt Darby intercepted O'Donnell. But on the next play, Kelly fired his third interception of the game, and Steelers linebacker Levon Kirkland returned it to the Buffalo 4-yard line. Morris finished off the Bills with a 2-yard touchdown run, and a 40–21 Pittsburgh victory. Buffalo's season was over. The Bills would not reach the AFC championship game or qualify for their fifth Super Bowl in six years.

The Steelers beat the Indianapolis Colts the next week 20–16 to advance to Super Bowl 30, where they lost to the Cowboys 27–17.

The Bills defense played its worst game of the season, giving up 409 yards and 40 points. The offense also contributed significantly to the defeat with four turnovers, and even the special teams unit had a bad punt snap. Between the Bills' all-around poor play and the two bad officiating calls, a fifth Super Bowl appearance was not in the cards in 1995, as the Curse continued its contributions in keeping Buffalo away from a championship.

The Bills' 1996 season brought optimism, though the team's core players were aging. Buffalo thought it had another great shot to return to the Super Bowl and finally win it. With the addition of All-Pro linebacker Chris Spielman, wide receiver Quinn Early and rookie wideout Eric Moulds, nobody doubted that the Bills were one of the favorites.

Buffalo lived up to its preseason hype, sprinting to a 9–3 record and first place in the AFC East. However, the Week 13 win over the Jets was costly as the Bills lost Kelly, Thomas and Tasker to injury. Though the injuries were all short in duration, the trio missed the next week's game against the Colts, its 13–10 overtime loss. That defeat put the Bills on a three-game losing streak, despite the return of the team's three stars, and their grip on first place in the AFC East disappeared as a result. The Bills had to win their final game of the season against the Kansas City Chiefs at Rich Stadium to qualify as a wild card. The Patriots, with coach Bill Parcells and quarterback Drew Bledsoe, won the AFC East title.

Buffalo defeated the Chiefs 20–9 behind its stingy defense, as the group made two goal-line stands, forced three turnovers and did not allow a touchdown in the critical victory. With the win, the Bills also secured a home playoff game, thanks to the Colts' loss and a Jacksonville win in the final week of the season. The Bills were set to host the young and rising Jaguars.

Jacksonville, in only its second season in the league, was 9–7 and was playing the veteran Bills in its first playoff game on Dec. 28. Buffalo came into the game with a perfect 9–0 all-time playoff record in Rich Stadium. The game was exciting throughout, with back-and-forth scoring. The Bills scored on their first offensive possession on a 7-yard touchdown pass from Kelly to Thomas, finishing off an impressive 57-yard drive. The Buffalo offense also was instrumental in the second touchdown of the game, this time on an interception thrown by Kelly to Jacksonville's Clyde Simmons. The linebacker sprinted 20 yards for a touchdown, tying the game at seven. Kelly immediately bounced back, driving the Bills 68 yards in 10 plays. Thomas scooted 2 yards for the score, putting Buffalo back in front 14–7.

The Jaguars answered on what would be an inauspicious play for the Bills, as running back Natrone Means ran 62 yards to the Bills 5-yard line. Though Buffalo held the Jaguars to a field goal, it was a harbinger of what was to come. In the second quarter, the Bills put together another nice drive, moving the ball from their own 20 to the Jaguars 16. On fourth down and less than a yard to go, the Bills decided to go for it instead of settling for a field goal. Jaguars linebacker Jeff Lageman made a great play, stopping Kelly for no gain, and Jacksonville took over on downs. It was a crucial moment in the game. The Jaguars immediately took advantage, driving for the go-ahead touchdown and Means finishing it off with a gashing 30-yard scoring run. The Bills responded with a field goal, and the teams went to the half tied at 17.

The Bills and Jaguars traded field goals in the third quarter. Bills corner-back Jeff Burris picked off Mark Brunell's pass early in the fourth quarter and returned it 38 yards for a touchdown and a 27–20 Buffalo lead. All looked good for the home team. But Brunell and Means teamed up to drive the Jaguars 65 yards in 10 plays and finished it off with a 2-yard touchdown pass from Brunell to Jimmy Smith. That tied the game at 27–27 with 8:30 remaining. Means converted a key fourth-down play to go along with his other six carries on the scoring drive.

On the penultimate drive of the game, Kelly moved the Bills to midfield and on third and 7, he dropped back to pass. The pocket collapsed around him as Chris Hudson and Simmons viciously hit Kelly, forcing a fumble that was recovered by Jaguar Aaron Beasley at the Bills 42-yard line. Even more important, Kelly had suffered a concussion that forced him to leave the game.

The Jaguars, behind the pounding runs by Means and two Brunell completions, positioned kicker Mike Hollis for a field-goal attempt. The 45-yard kick was aided by a 13 mile-an-hour wind. Hollis struck the kick well, but it appeared to fade to the right. Even so, the ball struck the goal post and bounced inside the post, to a huge sigh from the Rich Stadium crowd.

With the Jaguars leading 30–27, the Bills had two offensive possessions with Todd Collins at quarterback, but he was unable to move the team. Collins fumbled the ball on his final play, securing the upset victory for Jacksonville. Means rushed for 175 yards on 31 carries with several big plays, including the 30-yard touchdown run.

It was an especially disappointing outcome for Buffalo, losing on a field goal that bounced off the upright, not having its star quarterback able to play on the last two drives and forgoing a field goal earlier in the game that proved immensely costly at the end. Four weeks later, Kelly announced his retirement from the NFL, and the Bills spent the next 20-plus seasons looking for a franchise quarterback. Not by coincidence, the Bills did not win a single playoff game in that span. And the Curse continued!

In 1997, Buffalo suffered through a rare subpar season (at least by their standards at the time), finishing 6–10 and missing the playoffs for only the second time in 10 seasons. The 1998 team bounced back, behind the sterling play of quarterback Doug Flutie and a dominating defense.

The Bills began the 1998 season with the highly acclaimed acquisition of Rob Johnson at quarterback. Buffalo traded for the talented prospect in the offseason, acquiring Johnson from Jacksonville. The team then rewarded him with a massive $25 million contract. The Bills had their franchise quarterback, or so they thought. However, between Johnson's injuries and his poor play, Buffalo started a dismal 1–3. In Week 5 versus the Indianapolis Colts, Johnson was injured again, this time a little more seriously as he suffered separated rib cartilage that would keep him out of action for three weeks. Flutie replaced Johnson as the starting quarterback during his injury. The Bills had signed the diminutive, exciting Heisman Trophy winner from Boston College as a free agent in the offseason from the Canadian Football League before the Johnson trade was completed.

Flutie spearheaded the Bills to a surprising 31–24 comeback victory over the Colts. He completed 23 of 28 passes for 213 yards and two touchdowns along with 23 yards rushing on three attempts. The next week Flutie directed an improbable upset of the undefeated Jaguars 17–16 at Rich Stadium. In his first NFL start since 1989, Flutie scored on a 1-yard bootleg on fourth down and goal with 13 seconds remaining to tie the score. Steve Christie's extra point put the Bills ahead. They had taken the ball from their 30-yard line with 1:50 remaining, driving 70 yards for the winning score. Before the touchdown, Flutie had thrown a strike to Moulds for an apparent score, but an official overruled the original call and placed the ball at the 1. The Bills failed on the next three plays, setting up Flutie's bootleg on fourth down. The final play was intended to have been a pitchout to Thurman Thomas, who ran the wrong way, forcing Flutie to improvise. The quarterback came through and provided one of the most joyful moments in team history. Flutiemania was born!

Flutie and the Bills won four of their next five games, improving to 7–4 and putting Buffalo in the middle of the AFC East race. When Johnson was ready to return from his injury, head coach Wade Phillips decided to stick with Flutie. The quarterback's sparkling play caught the fancy of Bills fans, and No. 7 Flutie jerseys were popping up throughout the region. A new cereal even was introduced in Western New York: "Flutie Flakes."

Buffalo faced a pivotal game versus the New England Patriots in Foxborough, Massachusetts, on Nov. 29. The Bills were in a three-way tie for first place in the AFC East with the Miami Dolphins and New York Jets, with the Patriots just one game behind. Also, this was Flutie's return to Foxborough for the first time in almost 10 years. It was an especially important game for him personally, as he returned to a stadium where he had success as the Heisman Trophy quarterback at Boston College and struggled as a professional quarterback with the Patriots from 1987 to 1989.

The Bills came back from a 14–0 second-quarter deficit to take the lead 21–17 in the fourth quarter. Two Flutie touchdown passes, one of 84 yards to Moulds and a 4-yarder to Andre Reed, along with three Christie field goals, had given the Bills the lead. The Patriots had one final chance at victory as they started a drive at their own 18-yard line with 1:52 remaining.

New England quarterback Drew Bledsoe moved his team to the Bills 36-yard line with 11 seconds left. The Patriots faced a fourth down and 9 with no timeouts remaining. Bledsoe fired a pass to wide receiver Shawn Jefferson on the sideline, and it appeared he caught the ball out of bounds and short of the first down. However, the two officials closest to the play seemed confused and after some discussion, as Reed said after the game, one official said, "Just give it to 'em." And the Patriots were awarded a first down at the Bills 26-yard line with six seconds left. Replays clearly showed Jefferson was short of the first down and had one foot out of bounds, which ordinarily would have resulted in the pass being ruled incomplete.

On the ensuing play, Bledsoe threw a Hail Mary pass toward wide receiver Terry Glenn in the end zone. The pass fell harmlessly incomplete, and the Bills appeared to have won a hard-fought victory — but wait, a flag had been thrown for pass interference against Bills safety Henry Jones. For one of the only times in NFL history, a pass interference penalty was called on a Hail Mary pass, giving the Patriots a first and goal at the 1 with no time left. A game cannot end on a defensive penalty, so New England had one more chance. With the ball now at the goal line, Bledsoe tossed a touchdown pass to Ben Coates for the stunning Patriots victory.

The Bills and owner Ralph C. Wilson Jr. were incensed. After the game, Wilson said, "This was the worst. It is embarrassing to the league. We got robbed." The Bills completely outplayed the Patriots, piling up 428 yards to 259, but the game ended in controversy and a costly defeat for Buffalo.

The Bills finished the season winning three of their last four games to finish 10–6. However, with the New England loss, Buffalo finished in a tie for second place with Miami. The Dolphins won the fifth tiebreaker, net points in divisional games, and therefore hosted the wild-card playoff game between the two teams on Jan. 2.

The teams had split their season series, although the Bills' loss had come early in the season with Johnson at quarterback. The Bills attacked the Dolphins defense immediately. On the first play from scrimmage, Flutie fired a bomb to Moulds for 65 yards, but Dolphins cornerback Terrell Buckley stripped him of the football and Miami recovered the fumble. The Dolphins took advantage of the Bills' miscue, marching 57 yards for an Olindo Mare 31-yard field goal and a 3–0 lead.

On the Dolphins' next possession, aided by two pass interference penalties against Buffalo, they drove for another field goal and an early 6–0 lead. Miami attempted an onside kick, but it failed and gave the Bills the opportunity to take advantage of Dolphins head coach Jimmy Johnson's aggressiveness. Flutie fired a 37-yard pass to Moulds, followed by a 4-yard run by Antowain Smith, and the Bills capped off the quick touchdown drive on a 1-yard run by Thomas. The game went to halftime with Buffalo leading 7–6.

Miami scored a third-quarter touchdown by running back Karim Abdul-Jabbar and scored a successful 2-point conversion that staked them to a 14–7 lead. Meanwhile, Moulds was proving to be uncoverable by the Dolphins. On the Bills' next drive, he caught a pass for 23 yards and soon added a 32-yard touchdown pass to tie the game at 14. He garnered 55 of the Bills' 81 yards on the drive.

The game entered the fourth quarter knotted at 14. Miami put together a solid 77-yard drive in 11 plays, assisted by a Bills 15-yard facemask penalty. The drive resulted in Mare's 23-yard field goal. After a Reed fumble, Miami scored a touchdown on a Dan Marino pass and took a commanding 24–14 lead with only 3:42 remaining.

However, the Bills would not quit. Flutie drove the Bills 70 yards to the Dolphins 10-yard line at the two-minute warning. With a first and 10, Flutie fired a strike to Reed, who caught the pass and fought his way toward the end zone. It appeared that he had crossed the goal line for a touchdown; however, the officials ruled him down at the 1. Reed was incensed — and bumped the official while arguing with him. He was immediately ejected from the game and the Bills were assessed a 15-yard unsportsmanlike conduct penalty. Instead of having a second and goal at the 1, they were now facing a second down from the 16. This was a critical sequence as Buffalo settled for a field goal instead of getting a touchdown. The Bills now trailed 24–17 instead of potentially 24–21.

Christie converted a successful onside kick, with Buffalo recovering the football at its own 31-yard line. The team was in business with 1:33 left and with the magic of Flutie on their side. He successfully guided the Bills down the field to the Dolphins 4-yard line in 10 plays using 1:16 off the clock. With 17 seconds remaining, Flutie searched for an open receiver, pumped to throw once and cocked his arm a second time. Dolphins defensive end Trace Armstrong came around the end and hit Flutie to force a fumble. The Dolphins recovered, ending the Bills' hopes and their season.

It was a big disappointment for the Bills and their fans. This is a game Buffalo should have won. The Bills committed five turnovers, by far their most of the season in a single game, and had several key penalties called against them. They also were the victim of the non-touchdown call on Reed and subsequent penalty.

Moulds had a game for the ages, breaking the Bills' mark for most receiving yards in a game with 240 on nine catches and a touchdown. However, Buffalo could not overcome its turnovers and the officials' calls to pull out the victory. It was a crushing end to a fun and successful season for the Bills.

The only consolation to the season was that it regenerated interest in the team. That was important, because the franchise's lease for Rich Stadium was expiring, and there was talk that the team might be tempted to look elsewhere. It could be argued that Flutie's heroics in 1998 guaranteed that the Bills would be back in Buffalo in succeeding seasons.

The Bills entered the 1999 NFL season full of optimism coming off their playoff year of 1998 and with Flutie firmly entrenched as the starting quarterback. Buffalo lost its season opener to the Colts in Indianapolis but then won four games in a row. After two consecutive losses, the Bills won the next three games and stood at 7–3. Buffalo split its next four games and entered its Week 16 game at Foxborough with a 9–5 record. This year, the Bills were able to sneak away with a 13–10 overtime victory to clinch a wild-card playoff spot for the second consecutive season.

Buffalo had some signature wins in 1999, including a sweep of the Dolphins (23–18 in Miami and 23–3 in Buffalo), a 24–21 win over the Steelers, a 13–10 thriller in Baltimore as Flutie's heroics led to a touchdown in the final two minutes for the victory, a 34–17 pounding of the Redskins and a season sweep of the Patriots.

The Colts, since their opening-day victory against the Bills, stormed to a 13–2 record and the AFC East title. In a meaningless Week 17 game, the Bills rested Flutie, and Johnson started his first game of the season. Buffalo pounded Indianapolis' reserves 31–6. Johnson played extremely well on 24 of 32 passing for 287 yards and two touchdowns in the lopsided win.

As Buffalo prepared to play the Tennessee Titans in Nashville in the wild-card playoff round, the team's front office — including Wilson and head coach Phillips — made the mind-numbing decision to switch starting quarterbacks for the playoff game. Johnson was named the starter, despite having started only one game, mostly against second-stringers, that season. It is the only time in NFL history that a quarterback who started throughout the season was replaced on the eve of a playoff game for reasons other than an injury. Flutie was shocked, as were other players and fans.

The Bills came into the game with the No. 1-ranked defense in the NFL. The Titans had a ferocious pass rush, making the Johnson decision even more curious, since most of his struggles stemmed from not getting rid of the ball quickly enough and taking the highest percentage of sacks per pass play in pro football.

The game was a defensive struggle throughout the first quarter as neither team could mount much offense. Early in the second stanza with the Bills on their own 8-yard line, Johnson was sacked in the end zone by Titans all-everything defensive end Jevon Kearse for a safety.

On the ensuing kick, Tennessee returner Derrick Mason raced 42 yards to the Bills 28. After two Bills penalties and three rushing plays, Titans quarterback Steve McNair capped off the drive as he raced around the right end for a 1-yard touchdown and a 9–0 Tennessee lead. The Bills were unable to mount any kind of offense against the aggressive Titans defense in the first half, gaining only 64 yards on 27 plays and a pitiful three first downs.

The Titans added to their lead with a 12-play drive to end the half, with kicker Al Del Greco hitting a 40-yard field goal as time expired. Tennessee appeared to be in complete control, with a 12–0 lead. Johnson was 5 of 12 for 64 yards and had taken five sacks. With the aggressiveness of the Titans defense, it was surprising that Phillips did not go to Flutie in the second half.

Buffalo came out of the locker room a different team. On the first play after the kickoff, Antowain Smith broke through the Titans line and raced 44 yards to the Tennessee 18. Four plays later, Smith cracked over from the 4-yard line, putting the Bills on the scoreboard and back in the game at 12–7. The defenses again took control of the game for the remainder of the third quarter.

Early in the fourth period, Buffalo mounted its best drive of the day, highlighted by a 37-yard pass-and-run by Moulds. The Bills concluded the nine-play, 65-yard scoring march with Smith's second touchdown of the game, a 1-yard run off left tackle. The Bills were in the lead for the first time 14–12. Neither team moved the ball on their next possession. The Titans got the ball back with 6:15 remaining and put together a solid 10-play, 27-yard drive. It ended with a 36-yard Del Greco field goal with 1:48 remaining and a 15–14 Tennessee lead.

The Bills would not give in and began what probably was Johnson's best and gutsiest drive as a Buffalo quarterback. The Bills started at their own 39-yard line. On first down, Johnson fired a 14-yard pass to Peerless Price. After an incompletion, Jonathan Linton scampered for 12 yards, and then Johnson ran for 3 to the Tennessee 32-yard line. With his shoe falling off as he hurried to the line of scrimmage, Johnson fired a 9-yard pass to Price for a first down at the Titans 23-yard line. Tennessee called a timeout with 20 seconds left.

The Bills then elected to kick a field goal rather than run another play, spike the ball and kick with only a few seconds remaining. It seemed like a less-than-crucial decision at the time, but the choice not to run another play would come back to haunt the Bills. Christie nailed the 41-yard field goal in the damp, dreary conditions at Adelphia Coliseum. Buffalo celebrated on the sidelines as it had taken a 16–15 lead with only 16 seconds remaining and an apparent playoff victory. What could go wrong?

Buffalo decided to kick the ball short — but not too short, as they were worried that the Titans, who had two timeouts left, could move into field-goal range on one quick pass off a squibbed kick. Christie booted the ball high to Tennessee's Lorenzo Neal, who caught the ball on the Titans 25. Neal took a couple of steps to his right and handed the ball to Frank Wycheck, who took a couple of steps to the right hashmark. Wycheck then turned and threw a pass to Kevin Dyson, who was near the left sideline. The ball looked to most television viewers like a forward pass, perhaps because Wycheck threw the ball around the 25-yard line, and Dyson clearly was outside the Tennessee 25 when the ball approached.

Dyson nearly dropped the ball but hung on and began running down the sideline. The Bills kicking team had converged toward the middle of the field on Neal and Wycheck, so the pass to the other side of the field caught them completely off guard. As Dyson sprinted down the sideline with a flood of blocking escorts, there were no Bills who could stop him. It was clear sailing to the end zone for a stunning touchdown.

The Titans fans erupted immediately. However, a forward pass on a kick return is an illegal play. In 1999, the NFL had instituted instant replay, so the play was reviewed. As the video scoreboard in the stadium displayed the replay, it was apparent that the pass appeared forward. The Bills fans watching at home probably had the same reaction — although it was clearly a close call. However, it would have taken a lot of guts to overturn the call on the field, because the stadium crowd was in a frenzy and the officials probably did not think they would get out of Tennessee alive. After a four-minute delay, head official Phil Luckett announced that the play would stand.

The Bills were stunned. They saw it as a complete injustice. Phillips went crazy, but to no avail. The Bills' season was over. Tennessee not only went on to the next playoff round but all the way to the Super Bowl. The play has become famously known as the "Home Run Throwback," since that was the Titans' name for the trick play, while others have referred to it as the "Music City Miracle."

After the game, Phillips said, "I thought we won, and they took it away from us." Buffalo News sports columnist Larry Felser wrote the next day, "Frankly, I think the Bills got jobbed." And even ESPN announcer and Lackawanna native Ron Jaworski said after the game, "I think it was an illegal forward pass." It was a devastating loss for the Bills — especially since Buffalo had a clear path to the Super Bowl, as the Titans were the toughest matchup for it in the AFC. The Bills had beaten the Jaguars and Colts during the regular season, and there was no reason to think they could not have done it again.

Photo 26. Tennessee Titans wide receiver Kevin Dyson returns a kickoff for a touchdown in the fourth quarter of an AFC wild-card game against the Buffalo Bills at Adelphia Coliseum in Nashville, Tennessee. Dyson sped 75 yards down the left sideline with a lateral from Frank Wycheck on a kickoff for the winning touchdown with three seconds remaining, lifting the Titans to a miraculous 22–16 playoff victory over the stunned Bills.

(AP Photo/Wade Payne)

What made the loss even worse was that the Bills did a salary cap purge after the 1999 season. Buffalo let go its big three of Reed, Bruce Smith and Thomas. It would be 17 years before the Bills would participate in another playoff game.

It was a painful two years for Buffalo. First came the woes of 1998, when two controversial officials' calls in New England cost them a home playoff game, followed by five turnovers proving deadly in a postseason game with the Dolphins. Then in 1999, fans suffered through the surprise benching of Flutie and the agony of the "Home Run Throwback." It sure felt like something sinister was at play. That "something sinister" also goes by the name of the Buffalo Sports Curse.

Flutiemania, which had captured the hearts and minds of Western New Yorkers in 1998 and 1999, could only be stopped by the Curse. The next season, the Bills made the decision to go with Johnson as the starting quarterback. He was 4–7 in his 11 starts, and Flutie was 4–1 in his five starts. In 2001, the Bills released Flutie and went with Johnson as the quarterback of the future for Buffalo. The future lasted all of eight games as Johnson went 1–7, was injured again and saw his career in Buffalo end abruptly. Johnson finished his Bills career with a 9–17 record; Flutie was 21–9 with the same team. Yet the Bills in their infinite wisdom decided on Johnson. The Curse even appeared to affect the Bills' own decision-making.

Chapter 15
NO GOAL!

The Buffalo Sabres entered the 1997–98 season with a lot of on-ice optimism. The team had a new general manager, Darcy Regier, and a new head coach, Lindy Ruff, along with a solid nucleus of talented players, including NHL MVP goaltender Dominik Hasek, center Michael Peca, wingers Miroslav Satan and Donald Audette, defenseman Alexei Zhitnik and tough guy Rob Ray. However, the ownership situation was tentative as the Sabres had lost $32 million during the previous three seasons. The Knox brothers and partners had owned the team since its inception, and this had become the most serious financial situation of that time period.

The Sabres were coming off a first-place finish in the Northeast Division in 1996–97 with a 40–30–12 record and a thrilling seven-game playoff series victory over Ottawa. Game 7 was won on an overtime goal by Sabres center Derek Plante — the only seventh-game win in the first 50 years of the team's history. Buffalo was eliminated in the next round by the Philadelphia Flyers, four games to one. It was the Sabres' first division crown since 1980–81 and only their second playoff series victory of more than three games since 1979–80. The team had made progress and the future looked bright.

Buffalo got off to a slow start and was in last place at 12–17–6 heading into Christmas. Rumors were swirling that John Rigas, founder and chief executive officer of Adelphia Communications Corp., was negotiating with the Knoxes to become the majority shareholder of the team. The Associated Press reported on Jan. 2 that Rigas had signed an agreement with Northrup Knox, the Sabres' chairman, to take over controlling interest of the team — subject to approval by the NHL Board of Governors. In March, Rigas officially took over as majority owner and quickly infused the franchise with millions of dollars.

As the ownership situation stabilized, the on-ice performance also improved. From Christmas through the end of the season, the Sabres were 24–12–11, finishing third in the Northeast Division with 89 points. Hasek had an outstanding season, winning his second consecutive Hart Memorial Trophy as league MVP. He was the first goaltender in NHL history to ever win the award twice. He also won his fourth Vezina Trophy, as the league's most outstanding goaltender. He led the league in shutouts with 13, the most by any NHL goaltender in 27 years. From December through the end of the regular season, he was nothing short of spectacular, boasting an eye-popping 1.70 goals-against average in 52 games with a .944 save percentage. In the middle of that run, he led the Czech Republic to a gold medal at the 1998 Winter Olympics.

Satan led the team in scoring with 46 points, followed by Zhitnik with 45. Audette led the team in goals with 24, and Satan chipped in with 22. The team's success was built on Hasek and a solid defense, as the offensive team leaders had the fewest points and goals of any single season in Sabres history.

Buffalo was matched up with the Flyers in the first round of the playoffs, and Philadelphia was a heavy favorite to win. The Sabres opened the series at the CoreStates Center in Philadelphia and took a 2–0 lead into the third period, behind goals from Michal Grošek and Wayne Primeau. In one of Hasek's few lapses, he allowed two goals only 19 seconds apart in the third period, and Philadelphia tied the game. But the Sabres' smallest player came up big, as the 5-foot-8 Audette pounced on a rebound at the side of the net and swatted the puck past goaltender Sean Burke with 8:17 left. Hasek made it hold up for a 3–2 Sabres victory.

The Flyers bounced back in Game 2 with a hard-fought, tight-checking 3–2 win. Despite 35 saves from Hasek, the Sabres could not pull out the victory. Philadelphia scored the game-winning goal on the power play with 3:32 remaining, as John LeClair jammed in a cross-crease pass from Eric Lindros.

The Sabres came home to a packed and enthusiastic crowd of 18,595 at Marine Midland Arena. Buffalo dominated the two games at home, winning 6–1 in Game 3 and 4–1 in Game 4. Satan scored twice and the Sabres netted four goals in the second period on their way to the Game 3 victory. Hasek lost his shutout with 6:09 left. In Game 4, Buffalo scored four goals in the span of 7:39, bridging the first and second periods, and Hasek was outstanding, turning away 44 of 45 shots, en route to the 4–1 win and a 3–1 series lead.

Game 5 was back in Philadelphia, and it took overtime to decide the contest. The Sabres opened the scoring with a Matthew Barnaby power-play goal only 2:29 into the game. The Sabres again took the lead with the extra man at 8:26 of the third period, with Audette doing the scoring. But the Flyers tied the game at 13:08 of the period behind a goal from Dave Babych, sending the game to overtime. Buffalo scored the game-and series-winner on another power play, as Grošek rang a slap shot off the post and in with 5:40 gone. The Sabres celebrated as it was only the franchise's second triumph in their previous 14 playoff series. Hasek again was outstanding with 35 saves.

It had been an amazing first round in the Eastern Conference, as the top three seeds all lost. The Montreal Canadiens upset Pittsburgh, four games to two, giving Buffalo home-ice advantage in the second round. The Sabres finished 2 points ahead of Montreal in the regular season. Montreal winger Martin Ručinský caused a bit of a stir before the series started when he said, "They're an average team. It's all the goalie, it's all Dominik." The fact that Ručinský probably wasn't wrong didn't matter.

The motivated Sabres jumped to a quick 2–0 lead in the first period of Game 1 as Brian Holzinger and Geoff Sanderson scored goals. From that point on, Montreal dominated play, and if not for Hasek playing incredibly well, the Sabres would have easily lost the game. Buffalo was outshot 33–10 throughout the second and third periods, and 48 to 26 for the game. However, Hasek made at least eight unbelievable saves in keeping the Sabres in the lead. The Canadiens finally broke through, scoring two goals in succession only 10 seconds apart, tying the game with only 5:34 left. The contest went to overtime, and at 2:37 of the extra session, Sanderson grabbed a loose puck that was not cleared by the Montreal defense and snapped a quick wrist shot past Andy Moog for the 3–2 victory. After the game, Buffalo captain Michael Peca said, "We really had no right winning that hockey game."

The Sabres played much better in Game 2 and, behind an unlikely hat trick from Barnaby, Buffalo won 6–3. Barnaby scored Buffalo's last three goals after Dixon Ward tied the game for the Sabres in the second period. Grošek and Audette also scored for the Sabres, securing the team's record fifth consecutive playoff game win.

Game 3, played at the Molson Centre in Montreal, was a back-and-forth affair. Buffalo scored three first-period goals, staking them to a 3–2 lead. The Canadiens responded in the second period, tying the game at four heading to the third period. Montreal outshot the Sabres 16–0 to start the third period, but Hasek was at his best, not allowing a goal. The first overtime was back and forth without either team scoring. Early in the second overtime, Ward gained control of the puck in the left circle and passed it across the ice to Peca, who fired a slap shot that eluded Canadiens goalie José Théodore for the game-winner and a 3–0 series lead for the Sabres.

Buffalo finished off the frustrated Canadiens a couple of nights later with a 3–1 victory, as Hasek stopped 37 of 38 shots. Barnaby and Audette scored goals for Buffalo, staking them to a 2–0 lead that Hasek made stand up for the victory. Barnaby and Audette led the team in scoring in the series with 10 points each. The Sabres qualified for their first conference final series since losing to the New York Islanders in 1980.

The Washington Capitals, the Sabres' opponent, finished third in the Atlantic Division and had a regular-season record similar to the Sabres' (92 points). The Capitals were led by 52-goal scorer Peter Bondra, winger Adam Oates and goaltender Olaf Kölzig. It appeared to be a very even matchup between two teams, with one appearance in the Stanley Cup Final between them.

The series opened at the MCI Center in Washington, DC, and the Sabres got off to a great start. Hasek continued his outstanding play, pitching a 2–0 shutout with 19 saves. The Sabres played an excellent checking game in front of Hasek, and goals from Grošek and Satan secured the 2–0 triumph. The Capitals won Game 2, 3–2 in overtime, tying the series at 1–1. However, the officials made two controversial calls against Buffalo that cost the Sabres two goals and the game.

The Sabres led 1–0 on a goal by Václav Varaďa in the first period, when Bondra scored at 19:55 of the second stanza to tie the game. However, Bondra's skate was in the crease when he deflected Phil Housley's shot past Hasek. The Sabres immediately protested and requested that official Kerry Fraser review the replay. He refused and let the goal stand. Ruff was incensed and said after the game, "Satisfy us — go upstairs, prove you made the right call." The replay showed Fraser had made the wrong call, but it did not matter. The Capitals scored a legitimate goal in the third period by Joe Juneau, taking a 2–1 lead with 5:54 remaining. However, Barnaby again came through for the Sabres, scoring the tying goal with only 57 seconds left on a soft shot that was inadvertently redirected by Washington's Esa Tikkanen past Kölzig.

Todd Krygier, a native of Orchard Park in suburban Buffalo, broke the hearts of Western New Yorkers by scoring the game-winning goal for the Capitals 3:10 into overtime. However, it came with a lot of controversy. The Sabres said it should not have counted. Before the goal, the Capitals' Andrei Nikolishin fired a pass from behind the center red line intended for Bondra, but he missed the puck at the blue line and it slid behind the Sabres' net, which meant icing should have been called. Hasek did not go after the puck and directed Sabres defenseman Darryl Shannon to touch it up. Shannon got the puck in the corner but lost it to Nikolishin, who then passed to Krygier, and he fired in the winning goal. Hasek was furious in the postgame locker room. "I know it was icing, I don't even have to look at the replay," he said. The no-call was very costly to the Sabres, as they had a chance of taking a 2–0 series lead in Washington. Instead, the series was tied.

The Sabres were outplayed in Game 3, losing a second consecutive overtime game to the Capitals 4–3. "From my point, it looked like we didn't play a playoff game," Hasek said. Bondra won the game for Washington on a partial breakaway as he fired a low slap shot that bounced off Hasek's glove and into the net for the game-winner. Then Buffalo was completely shut down in Game 4 in Marine Midland Arena as Kölzig pitched a 2–0 shutout, giving the Capitals a commanding 3–1 series lead.

The Sabres fought back against the odds in Game 5 at the MCI Center. Hasek played one of his otherworldly games as Buffalo was outshot 35–16 yet found a way to get the game to overtime tied at 1–1. Shannon scored at 6:33 of the first period to give the Sabres an early 1–0 lead, but Nikolishin answered later in the period. From that point forward, it was the Hasek show. Time and again he made brilliant save after brilliant save. During one sequence of the second period, he dove across the crease to stop a point-blank shot by Oates; after the rebound bounced to the other side of the crease, Juneau took a shot on the open net, and the sprawling Hasek knocked the puck away with his blocking glove. Later in the game he denied Bondra on a breakaway, keeping the Sabres in the game against all odds. In the overtime, defenseman Jason Woolley made an end-to-end rush and scored the game-winning goal for Buffalo, keeping them alive in the series.

In another do-or-die game for Buffalo, the Sabres played their hearts out in Game 6. Twice they took the lead — first on Peca's goal at 13:04 of the first period, and then on Paul Kruse's score at 7:40 of the second period. Each time, the Capitals responded, and the teams again headed to overtime after a frantic but scoreless third period.

It was Washington's turn to win on the other team's ice. Brian Bellows raced down the left wing and fired a shot on Hasek, who saved it. The Capitals took two more unsuccessful whacks at the rebound before the puck squirted to Juneau around the crease. With no Sabre near him, he planted the puck into the back of the net at 6:24 into the extra session. The game was over, and so was the series. The Capitals were 3–2 winners, leaving the Sabres heartbroken.

Buffalo played evenly with the Capitals and easily could have beaten them. Each team won a 2–0 shutout, and all the remaining games were decided by one goal. The poor officiating in Game 2 proved very costly for the Sabres. They would have been up two games to zero and could have put the series away at home. At the least, it could have had a ripple effect on how the entire series was played.

What other explanation is there to this series than the Curse had struck again? Three overtime losses by the Sabres, and another game ending with officiating controversy in an extremely close and tight series. Ruff said after the series, "It's a tough pill to swallow. But I am extremely proud of the way we played. It was obviously not to be." Another championship opportunity had gone wanting, thanks to the Curse. But the Sabres would be back. With Hasek in net, anything was possible for this team.

The Sabres were confident heading into the 1998–99 season. With the all-world goalie play of Hasek and the nucleus of the team back, Buffalo fan expectations were much higher. A Stanley Cup seemed very possible. The regular season was similar to 1997–98, with a lot of inconsistency throughout the year and a lack of overall scoring. However, the team continued to see outstanding play from Hasek, which propelled them to many victories. The Sabres did fall a notch to fourth as the division had gotten stronger. Ottawa won the Northeast Division with 103 points. The Sabres finished with a 37–28–17 record and 91 points. Hasek won his fifth Vezina Trophy as the league's best goaltender.

Buffalo was seeded seventh in the East and matched with No. 2 Ottawa in the first round of the playoffs. The Senators were led by center Alexei Yashin, winger Daniel Alfredsson, defenseman Wade Redden and goaltender Ron Tugnutt. The series opened in Ottawa at the Corel Centre and Hasek led the Sabres to a 2–1 victory. He was fantastic, as Buffalo was outshot 41–15, with many of his saves being of the acrobatic variety. Peca got the Sabres off to a good start, scoring the first goal of the series at 4:32 of the first period. The Senators tied the game as Redden beat Hasek on a power play about 10 minutes later. Curtis Brown gave the lead to Buffalo for good at 11:24 of the second period with a power-play goal. Hasek made several spectacular saves, especially in the third period when Ottawa outshot the Sabres 17–6.

Satan stunned the 18,500 in the Corel Centre for Game 2, as he whacked in the rebound of a Woolley shot at 10:35 of the second overtime. The 3–2 victory gave the Sabres a 2–0 series lead, heading home for the next two games. Hasek was solid again, making 45 saves on 47 shots. He gave up two power-play goals to Ottawa, but that was it. Satan had tied the game 6:43 into the third period when he dove into the crease to poke in a Peca shot, setting up his game-winner.

Buffalo returned home to a raucous sellout crowd of 18,595 and dominated the Senators in the next two games. Holzinger scored two goals and Hasek turned aside all 31 shots in the Sabres' 3–0 win in Game 3. In Game 4, Buffalo jumped to a quick 2–0 first-period lead behind goals from Erik Rasmussen and Varad'a in a 4–3 win. Hasek had another stellar performance with 40 saves as the Sabres stunningly swept the Senators out of the playoffs. Hasek allowed only six goals in the series on 162 shots for a fantastic .962 save percentage. "Sometimes it's ugly hockey, but we have the greatest goaltender in the world, and goaltending is important in the playoffs," Peca said.

The Boston Bruins dispatched the Carolina Hurricanes in the first round of the playoffs and hosted Game 1 of the second-round series versus Buffalo.

The Sabres had an eight-day layoff between the two matchups, and it appeared to have an effect. The first game was one of Hasek's only poor outings in the playoffs, as the Bruins scored four goals on only 21 shots in their 4–2 victory. Buffalo and Hasek bounced back in Game 2, with the Sabres playing an aggressive style throughout. Peca got Buffalo on the scoreboard early with a goal at 1:51 of the first period and Brown, on a power play, gave the Sabres a 2–0 lead at 5:57 of the second stanza. Hasek kept the Bruins at bay until Don Sweeney scored a goal late in the third period. Ward's empty-net goal in the final minute secured the Sabres' 3–1 victory to even the series.

In Game 3, the Sabres scored in the second minute of the game on a Woolley goal and then seemed to fall asleep through the end of the second period. Buffalo only generated six shots on goal as Boston responded, scoring twice to take a 2–1 lead heading into the final period. The Sabres awoke from their slumber, banging 17 shots on the Bruins net as Rhett Warrener and Ward scored two minutes and 54 seconds apart to save the Sabres, sending the crowd home elated with a 3–2 victory.

Buffalo dominated Game 4 with 39 shots on beleaguered Bruins goalie Byron Dafoe while Hasek was impenetrable for the Sabres in the 3–0 shutout. Buffalo scored first with a power-play goal from Zhitnik midway through the second period. Varad'a scored the Sabres' second goal with only 17 seconds left in the second for a 2–0 lead. Buffalo scored the backbreaker, a short-handed goal by Peca at 11:39 of the final period. The shutout was the fifth of Hasek's career, a Sabres record.

The Bruins faced elimination in Game 5 and put forth their best game of the series. They scored three goals in the second period off Hasek to break a 1–1 tie on their way to a 5–3 victory. The Sabres came home to Marine Midland Arena, where they had not lost all season to Boston, and they continued that streak in Game 6. Peca took advantage of the Sabres' first power play in the game, firing a slap shot between the legs of Dafoe for a 1–0 Buffalo lead. The Bruins tied it later in the first period, but Wayne Primeau gave the Sabres the lead back, burying a rebound off the stick of Sanderson at 17:29. Brown scored in the second minute of the second period, giving Buffalo a 3–1 lead. From there, Hasek and the boisterous Sabres crowd took over, carrying Buffalo to a 3–2 victory. The win clinched the series, four games to two and sent the Sabres onto the Conference finals for the second straight season. That had never happened in the team's history.

Their opponent was arch-rival Toronto. Known as the QEW Series, for Queen Elizabeth Way, the Canadian highway connecting Buffalo and Toronto, it was the first (and of this writing still the only) playoff series between the Sabres and Maple Leafs. Fourth-seeded Toronto finished 6 points ahead of the Sabres in the regular season with 97 points. The Maple Leafs were led by center Mats Sundin, wingers Steve Thomas and Sergei Berezin and goaltender Curtis Joseph. Hasek was unable to play in the first two games of the series because of a nagging groin injury. The Sabres turned to backup Dwayne Roloson, who had played in only 18 regular-season games. Buffalo somehow pulled out a win in Game 1 at the Air Canada Centre 5–4. The Sabres rallied from a 3–2 second-period deficit behind goals from Stu Barnes, Brown and Sanderson. Buffalo was blown out in Game 2, 6–3, as the Maple Leafs scored two goals 18 seconds apart in the first period and tied the series.

Hasek returned for Buffalo in Game 3, and the Sabres took over the series. In the final three games, Toronto scored only two goals in each game. The Sabres won all three, by scores of 4–2, 5–2 and 4–2. In Game 3, Buffalo fell behind 1–0 but then scored three consecutive goals in the second period, from Satan, Juneau and Barnes, to pull ahead by two goals. Ward scored a short-handed goal for the Sabres in the first period of Game 4. Then they peppered Joseph in the second period by scoring four goals, taking a 5–0 lead and coasting home with the 5–2 win. Buffalo traveled up the QEW on May 31 for Game 5 and came home with the Eastern Conference championship. With the score tied at 2–2 in the third period, Rasmussen backhanded a rebound past Joseph for the game-winner at 11:35. With the Sabres hanging on late in the game and playing short-handed, Ward clinched the conference title by scoring an empty-netter from about 150 feet with 1:02 remaining. Buffalo was returning to the Stanley Cup Final for the second time in franchise history and the first time since 1975.

Ruff's reaction to the Sabres going to the Stanley Cup Final was, "It's awesome. After 24 years, Western New York deserves it." Hasek said, "I can not wait for it to start. Of course, I'm very, very happy. It's a great feeling to be in the final." Dixon Ward commented, "It means everything to us. We're on the course we set for ourselves … our goal was to get to the finals and win it. We've proved we're a very good hockey team. We can prove we are a great hockey team in the next series." Sabres fan reaction can be summed up by Mike Szpylman, who, while trying to secure tickets, said, "I've been waiting my whole life to go." Members of that Sabres team still say the joyous bus ride back to Buffalo after the game was one of the highlights of their hockey careers.

The Sabres' opponent in the 1999 Stanley Cup Final was the Dallas Stars, the No. 1 seed in the playoffs. They led the league with 51 wins and 114 points while outscoring their opponents by 68 goals in the regular season. The Stars advanced to the Final with wins over Edmonton, St. Louis and Colorado. Dallas had a star-studded lineup that included centers Mike Modano and Joe Nieuwendyk, wingers Brett Hull and Sergei Zubov and goalie Ed Belfour. The Sabres were decided underdogs.

Even so, Buffalo didn't look like an inferior team in Game 1, stunning the Stars in Dallas 3–2 in overtime. Dallas controlled the tempo in the first two periods and held a 1–0 lead on a power-play goal by Hull. But the Sabres regrouped in the third period, pressing the action throughout and being rewarded with two goals by Barnes and Primeau that gave Buffalo a 2–1 lead. However, as the Sabres were trying to kill the clock and Dallas had a sixth attacker on the ice, Modano found Jere Lehtinen alone in front of the Sabres' net, and Lehtinen beat Hasek to force overtime. In the extra session, Woolley scored the game-winning goal for the Sabres, firing a low shot that eluded a sprawling Belfour for a 3–2 victory. Hasek had 35 saves for Buffalo to Belfour's 21 for Dallas.

Game 2 was evenly played. There was no scoring in the first period, and the teams traded goals in the second stanza. Dallas scored early in the third to take a 2–1 lead, but only 1:11 later Zhitnik netted a power-play goal for Buffalo. Both teams played solid defense, and the goalies were sharp as time ran down in the final period. Seemingly out of nowhere came Hull as he skated into the Sabres' zone with the puck. He fired a blistering slap shot that Hasek, who was screened on the play, did not see as the rubber disk clanged off the right goal post and fell into the net with only 2:50 remaining. It gave the Stars a 3–2 lead. Derian Hatcher scored an empty-net goal for Dallas, securing its 4–2 victory to even the series at one game apiece.

The two teams came to Buffalo for Game 3 and the first Stanley Cup Final game in that city since 1975. At the start of the game, the crowd was incredibly loud and the building seemed to shake at times. However, Dallas played suffocating defense, using its strength and size advantages to shut down the Sabres offense. Buffalo had some great opportunities in the first period with four power plays but could not convert and even struggled to get shots. Late in the first period the Sabres had a two-man advantage, but three Buffalo players broke their sticks in a matter of seconds, foiling any hopes of scoring. Despite all the power plays, Buffalo managed only three shots on goal.

Buffalo did take a 1–0 lead on a Barnes goal at 7:51 of the second period. Dallas bounced back as Nieuwendyk tied the game at 15:33. The Stars again came up with the big goal when it mattered most, as Nieuwendyk took a pass from Jamie Langenbrunner and scored the game-winning goal midway through the final period. The Stars defense clamped down on the Sabres, and Buffalo was unable to create even a good chance to tie, losing the game 2–1 and finishing with only 12 shots on goal.

The Sabres faced an almost must-win situation in Game 4, and Hasek came up big for Buffalo, steering aside 30 of 31 shots. The Sabres used a first-period goal by Sanderson and a second-period marker from Ward to offset the Stars' lone goal on a power play by Lehtinen in the first period to sneak away with a 2–1 victory.

Game 5 back in Dallas at Reunion Arena was almost a repeat of Game 3 as the smothering Stars defense kept the Sabres at bay. Buffalo could only generate 23 shots on Belfour, and very few of them were good scoring chances. Belfour played well with the strong defense in front of him and shut out the Sabres 2–0. The Stars took a 3–2 lead in the series heading back to Buffalo.

The result left the Sabres with no margin for error. A win would send them back to Dallas for Game 7 and a chance to come home with the Stanley Cup. A loss would send them to the golf course. The evenly matched teams had battled to something close to a draw, with every game in doubt late into the third period.

Marine Midland Arena was sold out for Game 6, and 10,000 additional fans watched on the video scoreboard in Dunn Tire Park, home of the Triple-A baseball Buffalo Bisons, a few short blocks from the arena. Dallas struck first as Lehtinen scored his 10th goal of the playoffs. The Sabres fought back and Barnes scored a goal at 18:21 of the second period to tie the game at 1–1. The teams battled through the third period but neither team could convert its chances into the decisive goal. The first overtime was scoreless, although James Patrick's shot from the right point went through a crowd and hit the goal post — only to bounce away from the net instead of into it. A quarter-inch difference might have been enough to give the Sabres the win. There was also no scoring in the second overtime as both goaltenders refused to allow a goal.

The third overtime period began after 1 a.m., and neither team had the energy to generate many scoring chances. Suddenly, the Stars put pressure on Buffalo in its end of the rink. The puck slid in front of the goal off Hasek, Hull played it with his foot, avoided a check by Holzinger and — *with his left foot still in the goal crease* — guided the puck into the net for the Cup-winning goal.

The problem was that the league had been disallowing goals throughout the season when a player's skate was in the crease. The relevant rule had been so confusing that the NHL had to issue guidelines during the season on how such plays should be called. Those guidelines didn't help the officials in this situation since the play fell between two of the listed examples.

Photo 27. Dallas Stars winger Brett Hull (22) jams the puck lose from Buffalo Sabres goalie Dominic Hasek before scoring the series-winning goal in the third overtime of the Stanley Cup Final in Buffalo on June 19–20, 1999.

(AP Photo/Kevin Frayer)

The Stars quickly began to celebrate, and photographers streamed onto the ice to add to the confusion. However, the Sabres were left in a state of bewilderment. They argued that the goal should have immediately been disallowed. For some reason, the on-ice officials did not call it, and neither did the replay official, who should have immediately phoned down to the on-ice referee and disallowed the goal. Instead, commissioner Gary Bettman awarded the Stars the Stanley Cup. Ruff came out of the locker room after seeing a video replay and shouted at Bettman while he was awarding the Cup. Ruff later said, "I wanted Bettman to answer the question. 'Why is that not reviewed?' He turned his back on me. He almost looked to me like he knew this might be a tainted goal, and there was no answer for it." Ruff called the outcome "our worst nightmare!"

Juneau added, "I believe everybody will remember this as the Stanley Cup that was never won in 1999. … The goal was not a legal goal. I think because it was a goal that gave them the Stanley Cup, everybody jumped on the ice, and they were afraid to make the call." Sabres defenseman Jay McKee said, "If there's a guy in the crease before the puck goes in there, the goal doesn't count. It has happened all season long. We are not whining, that's the rule. To have it end that way is devastating to us."

It was a complete travesty to end the series with a blown call — and certainly ranks as one of the most controversial endings to a championship game in the history of professional sports. It was an outstanding series with two very evenly matched teams. There was no guarantee that the Sabres would have won the sixth game had the goal been waved off, but they never had a chance the way the contest was decided. Had they won Game 6, the Sabres could have gone to Dallas and won the Stanley Cup — especially with the way Hasek was playing. The Curse ruled the day on June 20, 1999.

Sabres defenseman Rhett Warrener missed the game with a broken ankle and watched from the locker room. More than 20 years later, he was still waiting for an apology. "Whether you agreed with it or not — and I thought it was a goofy rule to begin with — it was called so strictly all year," he said. "One of the guys from the Calgary media was at the game, and he said to me, 'Everyone knew it wasn't a goal, but everyone was on the ice. It was too late.'"

Hasek said years later, "It was a huge disappointment. We were upset, so upset. We were so close. We give up a goal in overtime. Maybe we were a better team. We don't know. It was Game 6. So close. We've worked so hard for so many years and now it's all over."

The city of Buffalo still staged a rally for its hockey heroes in Niagara Square despite the loss. Ruff added the punctuation mark for the season when he ended his speech with two words: "No Goal."

The Sabres had fallen *oh so close*, but this group of players would not get anywhere near the Stanley Cup again. The 1999–2000 season ended in major disappointment as Buffalo was ousted in the first round by Philadelphia, four games to one. In 2000–2001 they were eliminated in the second round by Pittsburgh in the seventh and deciding game on an overtime goal — after coming within 78 seconds of eliminating the Penguins in Game 6. It was another cursed season that ended in frustration.

After the 2001 season, the Sabres dismantled their team as they let Dave Andreychuk become a free agent, traded Peca and granted Hasek's wish to go elsewhere with a one-sided trade to Detroit. Hasek went on to win two Stanley Cup titles as a Red Wing before retiring, just rubbing salt in the wounds of Sabres fans. Buffalo's ownership under Rigas completely fell apart in 2002, placing the future of the team in serious jeopardy after he was indicted for bank fraud, wire fraud and securities fraud. The NHL had to step in and take control of the franchise. Rigas was later convicted and sentenced to 15 years in prison.

"No Goal" was an incredibly sad end to a great Sabres run with back-to-back Eastern Conference finals appearances, a conference title and a Stanley Cup Final appearance with a tainted ending. However, because of the Curse, no league championship was won.

Chapter 16
THE LEGEND OF "BABY JOE" MESI

Think about it: undefeated Buffalo heavyweight boxer "Baby Joe" Mesi taking on Mike Tyson at Ralph Wilson Stadium in front of 73,000 partisan fans. It figured to be an event unmatched in Buffalo's long sports history. And it appeared to be only one small step from happening in the summer of 2004.

Mesi, a top heavyweight contender at the time, was on the verge of getting that bout. The thinking was that if he defeated Tyson (the undisputed heavyweight champion from 1987–1990 and 1996–97 and considered one of the most devastating punchers of all time), Mesi would be positioned for a World Boxing Council heavyweight championship fight with Vitali Klitschko. There was one detail in the way: a bout with Russian cruiserweight champion Vassiliy Jirov on March 13 in Las Vegas. Win, and Tyson would be the next step on the ladder.

Mesi, a 6-foot-1, 230-pound phenom who was born and raised outside of Buffalo in Tonawanda, became known as Western New York's "Third Franchise" (with the Bills and Sabres being the other two) as he pursued the heavyweight championship of the world. A relatively unknown heavyweight contender outside of Western New York, Mesi amassed a 26–0 record with 24 knockouts from 1997 to 2003 against increasingly better competition. He was extremely popular in his home region and had begun to be noticed nationally.

Mesi was born Nov. 27, 1973, and graduated from Sweet Home High School in Amherst. He started his boxing career at a late age, after being motivated by listening to his grandfather Tom and uncle Russell reminisce about their boxing adventures. In 1992, at 19, a very determined Mesi walked into a Police Athletic League gymnasium and put on boxing gloves for the first time.

Though he had some early success as an amateur, winning the New York State Golden Gloves super heavyweight division and an Empire State Games gold medal in 1993, Mesi lost interest and quit. He decided to pursue a career as an elementary education teacher and enrolled at D'Youville College in September 1994.

In January 1995, by happenstance, Mesi was reading a story about the upcoming boxing trials for the 1996 Atlanta Summer Olympics, and a new boxing spark was ignited. As far-fetched as it sounds, he was determined to compete for the heavyweight slot on the Olympic team and represent his country. At this point he was 60 to 80 pounds overweight and had been out of boxing for almost a year. But he was determined … or some might say manic.

As Mesi was looking to find a trainer, he met Juan DeLeon, a 30-year Buffalo police veteran detective who was considered a first-class boxing trainer known for his patience and technical skills. His brother, Sugar, was a four-time cruiserweight champion. Mesi worked with DeLeon throughout the Olympic trials and most of his professional career. DeLeon put Mesi through rigorous training in preparation for the Olympics. Amazingly, in less than 15 months, he fought all the way through the Olympic trials to the super heavyweight finals for the U.S. team. Mesi lost in the finals to U.S. nationals champion Lawrence Clay-Bey, who became the super heavyweight representative for the United States. Mesi was named an alternate to the U.S. Olympic team for his runner-up performance. In addition, he won the New York State Golden Gloves super heavyweight championship in both 1995 and 1996.

With help from his father, Jack, as well as DeLeon, Mesi made the decision to turn professional after the Olympics. His first pro fight was a second-round knockout of Dwane Cason on Nov. 1, 1997, in Harlem. Mesi won his first 21 pro fights with gradually improving competition. Jack and DeLeon were intentionally bringing him along slowly.

To generate more publicity for the rising boxer, Team Mesi signed a promotional contract with Sugar Ray Leonard Boxing on Feb. 20, 2002. Leonard and his company produced "Friday Night Fights" on ESPN2. This deal brought increased exposure for Mesi. His debut as a main event fighter on ESPN2 was April 5 at Alumni Arena in Buffalo. He scored a technical knockout of Keith McKnight at 1:07 of the sixth round, when the referee stopped the fight, to the pleasure of the 9,954 on hand.

Mesi returned to Buffalo, this time at HSBC Arena, to fight David Izon on Oct. 18. To the delight of the 15,940 in attendance, he knocked out Izon nine seconds into Round 9, raising his record to 24–0. On June 24, 2003, Mesi returned to HSBC Arena to fight Robert Davis for the vacant North American Boxing Federation heavyweight title. Mesi made quick work of Davis, knocking him down and then knocking him out 90 seconds into the first round to claim his first professional title. Mesi moved his undefeated record to 26–0 and vaulted into the Top 10 of the WBC rankings.

Mesi's impressive record led to a contract with HBO Sports that would significantly increase his national visibility and the quality of his competition. It was the next logical move for Mesi and his boxing career. His first fight under the HBO contract was in HSBC Arena on Sept. 27, 2003, as part of the "Night of the Young Heavyweights." There were three featured fights, all with up-and-coming heavyweight contenders squaring off. Four of the six fighters were undefeated and the other two only had one loss. Mesi's fight was the main event of the evening. The enthusiastic crowd of 13,813 saw two very impressive fights leading up to Mesi's, with both ending in unanimous decisions.

The crowd was anxiously anticipating Mesi's arrival in the ring. Suddenly, he appeared in the upper level of the arena, below a large banner of "Baby Joe" in a boxing pose. As he made his way down to the ring, a wild display of pyrotechnics and music accompanied his walk, and the crowd was stirred into a frenzy. It was a perfect scene for HBO's broadcast. Once in the ring, Mesi made stunningly quick work of DaVarryl "Touch of Sleep" Williamson, his opponent that night. Williamson had received the nickname for his knockout prowess in running up an 18–1 record. Mesi came out with a flurry and, as The Buffalo News reported the next day, "administered a blitzkrieg assault in the main event." He knocked Williamson out cold at 97 seconds of Round 1. It was an incredible scene with the crowd cheering and celebrating the stunning victory. After all, Western New York hadn't had a native son like this in the boxing world in decades. Mesi sent a statement that he was a legitimate contender for the heavyweight title.

Mesi was next headed to Madison Square Garden in New York City for a fight on Dec. 6 versus Monte Barrett. This was a big step up in competition for Mesi. He started the fight strong and was in command when he knocked

Barrett down in the fifth round. However, Barrett rebounded by knocking Mesi to the canvas with a left hook in the seventh round. Then Mesi rallied and hung on to win his first 10-round fight. Two officials scored the fight for Mesi and the third scored it a draw. It was by far Mesi's toughest fight to date, but he showed resilience and toughness after the knockdown, which are essential for a boxing champion.

One national boxing expert described Mesi's boxing ability around this time by saying, "He can hit, but he's also going to get hit. How he responds to those big punches will determine how far he can go."

Mesi (28–0) was on to Las Vegas, his first appearance in Sin City, for the Vassiliy Jirov fight on March 13, 2004. A win at Mandalay Bay almost certainly would mean a fight with Tyson in Buffalo and a path to the heavyweight title. Mesi dominated the Jirov fight from the opening bell with his quick hands, boxing prowess and power on full display. Through eight rounds Mesi was in complete control, although he was unable to put Jirov to the mat or end the fight. In the ninth round, he was a little sloppy with his defense, and Jirov came around the back of him. The Russian hit Mesi in the back of the head with a solid punch, stunning Mesi and knocking him to the canvas. He was able to get up and withstand the onslaught Jirov administered until the end of the round. Mesi was clearly dazed and admitted after the fight that he had no recollection of "what transpired after the first knockdown."

Mesi also barely hung on in the 10th round, going down twice more, but he was able to hold on to finish the fight. Luckily for him, despite the three knockdowns, he dominated the early rounds, which put him ahead on all three judges' cards and led him to win a unanimous decision 94–93. Mesi certainly displayed incredible grit and determination in withstanding the beating he took in the last two rounds to finish the fight. Tony Holden, Mesi's promoter, said after the fight that the second punch was "clearly an illegal blow behind the head."

Three days after the fight, in a post-fight medical checkup, an MRI scan showed two subdural hematomas, or areas of bleeding on the brain. That's a very serious injury for anyone, but especially for a boxer. His boxing license in Nevada was immediately suspended, awaiting further tests. This suspension effectively banned him from boxing in any state. Nobody is certain which punch caused the brain bleed, but a lot of speculation centered on the back-of-the-head punch — also called a rabbit punch — by Jirov in the

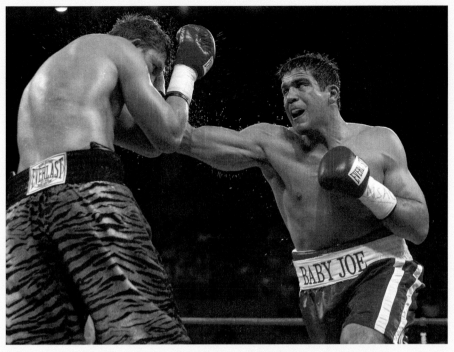

Photo 28. Joe Mesi, right, lands a right against Vassiliy Jirov
in the fifth round of their 10-round heavyweight bout on March 13, 2004,
at Mandalay Bay Resort & Casino in Las Vegas.

(AP Photo/Eric Jamison)

ninth round. This diagnosis and indefinite suspension ended any opportunity for the proposed fight with Tyson, effectively ending Mesi's professional boxing career.

For two years, Mesi fought to have his boxing license reinstated, going to many doctors and having several tests done, to no avail. He also pursued expert testimony of doctors, appearing in front of the Nevada boxing commission in 2005, but was turned down. He was never able to regain his Nevada license, though he did secure a boxing license in a few states, including Arkansas, Michigan and Rhode Island. He resumed his boxing career in 2006 after a two-year layoff. Mesi fought seven more times but was never able to regain his standing as a serious heavyweight contender. His last fight was on Oct. 12, 2007, a first-round TKO over Shannon Miller at the Twin River Events Casino in Lincoln, Rhode Island. Mesi ended his career with a 36–0 record.

Mesi pursued a political career after retiring from boxing. In 2008, he ran for the New York State Senate, representing Western New York. He was defeated in the general election by Republican Michael Ranzenhofer, who secured 53% of the vote to Mesi's 47%. Shortly after Mesi's defeat, Senate Majority Leader Malcolm Smith appointed him to serve as a community outreach liaison for his office in Buffalo, and he served in that capacity for a short time. Mesi has been involved in medical supply sales for several years and is a territory manager for Boston Scientific.

The end of his boxing story was an anticlimactic disappointment to Mesi and his many fans in Western New York. His once-promising boxing career and the chance to win the world heavyweight championship quite possibly ended on an illegal rabbit punch. The Curse usually only bothered teams from the area, but Mesi was an individual victim.

Chapter 17
SABRES ON THE BRINK

The Curse went into overdrive in 2002. The Buffalo Sabres were owned by Adelphia Communications Corp. owner John Rigas when he was charged with defrauding stockholders of billions of dollars. Rigas was later found guilty, and his illegal activities forced the Sabres into bankruptcy in 2003. The NHL had to step in and run the team, but there were no guarantees the Sabres would survive. Luckily, Tom Golisano and a group of minority investors purchased the team. Golisano, a native of Rochester, New York, was the founder of Paychex, a highly successful payroll and human resources services firm. The year before Golisano's ownership, the club lost $14 million. In his first season running the team (2003–04), he brought stability back to the franchise. Alas, the NHL owners implemented a lockout of the players in a labor dispute, an action that cost the league its entire 2004–05 season — a first in North American major sports history.

When the league resumed play in the fall of 2005, the Sabres had a great deal of good young talent and were positioned to compete with the NHL's best. Buffalo used the lockout year to develop many prospects in Rochester in the American Hockey League. Left wing Thomas Vanek, center Derek Roy, center Paul Gaustad, left wing Daniel Paille, defenseman Nathan Paetsch and goaltender Ryan Miller all played a full season in the AHL and were key elements to the 2005–06 season for the Sabres. They joined other players such as Daniel Briere, Chris Drury, Maxim Afinogenov, Ales Kotalik and Jochen Hecht. In addition, the league brought in new rules in 2005 that emphasized skill and speed — a good fit for Buffalo's revamped roster.

The Sabres played their first game in more than 18 months when they opened the regular season on Oct. 5 with a 6–4 victory over the New York Islanders. Briere and Afinogenov each scored twice while Miller became the team's No. 1 goalie. Buffalo followed up with a 4–1 win over the hated Bruins two days later, and the Sabres were off and running. They had a solid October with a 7–4 record and continued to improve throughout the season. The team put together Buffalo's first 50-win regular season (52) while amassing 110 points in one of the best regular seasons in Sabres history.

Afinogenov led the team in points with 73, and Drury was second with 67 while leading the Sabres in goals with 30. But this squad was known for its tremendous balance up and down the lineup, with six players scoring 20 or more goals and three other players contributing 18. Also, the Buffalo defense was solid, led by Toni Lydman, Teppo Numminen, Brian Campbell and Henrik Tallinder, along with excellent goaltending from Miller and backup Martin Biron.

Buffalo finished in second place in the Northeast Division, only 3 points behind Ottawa. The Sabres were seeded fourth in the East in the NHL play-offs and opened versus the Philadelphia Flyers. In the first Sabres postseason game in almost five years, the two teams showed the fans what they had been missing. Briere scored the game-winning goal on a pass from Hecht at 7:31 of the second overtime, giving the Sabres a 3–2 victory in Game 1. Buffalo had jumped to a 2–0 lead in the first 25 minutes, but Philadelphia responded with a goal in the second period and then a heartbreaking tying goal with only 1:51 left in regulation. The Sabres outplayed and outshot the Flyers 58–32 but nearly let the game get away.

Game 2 was completely different, as Buffalo scored five first-period goals on the way to an 8–2 destruction of the Flyers. J.P. Dumont and Jason Pominville led the way with hat tricks. It was the first time in team history that two players scored hat tricks in the same playoff game. The Flyers bounced back to win 4–2 in Game 3 behind two goals from one of the best players in the NHL, Peter Forsberg, and excellent goaltending from Robert Esche. Philadelphia evened the series at two with a 5–4 win in Game 4. Forsberg scored two more goals and R.J. Umberger netted the game-winner midway through the third period.

The Sabres regained their momentum at home, as Miller pitched a shut-out in front of 18,595 at HSBC Arena. Sabres center Tim Connolly scored the game's first goal and the backbreaking second goal in the last minute of the second period for a 2–0 Sabres lead. Miller completed the 3–0 shutout, as he steered away all 24 Flyers shots for the game. Buffalo left no doubt in Game 6 in Philadelphia, blowing out the Flyers 7–1 to win the series, four games to two. The Sabres scored three goals in the first period and the rout was on with three more goals in the second. Drury led Buffalo with two goals and Miller had 21 saves in spearheading the easy victory, sending the Sabres to play top-seeded Ottawa in the second round.

In a wild opening game at the Scotiabank Centre in Ottawa, the Sabres stunned the Senators 7–6 in overtime. The teams traded goals throughout the contest with neither team ever taking more than a one-goal lead. The game had an incredible finish. Buffalo's Derek Roy scored a short-handed goal with 1:37 remaining in regulation, tying the score at 5–5. On the same power play 24 seconds later, Ottawa's Bryan Smolinski beat Miller and scored what everyone in the Scotiabank Centre thought was the game-winner. In the final minute, the Sabres pulled Miller and, with six attackers on the ice, Connolly swatted the puck past Ottawa goalie Ray Emery to tie the game with only 10.7 seconds left in regulation. The overtime lasted all of 18 seconds with Drury scoring the game-winning goal to shock the Senators. It was an amazing victory for Buffalo and one of the most exciting games in team history.

Game 2 was quite different, with outstanding play from the goalies in a low-scoring affair. The Sabres scored twice in the second period from Hecht and Dumont to take a 2–0 lead and then put the game on Miller to win it for them, and he did. He was spectacular, especially in the second and third periods when Buffalo was outshot 32–8. Overall, Miller made 43 saves in the 2–1 victory, preserving the win with a tremendous save on a breakaway by Jason Spezza with 2:35 left. Surprisingly, the Sabres were heading home up two games to none. The one blemish in the night was that Buffalo lost starting defenseman Dmitri Kalinin with an ankle injury, and he would not return for the remainder of the playoffs.

Miller continued his outstanding play in goal for the Sabres in Game 3. Drury put Buffalo ahead with a first-period goal, and the lead stood up until the third period. Spezza tied the game for Ottawa early in the third, but Afinogenov gave the Sabres the lead back at the 10:15 mark. With Miller playing well, it seemed that they could hold on to the lead. But Spezza deflected a midair pass into the net after a Buffalo penalty to tie the score with 1:30 left and send the game to overtime. With 5:05 gone, Dumont stole a bouncing puck from Ottawa's Mike Fisher in the right faceoff circle and fired it like a knuckleball over Emery's right shoulder, winning the game for the Sabres 3–2. The victory gave Buffalo a commanding 3–0 series lead.

Buffalo had a chance to sweep the series at home, but Emery backstopped Ottawa to a 2–1 victory with the help of goals from Brian Pothier and Wade Redden. Game 5 was another one-goal game that was decided in overtime. With the score tied at two and the Senators on the power play, Pominville picked up a loose puck and raced down the left side of the ice. He then cut in front of Emery and tucked the puck past him for the series-winning goal. Tallinder had scored his first playoff goal for the Sabres in the first period and Drury scored a power-play goal in the second for the team's other goals. Miller made 34 saves as Buffalo upset the top-seeded Senators, four games to one, sending the Sabres to their first conference finals series since 1999.

The moment was caught perfectly by Sabres broadcaster, Rick Jeanneret, with a classic call.

"Pominville into Ottawa territory, Pominville goes around Alfredsson, cuts in front, scoooooores. Jason Pominville, shorthanded, oh now do you believe, now do you believe. These guys are good, scary good!...the Buffalo Sabres knock off the Senators in ooooooooovertime!"

The second-seeded Carolina Hurricanes — the former Hartford Whalers — defeated the New Jersey Devils in the second round, four games to one, to set up the conference final with Buffalo. As the Sabres did in each of their first two playoff series, they won a tightly contested Game 1, 3–2. Miller was outstanding again, knocking aside 29 shots, and Buffalo got goals from Tallinder, Briere and McKee in the victory. The Sabres lost defenseman Numminen in the first period to a lower-body injury.

The Hurricanes bounced back in Game 2 at the RBC Center. Carolina built a 4–1 lead, dominating the first two periods and early into the third. The Sabres mounted a furious comeback with two goals in the last nine minutes, but the Hurricanes held on and tied the series at one game each. A sellout crowd in HSBC Arena and thousands more in the plaza outside the rink witnessed an excellent contest by the Sabres in Game 3. Buffalo scored three unanswered goals in the second period, breaking a 1–1 tie. Briere scored twice and Kotalik netted the other goal during the Sabres' onslaught. Miller played well in the third period, keeping the Hurricanes at bay, and Buffalo held on for an exciting 4–3 win. The Sabres suffered another key injury as Tallinder, who had been their best defenseman throughout the playoffs, broke his arm and was lost for the remainder of the playoffs. The carnage was starting to add up.

Game 4 was a big disappointment for the Sabres and their fans, as Cam Ward stonewalled Buffalo with a 4–0 shutout, evening the series at two games. The Sabres played without three of their top six defensemen and could not overcome some penalties as the Hurricanes scored two goals before the game was 10 minutes old. After taking a 2–0 lead, Carolina dictated play and surrounded Ward with outstanding defense as the Hurricanes coasted to victory.

In Game 5 in Raleigh, Buffalo built a 3–1 lead early in the second period behind goals from Drury, Roy and Lydman. However, the short-handed Sabres could not withstand the pressure applied by the Hurricanes as Carolina scored twice in the second period to tie the game, 3–3. The third period was scoreless, with Buffalo missing on a couple of scoring opportunities, and the game went to overtime. Carolina put the Sabres on the brink of elimination when Cory Stillman scored a power-play goal at 8:46 into the extra session, giving the Hurricanes a 3–2 series lead.

Buffalo took a quick 1–0 lead in Game 6 as Dumont scored 4:56 into the contest. Numminen tried to return to the lineup but was re-injured in the first period, and the Sabres played with only five defensemen for the remainder of the contest. The defense held up as Miller played another outstanding game, but Carolina scored the tying goal with less than four minutes to play. The 1–1 game went to overtime. This time, Buffalo and Briere would not be denied. Briere took advantage of a Sabres power play in the extra session and beat Ward with a quick wrist shot at 4:22 of the overtime, sending Buffalo to a seventh and deciding game.

Buffalo received some additional bad news before Game 7: McKee, who had been outstanding in the series, would miss the contest because of a leg infection. The Sabres were about to play their most important game since "No Goal" in 1999 without four of their top six defensemen because of injury: Numminen (hip flexor), Tallinder (broken arm), Kalinin (ankle) and McKee. In addition, center Connolly was out with a concussion. Buffalo was once again victim of a curse, without a doubt.

The Sabres' effort in Game 7 was incredibly gutsy. They were forced to play with four defensemen who had been called up from their minor league team in Rochester: Rory Fitzpatrick, Jeff Jillson, Doug Janik and Nathan Paetsch (playing his first NHL game). Even so, Buffalo had the lead at the end of the second period. Carolina's Mike Commodore scored the first goal of the game in the first period. However, the Sabres played solid defense despite the group's significant inexperience, and Miller was at his best. Buffalo scored two goals late in the second stanza, topped off by Hecht's goal at 19:55 of the period. Stunningly, the Sabres went to the third period with a 2–1 lead. "It's in the hands of the hockey gods now," Ruff said in the pregame. It turned out to be in the hands of the Curse, which reared its ugly head at the most inopportune time.

Doug Weight scored the tying goal for the Hurricanes only 1:34 into the third period. The officials then made a questionable call on Brian Campbell, who was given a two-minute delay-of-game penalty for a clearing pass out of his end that went out of play. At that point in the game, it was a costly penalty against the Sabres, but by the rulebook it was the correct decision, and it had been called that way all season. It came down to the pass going up a little too high and missing the glass — a tiny adjustment in the angle would have made all the difference.

And, of course, everyone in Western New York worried that it would lead to the game-winning goal … and it did. Rod Brind'Amour stole the puck from Fitzpatrick and buried a shot over Miller's shoulder 64 seconds into the power play, giving the Hurricanes a 3–2 lead. Carolina clinched the game and the series with a goal in the final minute, sending the Hurricanes to the Stanley Cup Final.

Carolina went on to win the Stanley Cup, defeating Edmonton four games to three. The Sabres could not overcome the onslaught of injuries, though they fought the Hurricanes right until the end. With a healthy lineup, Buffalo was likely the better team. The series represented the franchise's best-ever chance to win the Stanley Cup. Years later, Briere had this to say: "When I look back, still to this day I felt we were the best team of the last four. To win a Stanley Cup, you need more than a good team. You need some breaks to go your way. It didn't happen. I wish we could have had a few more cracks together at it. Unfortunately, it didn't happen. That's definitely the year that I felt it was really close."

The Curse killed the Sabres' chances of winning, between the injuries and that questionable call in the final period of a tied Game 7. The injuries were too much to overcome. But a delay-of-game call probably shouldn't be made in the last 10 minutes of a tie game that decides who goes to the Stanley Cup Final. It was a cheap way for Carolina to have beaten a tough, resilient Buffalo squad.

Photo 29. Rod Brind'Amour (17) of the Carolina Hurricanes celebrates his game-winning goal during the third period against the Buffalo Sabres in Game 7 of the Eastern Conference finals on June 1, 2006.

(Getty Images, Grant Halverson)

Leo Roth, in his column in the Democrat and Chronicle on the day after the seventh game on June 2, wrote, "If you want to think Buffalo sports are cursed, go right ahead." With the loss, Buffalo was 1–5 in Game 7s in its history — another indication of a curse at play.

The Sabres' disappointment of 2006 turned into the greatest regular season in the team's history. The 2006–07 Sabres won the Presidents' Trophy, recognizing the NHL team with the most regular-season points, as the team amassed a franchise-record 53 victories. The Sabres started the season with 10 consecutive wins, a team record, and never looked back. They dominated the league, led by rising stars Miller, Campbell and Kalinin and their leading scorers Briere (95 points), Vanek (84) and Drury (69).

Buffalo entered the playoffs as the top seed and had home-ice advantage in every series through the playoffs. In April 2007, ESPN the Magazine ranked the Sabres as the No. 1 team among all professional sports franchises in entertainment value, citing affordable ticket prices, an exciting brand of hockey and player accessibility. It was a remarkable achievement for a team that only five years earlier had almost ceased to exist.

Buffalo's first playoff opponent was the Islanders. The Sabres dominated the less-skilled New Yorkers, winning the series in five games. Buffalo won the opening game 4–1 in Buffalo, behind two goals each from Drury and Campbell. New York captured its only victory in the series, 3–2, in Game 2. However, any hopes New York had of pulling an upset were quickly squashed when the Sabres went into Nassau Coliseum and won the next two games by scores of 3–2 and 4–2. Briere scored a power-play goal midway through the third period in Game 3, giving the Sabres the lead, and Miller made it stand up. In Game 4, Drury scored twice and Vanek and Pominville each chipped in with a goal in Buffalo's 4–2 win, giving the Sabres a 3–1 series lead. The Sabres came home to HSBC Arena and claimed the series with a 4–3 win. Afinogenov scored in the third period to give the Sabres a 4–1 lead, but Buffalo had to withstand a furious rally by the Islanders. New York scored two goals, four minutes apart, midway through the final stanza and was pressing for the tying goal, but the Sabres were able to hang on to clinch the series.

The New York Rangers were the Sabres' opponent in the conference semifinals. The Rangers were led by star center Jaromír Jágr, centers Michael Nylander and Martin Straka and winger Brendan Shanahan, along with goaltender Henrik Lundqvist. Rangers head coach Tom Renney gave the

Sabres some bulletin board material before Game 1 when he said they were not the cream of the crop of the NHL. Game 1 started slowly and was scoreless well into the second period when the highest-scoring team in the NHL during the regular season exploded for three goals in a little more than four minutes. Vanek scored to start the onslaught, and in quick succession Kotalik and Vanek again. Buffalo's burst propelled it to a 5–2 victory.

In Game 2 at HSBC Arena, the Rangers controlled the first two periods, outshooting the Sabres 22–9 and outscoring them 2–1. However, Buffalo came to life in the third as Drury revived the home fans 24 seconds into the period by deflecting a shot from Lydman into the goal, tying the score at 2. Vanek sent the fans into delirium less than 10 minutes later on a beautiful behind-the-back feed from Drew Stafford. Vanek fired a slap shot over the glove of Lundqvist into the back of the net for a 3–2 Sabres lead. In the final two minutes, the Rangers were all over the Sabres, keeping the puck in the Buffalo zone and firing shot after shot at Miller. The goalie made a terrific save on a blistering slap shot by Jágr, sprawled to stop Paul Mara's wrister and turned away several other Rangers' chances to preserve the win for Buffalo. The Sabres headed to Madison Square Garden in New York ahead 2–0 in the series.

Game 3 was a goaltending duel between Lundqvist and Miller that needed more than 96 minutes before a winner was determined. Jágr scored a second-period goal and Briere tied it for Buffalo midway through the third, but that was all the scoring in regulation. Miller turned away 44 Ranger shots, and Lundqvist had 38 saves in the opening 60 minutes. Goals remained scarce until 16:43 of the second overtime, when Michal Rozsíval's shot sailed past a screened Miller, hit the post and bounced into the goal. Lundqvist was again spectacular in Game 4, outdueling his goalie counterpart in a 2–1 victory. Jágr and Shanahan scored for the Rangers while Lundqvist steered aside 29 Sabres shots, allowing only a single goal by Kotalik in helping the Rangers tie the series at 2–2. Buffalo thought Briere had scored the game-tying goal with 17 seconds left, but after a lengthy video review the officials ruled the puck had not crossed the goal line. It was yet another questionable call.

As the Sabres headed home for Game 5, the pressure was on Buffalo to find a way to solve Lundqvist and score more than a single goal. Lundqvist was outstanding again and when Straka scored with only 3:19 left in the third period to give New York a 1–0 lead, all seemed lost for Buffalo. With only 16 seconds left in regulation, the Sabres won a faceoff to the left of Lundqvist. A couple of quick passes set up Connolly, who fired a shot on goal. Lundqvist made the save but did not secure the rebound as it bounced off his shoulder to the left of the goal. Drury came from behind the net and fired the bouncing puck past Lundqvist, tying the game with only 7.7 seconds remaining. It was one of the most memorable moments in franchise history.

At 4:39 of overtime, Afinogenov, who had been benched in Game 4, fired the puck from the top of the faceoff circle. Lundqvist did not see the shot as it flew past him into the net for the improbable game-winning goal. Afinogenov sprinted down the ice and dove on his belly, sliding across the ice in celebration. After the game, he said, "It's the biggest goal of my career."

The win gave the Sabres a 3–2 lead in the series. Buffalo rode the momentum all the way to New York for Game 6 and came away with an impressive 5–4 win and the series, four games to two. After spotting the Rangers a 1–0 first-period lead, Buffalo exploded for four goals in the second stanza, highlighted by goals from Drury and Pominville. Hecht scored his second goal of the game with 5:10 remaining in the third period, giving the Sabres a two-goal lead. Although the Rangers pulled within one, they were not able to secure the tying goal.

For the second season in a row, the Sabres were in the Eastern Conference finals. This time, division rival Ottawa was the opponent, a team the Sabres had vanquished in the NHL playoffs in 2006. Ottawa silenced the frenzied Buffalo crowd in Game 1, scoring two goals in the first period to take a 2–0 lead. The Sabres responded with two goals of their own (from Afinogenov and Lydman) to tie the game going into the third period. Ottawa dominated the final stanza, scoring three goals against a shoddy Sabres defense and pulled away for a 5–2 win.

Game 2 was critical for the Sabres as they could not afford to lose the first two games on home ice. Buffalo, fueled by the energy from the crowd, stormed to a quick 2–0 lead in the first 6:13 behind goals from Vanek and Hecht. The Senators methodically settled the game down and got themselves back into it. Daniel Alfredsson scored a goal before the end of the first period. Mike Fisher scored on a power play for Ottawa to tie the game at 6:08 of the second. Then before the period was over, Redden scored on another power play, giving the Senators a 3–2 lead heading to the third stanza. Ottawa controlled the tempo throughout the third period, and things were looking bleak for Buffalo.

In the final minutes, the Sabres pulled Miller and attacked with six players. With 5.8 seconds left in regulation, Briere stuffed a rebound past Emery to tie the game. It was easy to expect that the Sabres would carry that momentum into the opening minutes of overtime, and the fans in the arena never sat down in anticipation of that finish. However, the first extra session ended scoreless. With slightly less than five minutes gone in the second overtime, Spezza beat Drury on a faceoff in the Buffalo zone and pulled the puck back to Joe Corvo. The defenseman's slap shot darted and dipped toward the goal, more like an end-over-end kick in football. Just before getting to Miller, the shot broke under his glove and into the net. It was a heartbreaking 4–3 defeat for the Sabres.

Ottawa scored another fluky goal in Game 3. The Senators' Dany Heatley fired a slap shot that caromed off the back wall toward Miller. The puck bounced off his glove and into the crease where Alfredsson was standing all alone, and he just tapped it into the empty net. It was the only goal of the game as the Senators took a commanding 3–0 lead in the series. The losses in Games 2 and 3 were cases of sheer bad luck for Buffalo. In both games they played well enough to win, only to lose on two bad bounces. There was that Curse again. Everything that went the Sabres' way in the 2006 series with Ottawa reversed itself in 2007 to favor the Senators.

At least Buffalo didn't go away quietly. The Sabres built a 3–0 lead in Game 4 and hung onto it to win 3–2 behind some outstanding goaltending from Miller. Roy scored nine seconds into the game, setting the tone for Buffalo. Afinogenov and Drury scored goals in the first half of the second period, and Miller pushed aside 31 Ottawa shots.

Game 5 was evenly played. Afinogenov scored a power-play goal at 10:58 of the third period to tie the game 2–2, ultimately sending the game to overtime. But in extra time, Alfredsson broke the hearts of Sabres fans by scoring the series-clinching goal at 9:32 and ending Buffalo's quest for the Cup. For the second straight season, the Sabres came up short of advancing to the finals, although this exit was much more definitive than the one that had come the year before. Briere, who didn't know that he had just played his last game as a Sabre, said in the postgame locker room, "It's disappointing that such an awesome season ends like that. It's tough to swallow and we feel like we let the fans and the city down. I really thought it was our year, but we weren't able to get it going against the Senators."

Photo 30. Daniel Alfredsson (11) of the Ottawa Senators celebrates scoring the game-winning and series-winning goal past Ryan Miller (30) of the Buffalo Sabres during overtime in Game 5 of the Eastern Conference finals on May 19, 2007.
(Getty Images, Bruce Bennett)

It was a disheartening end to a great season for Buffalo. Ruff said many years later he felt this was the best team he coached, and it was his fourth conference finals team. He thought this squad had the best chance to win the Cup. However, it appeared the team ran out of gas against Ottawa. Maybe all those games over two years did them in. Or maybe it was the Curse that again had to interfere with Buffalo winning a championship.

The Sabres still had a young, dynamic and exciting team built for the new faster-paced NHL. However, Sabres management misread the free-agent market and the value of its best players. In July, Buffalo lost two major cogs in its offense in Drury and Briere. On the opening day of free agency, the Flyers signed Briere to an eight-year, $52 million contract. The Sabres had offered him a five-year, $25 million deal. Shortly after Briere signed, Drury inked a five-year, $35.25 million contract with the Rangers. In a matter of a few short hours, Buffalo had lost its two co-captains and the heart and soul of the team. It was the beginning of a slow but precipitous decline for the franchise.

The Sabres missed the playoffs in the 2007–08 season. The highlight of the year was Buffalo hosting the first NHL Winter Classic. On Jan. 1, the Sabres played the Pittsburgh Penguins at Ralph Wilson Stadium. The game was outdoors in front of an NHL-record crowd of 71,217. The Winter Classic was something of an experiment that topped any predictions about its success. Tickets were extremely difficult to get, as Buffalo fans showed their passion for hockey and the Sabres. Many relived their childhood hockey memories of playing outdoors. The stadium parking lots were electric with fans tailgating and light snow falling, making for a perfect backdrop for the game. What's more, the game lived up to the hype. The contest went to overtime and was won on a shootout goal by Penguins star Sidney Crosby. Of course, the Sabres lost, and in heartbreaking fashion. Why should the Curse not apply to a regular-season game? But the Winter Classic was a tremendous success and would become the NHL's most popular regular-season event, one that continues today.

Buffalo also did not qualify for the playoffs at the end of the 2008–09 season. The team rebounded in 2009–10 by winning the Northeast Division with 100 points but was eliminated in the first round of the playoffs by the Boston Bruins 4–2. In March 2011, Golisano sold the Sabres to Terry and Kim Pegula for $189 million. Golisano had turned down a more lucrative offer to ensure that the team stayed in Buffalo.

Terry Pegula founded East Resources, Inc. in 1983, an oil and gas exploration company. Kim joined the firm in 1991. The company profited heavily from the discovery of deep layers of natural gas on property owned by the firm, and the use of hydraulic fracturing. Terry first sold the New York, Pennsylvania and Rocky Mountain reserves for $4.7 billon to Royal Dutch Shell. Then in 2014 he sold the Ohio and West Virginia reserves for $1.75 billion.

In 1983, Terry told his business partner, "If I ever have more than two nickels to my name, I'm going to buy the Buffalo Sabres one day." Less than 30 years later, Terry's dream came to fruition.

There was excitement in Sabreland as the Pegulas took over, especially when Terry said he was committed to spending money to bring a Stanley Cup to Buffalo. As of 2022, the Pegulas also owned the Buffalo Bills, which they purchased for $1.4 billion on Oct. 10, 2014, following the death of Ralph C. Wilson Jr.

The Sabres played excellent hockey down the stretch after the ownership change, finishing with a 10–3–2 run. Buffalo placed third in the Northeast Division and qualified for the playoffs. However, the Sabres lost in the opening round, in a seven-game series to the Flyers and former teammate Briere. Buffalo led the series 3–2 and had a chance to win it with a victory at home in Game 6. Buffalo led 4–3 in the third period but surrendered the tying goal with 9:17 left in regulation. The game went to overtime, and Philadelphia's Ville Leino — who later became known as one of the worst free-agent signings in Buffalo's hockey history, with a six-year, $27 million deal that came to an early end when he was put on waivers three years in — scored the game-winner at 4:43 of the extra stanza. Briere, just for cruel irony, scored two of the Flyers' goals, keeping them in the game when Buffalo was threatening to pull away. The Sabres were blown out in Game 7 in Philadelphia, with the Flyers building a 4–0 lead and coasting to a 5–2 series-clinching victory. Briere scored another goal in the victory. As of 2022, Buffalo had not returned to the playoffs since losing to the Flyers.

The Sabres signed Leino that summer of 2011. With new ownership that had money and Terry having told the fans in his first press conference that money would not be a limiting factor to winning a Stanley Cup, Buffalo wanted to make a splash in free agency. When the Sabres lost out on signing Tampa Bay's star center Brad Richards in free agency, they basically bid against themselves, giving Leino a contract that no other team would have come close to offering him. It was the first of what would become many poor, maybe cursed, personnel decisions since the Pegulas have owned the team.

Ruff lasted another year and a half but was relieved of his duties as Buffalo head coach on Feb. 20, 2013. The era had come to an end. Ruff, the best coach in Sabres history, lasted almost 16 seasons and took his team to four conference finals and one Stanley Cup Final but could never get the team over the hump and win the Cup. Poor Lindy could never overcome the Curse.

Chapter 18
A GLIMMER OF HOPE

The decision to bench Doug Flutie on Jan. 3, 2000, sent the Bills into a downward spiral that lasted almost two decades. Call it the Flutie Curse, but really it is just another mutation of the Buffalo Sports Curse. Choosing Rob Johnson over Flutie was a monumental mistake, both going into the Tennessee playoff game and then making the more permanent decision a year later in keeping Johnson and releasing Flutie in the winter of 2001. It not only eliminated any real chance the Bills had of reaching Super Bowl 34, but it led to an entrenched losing culture with Johnson a perfect example of its outcome. It took until 2017, with the hiring of head coach Sean McDermott and general manager Brandon Beane, to rid the organization of that culture.

Johnson lasted just eight games in 2001, leading the team to a 1–7 record, and then he was again injured for the fourth time in his 26-game, four-year tenure, mercifully ending his career with the Bills. Alex Van Pelt started at quarterback the rest of the season and outplayed Johnson, steering the team to a 2–6 finish for an overall 3–13 record.

The Bills made a major splash on April 21, 2002, trading with division rival New England for quarterback Drew Bledsoe. The veteran had been an effective starting quarterback for the Patriots for eight years after being the first overall pick in the NFL draft in 1993. However, he lost his job to Tom Brady because of an injury during the 2001 season, and Brady led the Patriots to the Super Bowl championship — making Bledsoe expendable. It was a bold move by the Bills, but the team knew it desperately needed a quarterback.

Bledsoe put together the single best season by a quarterback in Buffalo's history (at least by some statistical standards up to that time) in 2002, improving the Bills' record to 8–8. Bledsoe combined with receivers Eric

Moulds and Peerless Price in throwing for a team-record 4,359 yards on 375 completions in 610 attempts. Moulds and Price put together the best single season for receptions and yards by a duo of receivers in team history. Moulds caught 100 passes for 1,292 yards, and Price contributed 94 receptions for 1,252 yards.

Buffalo took a step back in 2003, finishing with a 6–10 record after a 2–0 start that included a 31–0 thumping of the two-time defending NFL champion Patriots. The poor season led to the firing of head coach Gregg Williams after three years. Mike Mularkey took over as head coach in 2004. The team started the season with four consecutive losses before beating Miami 20–13 on Oct. 17. The Bills split their next four games and were sitting at a dismal 3–6. All of a sudden, Buffalo caught fire behind a rejuvenated offense, led by Bledsoe and running back Willis McGahee, along with a stout defense. The Bills ran off six consecutive wins, including thrashings of Seattle 38–9, Cleveland 37–7 and San Francisco 41–7. Buffalo went into the final week of the season with a 9–6 record, and a win over Pittsburgh would qualify them for the playoffs.

In front of a raucous home crowd at Ralph Wilson Stadium on Jan. 2, 2005, the Bills battled the Steelers, who were playing many second-string players as they had already clinched their playoff spot. The game was tight into the fourth quarter. Buffalo cornerback Nate Clements picked off a Tommy Maddox pass and returned it 30 yards for the go-ahead touchdown late in the third quarter to give the Bills a 17–16 lead. The Steelers drove for a field goal early in the fourth quarter and took the lead back at 19–17. The ensuing drive changed not only the game but also the trajectory of the Buffalo franchise. On third down and 6 from the Bills 24, Bledsoe dropped back to pass, was sacked by Ricardo Colclough and fumbled the ball. The fumble was scooped up by Steelers linebacker James Harrison, and he rambled 18 yards for a touchdown. The score put Pittsburgh ahead 26–17 on the way to a 29–24 win. The Bills were eliminated from the playoffs by the devastating loss.

The Buffalo front office overreacted in the offseason, as it decided to release Bledsoe and go with 2004 first-round draft choice J.P. Losman, who was not ready to take over. Losman went 1–7 as the starter in 2005, with the Bills stumbling to a 5–11 finish. Mularkey quit his job at the end of the season.

For the next dozen seasons, the Bills were stuck in mediocrity. The team went through myriad general managers, head coaches and starting quarterbacks. Buffalo had five general managers, eight head coaches, including Williams and Mularkey, and 11 starting quarterbacks, while only once achieving a winning record. Another problem was that they were also never really bad and thus did not secure picks at the very top of the NFL draft. They were 6–10 four times and 7–9 four times. Coach Dick Jauron was the epitome of mediocrity, as he led the team to three consecutive 7–9 seasons from 2006 through 2008. He was fired midway through the 2009 season.

Losman never developed in his five seasons, posting a 10–23 record as a starter. His shining moment was a game against the Texans on Nov. 19, 2006, when he led his only fourth-quarter comeback in a 24–21 win in Houston. The players whom the Bills funneled onto the field as so-called NFL starting quarterbacks from 2005 through 2018 can only be described as wannabes, has-beens or journeymen. The list included Losman, Kelly Holcomb, Trent Edwards, Ryan Fitzpatrick, E.J. Manuel, Kyle Orton and Tyrod Taylor. Most of them had some success with the Bills, creating a ray of hope for the team's fans, but then would come crashing back to earth. They consistently led Buffalo to 7–9 and 6–10 records, with a 4–12 or 5–11 thrown in for good measure. They never could sustain a high degree of competence at the game's most important position. They always came back to their level: players who should have been second-stringers in the NFL. The Bills also had other players under center for short stretches of time or for a single game who had absolutely no business starting for an NFL team. That list includes Jeff Tuel, Thaddeus Lewis, Nathan Peterman, Derek Anderson and Brian Brohm.

And for the Bills' one winning season between 2005 and 2016, the team coaxed Orton out of retirement, and he helped guide the team to a 9–7 record. However, on the most important play of the season, he came up short — literally — in an attempt to keep the team's playoff hopes alive. In a game against the Raiders, instead of diving for a first down on a fourth-down run, he slid to protect himself. Of course, Orton was short of the first down, and the Bills' playoff hopes ended. He went back into retirement at the end of the season. That year ended with a meaningless win over New England on the final day of the season, so that head coach Doug Marrone could say he had a winning record. After the season concluded, Marrone tried to leverage new owner Terry Pegula for more power and money (a clause in Marrone's contract allowed him to opt out if ownership of the team changed), and thankfully Pegula chose to let Marrone walk away.

During this period in Bills history, the team was highly effective at creating and selling hope to the fan base. They would do just enough in the offseason to generate interest through some big acquisition in free agency like Terrell Owens or Mario Williams, or through the draft with players like C. J. Spiller, Willis McGahee, Marshawn Lynch, Sammy Watkins and Marcell Dareus. Once the season began, the Bills often would tease their fans with a good start or would pull an upset victory that generated hope. But they always failed over the course of each season. Buffalo even hired a coach for hype when the team was enthralled with Rex Ryan. But that also did not work as he was out after two mediocre seasons while feuding with one of the worst general managers in the team's history, Doug Whaley.

In 2008, the Bills started 5–1 but finished 7–9. In 2011 they started 5–2 and finished 6–10. In 2016, Ryan's last season, they started 4–2 and finished 7–9. Get the idea? Buffalo was mired in mediocrity.

With the hiring of head coach Sean McDermott and general manager Brandon Beane, the Bills finally brought real hope to Buffalo fans in 2017. It didn't take long for them to show that they were solid professionals who knew what they were doing. After 17 years of no playoffs, the longest drought for any team among the four major sports leagues, McDermott remarkably brought the postseason back to Buffalo with the help of a miracle on the final day of the regular season — in a game that didn't even involve the Bills.

The Bills were 8–7 entering the final game of the 2017 season in Miami. Buffalo had to beat the Dolphins and wait for some help in the form of results from other games. The Bills played well in Miami, defeating the Dolphins 22–16. The victory was preserved by a final-minute interception by safety Jordan Poyer. The game was highlighted by a smashing touchdown run by a Bills fan favorite, defensive tackle Kyle Williams. It was his only career touchdown.

After the win over the Dolphins, the Bills went to their locker room and awaited the results of the other games. To sneak into the playoffs, the Bills needed one of two scenarios to play out: a) the Chargers losing to the Raiders *and* the Titans losing to the Jaguars; or b) the Bengals upsetting the Ravens. Eventually it all came down to the late game between the Bengals and Ravens in Baltimore. If Cincinnati won, the Bills were in. With less than a minute left, the lowly Bengals faced a fourth down and 12 from the Ravens 49-yard line trailing 27–24. Bengals quarterback Andy Dalton fired a pass down the field that barely sailed over the outstretched arms of a Ravens defender and was caught by Tyler Boyd. The receiver accelerated past two Baltimore players and sprinted into the end zone for an incredible, improbable touchdown with 44 seconds left, giving Cincinnati a 31–27 lead. The Bills locker room erupted in joy, but Baltimore still had a chance to come back. On the Ravens' ensuing possession, the Bengals stopped them in four plays. After Baltimore's last hope was extinguished, the Bills locker room exploded in celebration a second time, as the 17-year drought was over. McDermott had changed the culture and steered the team to a spot in the NFL playoffs.

One point should be noted here: Of all the best moments in Bills history, this was the only one in which Buffalo had nothing to do with the outcome on the field. The fans celebrated in a unique and wonderful way: They donated more than $415,000 to the Andy & JJ Dalton Foundation, supporting the Bengals quarterback's efforts to help seriously ill and physically challenged children.

The Bills traveled to Jacksonville to take on the Jaguars on Jan. 7, 2018. Jacksonville (10–6), winner of the AFC South, was led by a solid defense with All-Pro cornerback Jalen Ramsey, cornerback A.J. Bouye and defensive end Calais Campbell, along with a strong running game featuring Leonard Fournette. The game was a defensive struggle from the outset. Both defenses bottled up the opposing offense until the Bills put together a very impressive drive starting from their own 16-yard line in the second quarter. The Bills drove 71 yards in 18 plays, using up more than eight minutes on the clock. Buffalo had a first and goal at the Jacksonville 1, when McDermott outsmarted himself. Instead of running the ball, the Bills decided to pass. Taylor lofted the ball into the end zone for 6-foot-5 Kelvin Benjamin. However, as the play unfolded and the pass was slightly overthrown, the official threw a penalty flag for offensive pass interference on Benjamin. It was a critical penalty against Buffalo, as it moved them back to the 11-yard line. At best it was a questionable call, as both players pushed each other to try to gain leverage. It should have been a no-call. The Bills settled for a field goal for a 3–0 lead.

The Bills defense was containing the Jacksonville running game and Blake Bortles' passes throughout the first half. However, Bortles found a weakness in the Bills defense on the final drive before intermission. Jacksonville took over the ball at the 47-yard line. Bortles scrambled for 20 yards to the Buffalo 33 and then ran 12 more yards to the Bills 21. Those two plays positioned the Jaguars to kick a game-tying field goal to end the half. Bortles, not really known for his running, hurt Buffalo as he took off a few more times in the second half. His legs were Jacksonville's best offensive weapon.

Midway through the third quarter, the Jaguars put together their one good drive of the game. Jacksonville marched 86 yards in 15 plays and converted it into a touchdown. On fourth and goal at the 1 and everyone expecting a running play, Bortles crossed up the Bills and found tight end Ben Koyack in the back of the end zone for the touchdown and a 10–3 Jacksonville lead.

Buffalo had one final chance to tie the game with 1:51 remaining. The Bills took over at their own 37-yard line, and Taylor hit Charles Clay with a 5-yard pass on second down and scrambled for 2 yards on third down, setting up a fourth and 3. However, Taylor was injured on the play and did not return to the game. Nathan Peterman came in to replace him and scrambled for 4 yards and a first down at the 48-yard line. The following play, Peterman fired a 14-yard pass to Deonte Thompson to the Jacksonville 38-yard line, and the Bills still had a pulse with 1:07 left.

On another questionable call, Peterman was flagged for intentional grounding on the next play, a huge penalty moving the Bills back to the 48-yard line. Facing a first and 20, Peterman fired a pass to Thompson, and Ramsey, covering him tightly, ran through Thompson, pushing him to the side while intercepting the pass. The play was reviewed by the replay official, and he let the play stand. Bortles knelt on the next play, ending the game and the Bills' season. This is a game Buffalo probably should have won, as a few plays and a couple of questionable official calls went against them that ultimately decided the outcome.

The Bills brain trust determined that Taylor was not the quarterback to take the team to the next level. Buffalo traded him to Cleveland in March 2018 as they prepared to select a quarterback in that year's NFL draft. The Bills traded up to select Wyoming quarterback Josh Allen with the seventh overall pick.

Allen was a raw rookie, so McDermott started Peterman at quarterback to begin the season with disastrous results — a 47–3 loss to Baltimore. Allen, ready or not, had to step in and play right away. He was the starting quarterback in the Bills' Week 2 loss to the Los Angeles Chargers. Allen had his ups and downs in his rookie year while also missing a few games with an injury in the Bills' 6–10 season. He improved as the season went along and was 5–6 as the starting quarterback.

McDermott and Beane significantly strengthened the team during the 2019 offseason, adding free-agent wide receivers John Brown and Cole Beasley, center Mitch Morse, tackle Ty Nsekhe, guard Jon Feliciano and running back Frank Gore. In the draft they added defensive tackle Ed Oliver, tackle Cody Ford and running back Devin Singletary.

The Bills' 2019 season was their best since 1996, winning 10 games and clinching a playoff spot with a win over Pittsburgh on "Sunday Night Football" with two games remaining in the regular season. They qualified as a wild card, as they were still unable to beat nemesis New England. However, the Bills had some exciting wins throughout the season. They included a come-from-behind opening-day win over the New York Jets 17–16, a 28–14 victory over the New York Giants the next week, two wins over the Dolphins, a hard-fought 14–7 triumph over Tennessee and a dominating 26–15 beat-down of the Dallas Cowboys on Thanksgiving.

With a national television audience tuned in on Thanksgiving, and most expecting a Dallas victory over Buffalo, the Bills played their best game of the season — though it did not start that way. The Cowboys took the opening kickoff and marched down the field with Dak Prescott hitting Jason Witten for an 8-yard touchdown pass to cap off the drive. The Bills bounced back in the second quarter with a 25-yard Allen touchdown pass to former Cowboy Beasley to tie the game. Then the Bills shocked the Cowboys near the end of the first half. Buffalo drove to the Dallas 28-yard line at the two-minute warning. On first down, the Bills ran a double reverse with Brown throwing a pass to a wide-open Singletary, who waltzed into the end zone with the go-ahead touchdown.

The Bills had wrested the momentum from the Cowboys. They scored on their first two possessions of the second half: a 41-yard field goal by Stephen Hauschka and an Allen surprise 15-yard scramble for a touchdown. Those scores put the Bills in complete control of the game at 23–7. Buffalo's highly rated defense held the Cowboys at bay the rest of the way, only allowing a garbage-time touchdown in the Bills' dominant 26–15 victory.

Buffalo finished the regular season with the third-best defense in the NFL, and Allen improved significantly, throwing for 3,089 yards and 20 touchdowns, along with 510 rushing yards and nine scores. The Bills traveled to Houston to play the Texans in the wild-card playoff round on Jan. 4.

Buffalo jumped to a 13–0 first-half lead behind a razzle-dazzle pass play from Brown to Allen for a touchdown and two field goals from Hauschka.

The second-half kickoff created a major controversy as Texans returner DeAndre Carter threw his arms out parallel to the ground, caught the kick in the end zone, took a step forward and then tossed the ball to the referee. The official moved out of the way of the ball as it hit the ground. The Bills rushed in and recovered it, and the official ruled it a touchdown. Carter had taken a step and he did not kneel to give himself up; he just tossed the ball to the referee. By the NFL rules, that is a fumble, and the on-field official made the correct call.

However, the officials gathered for a discussion, which may have even included someone from the NFL's officiating office in New York via the headset. They soon ruled collectively that Carter gave himself up with the arm signal and showed with that gesture that he did not intend to return the kick. While some thought that the decision was a case of common sense prevailing, many others strongly believed that the returner had not made his intentions clear. If the play had been upheld as called on the field, it would have been a Buffalo touchdown and a 20–0 lead.

The Bills pulled ahead 16–0 later in the third quarter, but the Texans soon scored on a 20-yard Deshaun Watson run and a successful 2-point conversion to cut the Buffalo lead to 16–8. The Texans added a field goal to reduce the margin to 16–11 with 10:55 remaining and then took the lead on Carlos Hyde's 5-yard pass from Watson with only 4:37 left. The Texans stopped the Bills on their ensuing drive and needed only a single first down to win the game. Houston decided to go for a fourth and 1 from the Bills 30-yard line to salt the game away. However, the Buffalo defense stopped them short of the first down with 1:16 remaining. Allen, with no timeouts, scrambled for 20 yards and completed two key passes to gain first downs as he moved the Bills to the Texans 29-yard line with 10 seconds left. Hauschka made the clutch 47-yard field goal to tie the game and send it to overtime.

Houston received the ball to start the extra period, but the Bills, after giving up one first down, stopped the Texans to force a punt. Buffalo began a drive at its own 30. Allen engineered two huge third-down conversions, the first a 14-yard pass to Dawson Knox to the 42-yard line and the second to Singletary for 14 yards to the Houston 43. Again on third down, Allen improvised, scrambling 4 yards to the Houston 38 to set up a 55-yard game-winning field-goal attempt for Hauschka. However, a flag was thrown on the play and the official called a 15-yard illegal blindside block on Ford. It was a borderline call that had no impact on the play and the player was not at all blindsided. The questionable penalty took the Bills out of field-goal range, and they were forced to punt. A year later, the NFL admitted that it was the wrong call.

On Houston's ensuing possession, it converted a key third-and-18 play for a first down. Then after Watson somehow escaped a sack from two Bills defenders, ex-Bill Taiwan Jones caught a short pass and ran 30 more yards to the Buffalo 10, setting up the game-winning field goal. Texans kicker Ka'imi Fairbairn converted the 28-yard kick and the Bills' season was over. It was a heartbreaking 22–19 loss for Buffalo.

"We had opportunities to win and came up short," McDermott said later. "Not an easy pill to swallow this time of year. A lot of pain in that locker room." The Bills had several chances to win the game and did not, but the two officials' calls were especially brutal and had a direct impact on the outcome. The Curse struck again. Between the Bills' inability to make a few key plays and the two bad calls, Buffalo lost a game they should have won.

The Curse again played a role in denying the Bills an opportunity to win a playoff game and go to Kansas City to play the ultimate Super Bowl champions. And you never know what might have happened — another lost opportunity for Buffalo.

The Bills' 2020 season was a record-breaking campaign as the team won its first AFC East title since 1995 and had its best regular-season record (13–3) since 1991. In winning the AFC East and ending the stranglehold by the New England Patriots (with 11 straight such crowns), the Bills were 6–0 against their divisional opponents for the first time in their history. Of course the Bills picked 2020 to win the AFC East for the first time in 25 years, when no fans were allowed in the stadium during the regular season because of the Covid-19 worldwide pandemic. Can you say cursed?

The Bills broke many single-season records on offense. With the acquisition of wide receiver Stefon Diggs from the Minnesota Vikings and Allen's major improvement, Buffalo scored the most points in team history with 501. Diggs broke the Bills single-season record for receptions with 127 and yards receiving with 1,535. He also scored eight touchdowns, and his presence lifted the play of all the team's receivers. Allen broke several single-season team records including most passing yards, 4,544; most passing touchdowns, 37; most total touchdowns, 46; highest completion percentage, 69.2; and most

300-yard passing games with eight. Rookie kicker Tyler Bass broke the team's single-season scoring record with 141 points.

The Bills' regular season was highlighted by several thrilling victories: a 35–32 win over the Los Angeles Rams on a 3-yard touchdown pass from Allen to Tyler Kroft with 15 seconds left; a 24–21 victory over New England, preserved on a forced fumble by Justin Zimmer and recovered by Dean Marlowe on the Bills 13-yard line with 31 seconds left; a 44–34 shootout win over Seattle, as Allen outdueled Russell Wilson in throwing for 415 yards and three touchdowns; an AFC East title-clinching victory over the Broncos 48–19 in Denver; and the elimination of bitter rival Miami from the playoffs in a 56–26 beatdown.

The Bills' only regular-season loss after Week 6 was a 32–30 defeat at the hands of the Arizona Cardinals, dubbed "Hail Murray." Cardinal quarterback Kyler Murray threw a 43-yard desperation pass, with no time left, that DeAndre Hopkins caught in the end zone for the winning score as three Bills defenders were draped all over him. At the conclusion of the season, it was voted the NFL's Play of the Year.

The division title meant Buffalo would host its first playoff game since Jim Kelly's last game in 1996. The Bills defeated the Indianapolis Colts 27–24 in a hard-fought contest on Jan. 9, 2021. The game brought Curse thoughts to life late in the contest. The Bills were winning 27–24 with 50 seconds remaining, but the Colts were driving for a potential tying field goal or game-winning touchdown. Indianapolis faced a fourth and 10 from its own 37-yard line. Colts quarterback Philip Rivers fired a pass to a sliding Zach Pascal, who caught the ball and got up to run, and the ball was stripped by Bills safety Jordan Poyer. Buffalo cornerback Tre'Davious White recovered the fumble for the Bills. However, the officials ruled that Pascal was down by contact. It seemed clear that Pascal had fumbled the ball after he stood up after the catch.

However, the replay official did not overturn the call, which essentially would have ended the game in the Bills' favor. Instead, the Colts still had life with 26 seconds remaining from the Bills 46-yard line. Buffalo overcame whatever Curse might have been alive in that moment and shut down Indianapolis on its final four plays, including a Micah Hyde bat-down of a Hail Mary pass on the final play. The Bills secured their first playoff victory since 1995.

Photo 31. Buffalo Bills quarterback Josh Allen (17) celebrates with teammate Stefon Diggs after a touchdown during the first half of the Bills vs. Indianapolis Colts NFL wild-card playoff game on Jan. 9, 2021, in Orchard Park.

(AP Photo/Jeffrey Barnes)

The next week Buffalo earned its first divisional playoff victory since 1993 with a 17–3 win over the Baltimore Ravens. The game was a defensive struggle between two high-quality teams. The punishing contest turned in the third quarter. Allen led the Bills on a 66-yard drive, capped off by a 3-yard touchdown pass to Diggs, to start the quarter, giving the Bills a 10–3 lead. Baltimore responded, as Lamar Jackson led the Ravens on a 14-play, 66-yard drive to a third-and goal situation at the Bills 9-yard line with 58 seconds left in the quarter. Jackson fired a pass into the end zone intended for tight end Mark Andrews, but Bills cornerback Taron Johnson stepped in front and picked it off. Johnson hesitated for an instant and then raced out of the end zone and down the field, returning the ball 101 yards for a Bills touchdown. The play tied the record for longest interception return in NFL playoff history, and it represented a swing of up to 14 points.

Jackson was hurt on the next Ravens series and missed the remainder of the game while the Buffalo defense held the Ravens at bay to secure the victory and a berth in the AFC championship game. It appeared the Curse might be turning as Buffalo was fortunate to pull out this victory against a very solid Ravens team.

All the good feelings came to a crashing halt about a week later in the AFC championship game in Kansas City against the Chiefs. The Bills jumped to an early 9–0 lead as the team's first touchdown was set up on a fumbled punt that was recovered at the Chiefs 3-yard line. One play later, Allen hit Dawson Knox with a 3-yard touchdown pass.

With the Bills leading 9–7, the Curse victimized the Bills as the game turned on a miscue by Buffalo. Early in the second quarter, the Bills had a second down and 7 from the Kansas City 49-yard line. Allen faded to pass and read a blitz by the Chiefs. He lofted the ball over the onrushing defender into the hands of running back Singletary in the right flat. With open field in front of him, Singletary momentarily took his eye off the ball and it squirted through his fingertips and fell harmlessly to the ground. The play would have easily gone for a 20-yard gain and at a minimum put the Bills into field-goal range. Buffalo failed to convert on third down, as Kansas City cornerback Tyrann Mathieu blitzed Allen and the quarterback was forced to throw the ball away. The play resulted in a Bills penalty for intentional grounding, ending the drive. Buffalo was forced to punt.

Chiefs quarterback Patrick Mahomes led Kansas City on an 82-yard drive in five plays, highlighted by a 50-yard end-around run by Mecole

Hardman. It was capped by a 6-yard touchdown run by Darryl Williams. The Chiefs took the lead at 14–9 and never looked back, cruising to a 38–24 victory over the Bills and the AFC championship.

Buffalo was also victimized by its own conservative play-calling, which had not been a problem all year. Twice, with the Bills trailing by 15 points and facing fourth downs inside the Chiefs 10-yard line and with 3 yards or less to go for a first down or touchdown, Buffalo decided to settle for field goals. The Chiefs responded by scoring on both succeeding drives — in essence, salting the game away. Once again Buffalo was denied, this time one game short of the Super Bowl.

The Bills were able to bring back the team almost in its entirety for the 2021 season and were one of the preseason Super Bowl favorites. Buffalo did not look the part in the opening game, a 23–16 upset loss to the Pittsburgh Steelers. But the Bills bounced back and won their next four games, highlighted by a 38–20 thumping of Kansas City at Arrowhead Stadium.

It appeared the Bills were primed to earn home-field advantage in the playoffs, one of their stated preseason goals, however they quickly realized it would not come easily. After losing 34–31 to Tennessee the next week, when Allen slipped on a fourth and 1 at the Titans 3 with 22 seconds left, the Bills lost four of their next seven games to fall to a mediocre 7–6. The lowlights included a stunning 9–6 loss to last-place Jacksonville and a bewildering 14–10 loss to New England, when the Patriots threw only three passes in the windblown affair.

Buffalo recovered, behind the stellar play of Allen and the No. 1 ranked defense in the NFL, to win its final four games, including a commanding 34–21 win in Foxborough over those same Patriots. The Bills finished 11–6 and won their second consecutive AFC East championship. They clinched the division crown with a 27–10 win over the New York Jets on the final day of the season.

The Bills hosted the Patriots in a wild-card playoff game on Jan.15, which was the rubber match of their season series. Buffalo thrashed its arch-rival 47–17 in one of the most dominating offensive performances in NFL history, despite sub-zero wind chill temperatures. The Bills scored touchdowns on each of their first seven possessions, with only a kneel-down possession at the end of the game not resulting in a touchdown, a first in NFL history. Allen was 21 of 25 for 308 yards and 5 touchdown passes in helping the Bills

Photo 32. Buffalo Bills wide receiver Stefon Diggs stands on the field after their 38–24 loss to the Kansas City Chiefs in the AFC championship game on January 24, 2021 in Kansas City.

(AP Photo/Jeff Roberson)

finally bury the New England mystique that had hung over the franchise for 20 years.

The Bills, with their loss to the Jaguars, traveled to Kansas City in the divisional playoff round instead of hosting their nemesis in Buffalo. Many prognosticators felt these were the two best teams in the AFC, though they were playing in this round of the playoffs. The two combatants did not disappoint.

The Bills took the opening kickoff and drove 71 yards in 13 plays, scoring on a 1-yard run by Devin Singletary on fourth down. The Chiefs responded with a 74-yard drive of their own, capped off by an 8-yard scramble by Mahomes for the touchdown. The teams traded touchdowns in the second quarter and went to the half tied at 14. Gabriel Davis scored the Bills touchdown on an 18-yard pass from Allen.

It looked like the Chiefs were going to pull away in the third quarter as they outplayed Buffalo and after Mahomes hit Hardman with a 25-yard touchdown pass, despite a missed extra point, Kansas City led 23–14. But the Bills shocked the Chiefs, after the ensuing kickoff, with a 75-yard rifle shot touchdown pass from Allen to Davis to cut the Kansas City lead to 23–21.

The Chiefs added a field goal with 8:55 remaining in the fourth quarter to extend their lead to 26–21. Buffalo responded with its most methodical drive of the season. Allen directed them on a 17-play drive, converting three third downs and two fourth downs. At the 2-minute warning Buffalo faced a fourth down and 13 from the Kansas City 27 yard line. With the game on the line, Davis ran a perfect route and Allen threaded the needle with a 27-yard strike to put the Bills in the lead with 1:54 left. After the touchdown Buffalo went for two points. With Allen scrambling around for what seemed like eternity, he finally found Diggs in the back of the end zone for the critical two-point conversion and a 29–26 Bills lead.

The Chiefs responded almost immediately. After converting a third-and-10 pass to Kelce, Mahomes fired a short pass to Tyreek Hill, who turned on the jets and ran by the entire Bills defense on the way to an electrifying 64-yard touchdown reception, two plays later. The extra point was good, giving the Chiefs a 33–29 lead with only 1:02 left.

Buffalo began the penultimate drive from its 25-yard line. Allen shredded the Kansas City defense as he completed a 28-yard pass to Davis, followed by another pass to Davis of 12 yards, and then he found Emmanuel Sanders for 19 more yards to the Chiefs 16-yard line with 23 seconds left.

Allen and Davis had one big play left in them, as the pair teamed up on a 16-yard touchdown that gave the Bills a 36–33 lead with only 13 seconds left. It was Davis's fourth touchdown pass reception of the game, an NFL playoff record. Bills Mafia celebrated all across the country as if the nemesis Chiefs had been slain.

However, there was an unlucky 13 on the scoreboard. The Bills made the decision on the kickoff to boot the ball into the end zone, instead of squibbing the kick and forcing the Chiefs to use time off the clock on a return. Kansas City began its drive at the 25-yard line. After the Chiefs came to the line of scrimmage, the Bills used a timeout to set their defense. On first down, Mahomes dumped a short pass to Hill who scooted to the Kansas City 44-yard line for a 19-yard gain that took only 5 seconds off the clock.

Again, after the Chiefs came to the line, the Bills called timeout. For whatever reason Buffalo's linebackers and defensive backs were well off the ball and cornerback Levi Wallace was covering the boundary, despite the Chiefs having timeouts remaining. Mahomes looked over the Bills defense and noticed that nobody was covering Kelce. Kelce ran straight down the field, caught the easy pass from Mahomes and ran forward until the Bills defense came up to stop him. The problem for Buffalo was that it was 25 yards down the field before the star tight-end was brought to the ground. Inexplicably, the Bills had allowed the Chiefs to gain 44 yards in two plays as the ball now rested on the Buffalo 31-yard line, well within field goal range with 3 seconds remaining.

Kansas City kicker Harrison Butker nailed the 49-yard field goal attempt, and almost everybody was stunned that the Chiefs had tied the game and it was headed to overtime.

The two teams had combined to score 25 points in the final 1:54, the most points scored at the end of a game in NFL history. It was an incredible display of offensive prowess to go along with a few mind-boggling coaching decisions.

With the overtime ready to commence, Allen and Mahomes walked to midfield for the all-important coin toss that would decide which team would possess the ball first in overtime. Both defenses were exhausted, and each offense appeared unstoppable at that point in the game. It seemed likely that the winner of the coin toss would win the game.

Allen called tails as he had won every coin toss of the season calling tails. The coin came up heads, Chiefs ball.

After the Bills kickoff, Kansas City began its drive at the 25-yard line. The Chiefs then drove down the field like a hot knife through butter. Mahomes completed 6 of 6 passes and mixed in two runs, with his final dagger being an 8-yard touchdown pass to Kelce to win the game against a helpless Buffalo defense. In one of the most entertaining games in NFL history, Kansas City came back from the dead to pull out a miracle 42–36 victory over the Bills.

For Buffalo fans there was no explanation for how a game that was almost assuredly won, became a loss. Bills coach McDermott offered no explanation in the postgame press conference. There is only one, the Curse lives! Buffalo took the lead on what appeared to be the game-winning score with only 13 seconds left. That is right, an unlucky 13 seconds left. Inexplicably, a very astute coaching staff forgot how to coach, got brain cramps, or coached scared in those final 13 seconds, allowing the Chiefs' two best receivers to be uncovered for large gains. And then the Curse made the coin come up heads for the Chiefs after Allen had been 9 for 9 on coin tosses throughout the season. The Bills and Allen never got to touch the ball in overtime because the weary defense could offer no resistance and a touchdown on the first possession won the game. Allen had one of the greatest games in Bills history. He led the team to two go-ahead touchdowns in the last 2 minutes, only to come up short. Buffalo's Super Bowl dreams died in Arrowhead for the second year in a row. What makes the loss even worse is the Bills would have hosted the AFC championship game at Highmark Stadium against the Cincinnati Bengals. The Agony at Arrowhead lives on and the Curse lives on as well!

The outcry from fans, media members and league personnel was very strong after the game. Almost everyone watching on television wanted Allen and the Bills to get the football and see if they could match Mahomes and the Chiefs. The thought that Buffalo did not have the opportunity to possess the ball in overtime and that the game had pretty much been decided by the toss of the coin just seemed unfair, and not the proper way for a postseason game of this magnitude to be decided.

Three teams submitted proposed rule changes to the NFL's Competition Committee after the conclusion of the season. The Colts and Saints proposed a rule that would allow both teams to possess the ball in overtime and the Titans proposed a rule change that included a 2-point conversion option. The Competition Committee recommended to the NFL owners that they approve the Colts/Saints proposal. On March 28, the owners voted 29–3 to adopt the rule change, only for the postseason, that each team possess the ball, minimizing the impact of winning the coin toss.

"We always listen to the fans — that's an important thing," said NFL Commissioner Roger Goodell.

What appeared to sway the owners was that in 12 postseason overtime games, the team winning won the toss in 10 of those games, and seven of them were decided on the first possession. "When you see that, that's the type of thing that I think our coaches and everyone looked at — this is an issue in the postseason we should deal with," Goodell added.

For the 2021 Bills, it was two months too late.

The Bills have built a solid and young foundation with one of the best rosters in the NFL and have come close to getting to the Super Bowl two years in a row. Allen has grown into a superstar quarterback, setting Buffalo up for a period of sustained success. Just maybe, with the leadership of McDermott and Beane, this will be the team that can get Buffalo over the Curse and win that elusive championship. Only time will tell.

The Sabres, on the other hand, continued to struggle. As of the summer of 2022, they were on an 11-year drought without even a sniff of a playoff berth. As hard as this is to comprehend, the Sabres had not played a meaningful game in March or April since 2013 because they had been so far out of the playoff chase by March 1 of every season. It was an incredible string of futility in a sport designed for league-wide parity.

After the Sabres' stirring playoff runs in 2006 and 2007, front-office bungling led the team to lose the heart and soul of the franchise, Daniel Briere and Chris Drury, to free agency in the summer of 2007. Since that time, the Sabres have made two playoff appearances. They lost in the first round in 2009–10 (Boston, four games to two) and in 2010–11 (Philadelphia, four games to three). The Flyers' loss was particularly painful, since Buffalo couldn't hold a 4–3 third-period lead in Game 6 at home, and then was blown out in Game 7.

After finishing the 2011–12 season in third place in the Northeast Division with 89 points, three shy of the playoffs, and missing again in the shortened season of 2012–13 by 7 points, Sabres leadership made the incredibly short-sighted decision to completely rebuild — or "tank" — during the next two seasons. Buffalo's front-office brass was hoping to be in position to draft Connor McDavid in 2015. McDavid was considered one of the top prospects to ever come through the draft, with comparisons being made to Mario Lemieux and Wayne Gretzky.

The rebuilding had started the season before, as players such as Derek Roy, Jason Pominville and Jochen Hecht departed. Sabres management continued to dismantle the team and dealt Thomas Vanek in 2013. The capper came on Feb. 28, 2014, when Ryan Miller and Steve Ott were traded to the St. Louis Blues in exchange for Jaroslav Halák, Chris Stewart, William Carrier and two future draft picks.

If the idea was to lose, Buffalo succeeded. The Sabres accumulated only 52 points during the 2013–14 season and finished in last place by a wide margin. Their next closest competitor was Florida at 66 points. Despite the Sabres' last-place finish, they did not win the lottery for the No. 1 draft pick and selected second. The Panthers took Aaron Ekblad, a solid defenseman, and Buffalo chose Sam Reinhart. However, both teams missed on the third pick, Leon Draisaitl, who became one of the league's top scorers for Edmonton.

Buffalo was terrible again in 2014–15, finishing in last place with 23 wins and only 54 points. They were just barely worse than Arizona, which finished with 56 points. Again, the hockey gods were not with the Sabres, and the Curse was there to ensure that Buffalo would lose the lottery again and obtain the second pick in the draft. Edmonton picked McDavid first, and he has been as good as advertised, although he hasn't led the Oilers anywhere near the Stanley Cup. The Sabres' consolation prize was Jack Eichel, a very good player who wasn't able to carry the rest of the franchise on his shoulders. What was most disconcerting about the 2014 and 2015 NHL drafts is that Buffalo received little help from their picks outside of the first round. Victor Olofsson showed promise as a rookie in 2019–20, but the rest either were traded or did not pan out.

The idea behind tanking is to collect prospects and draft choices who will contribute down the road. However, that part of the process hasn't gone very well for the Sabres. Buffalo's drafting, trading and signing of free agents has been abysmal. When they did acquire talented players — such as Evander Kane and Ryan O'Reilly — they subsequently traded them away for less than equal value.

Since the two tanking years, the Sabres have only exceeded 80 points in a season once. In 2015–16, they had 81 but finished 12 points out of a playoff spot. Tanking also had a ripple effect on the organization. Buffalo drafted talented Casey Mittelstadt in the first round in 2017 but had to rush him to the NHL and may have slowed his development in the process. He spent much of 2019–20 with the Rochester Americans. The Sabres also got lucky when they added Jeff Skinner in a trade in 2018, as the winger broke the 40-goal mark in 2018–19. Buffalo needed to lure Skinner back to keep fans happy and signed him to a massive eight-year, $72 million deal in June 2019. Skinner suffered through a miserable 2019–20 season, scoring 14 goals and nine assists. That led to questions about whether he could ever live up to the expectations.

The Sabres could not catch a break during the pandemic-shortened 2019–20 season, even though the playoff format was expanded to include 24 teams. Little did the Sabres know when they traveled to Montreal on March 12, 2020, that their game with the Canadiens would be canceled as the league paused the season because of Covid-19. At that point, Buffalo was 3 points behind Montreal but with two fewer games played. When the NHL restarted the season a few months later, they made the decision to include 24 teams for the playoffs. Buffalo missed the cutoff by the 3 points they trailed Montreal, which was the last team in the Eastern Conference to qualify. Had Buffalo played that night or been able to make up the two fewer games they had played, might the team have qualified for the expanded playoffs? But it was not to be and the Sabres were left out.

Buffalo had high hopes with the hiring of Ralph Krueger as coach in 2019 (their sixth coach in eight years) and the promotion of Kevyn Adams to general manager in 2020. The duo engineered a much-heralded signing of left wing Taylor Hall, a former league MVP, as a free agent in October 2020 and also signed veteran center Eric Staal in September.

The Sabres' 2020–21 pandemic season could only be described as disastrous as they finished with the worst record in the NHL, 15–34–7, for the fourth time in the past eight seasons. They also broke the NHL record for consecutive losses since the advent of the shootout in 2005–06, with 18 straight. Some would say it was best that for most of the regular-season fans were not allowed to attend games.

The team was devastated by injuries for most of the season, losing star center Jack Eichel along with center Zemgus Girgensons, defenseman Jake McCabe and right winger Kyle Okposo. The Sabres' five top goaltenders missed time and by season's end, they were playing with the team's sixth-string netminder, who had never played an NHL game. Hall and Staal failed to live up to expectations and were shipped out at the trade deadline.

Photo 33. Buffalo Sabres forward Jack Eichel (9) skates during
the second period of an NHL hockey game against the
New York Rangers on Feb. 15, 2021, in Buffalo.

(AP Photo/Jeffrey T. Barnes)

In the midst of the 18-game losing streak, Adams fired Krueger and promoted Don Granato, who had no NHL head coaching experience but had been an assistant for both the Chicago Blackhawks and the St. Louis Blues and had minor league head coaching experience, to interim head coach. The team played better under Granato, finishing 9–16–3 but still well short of what had been expected.

During the latter half of the season under Granato, several young Sabres improved their play and provided some hope for the club. Adams removed the interim tag from Granato on June 29, 2021 and he was now charged with bringing along this young team.

Meanwhile the Eichel injury situation with the Sabres was worsening. He suffered a herniated disk in his neck in a March 7 loss to the New York Islanders. At first the Sabres thought he could return during the season and that rest and rehab was the best approach. Eichel almost immediately got a second opinion, and his doctor suggested a surgical procedure that had never been done on an NHL player — artificial disk replacement. The Sabres instead required Eichel to rehab the injury, hoping it would move back into place and it would be reevaluated in May. On May 10 the reevaluation determined that surgery was necessary, but the team and Eichel disagreed on the surgical procedure. Eichel wanted the artificial disk replacement while the Sabres wanted him to undergo fusion surgery. The two disagreed and the relationship's deterioration accelerated.

In July, Adams made the decision that the tanking rebuild begun in 2014 had failed and unloaded two of the three cornerstones. Rasmus Ristolainen was traded to Philadelphia on July 23 in exchange for defenseman Robert Hagg, a 2021 first-round pick and a 2023 second-round pick. The next day Adams traded Sam Reinhart to the Florida Panthers for goalie prospect Devon Levi and a first-round pick in 2022.

The Eichel situation continued to fester and the Sabres looked more incompetent with each passing day. On Sept. 23, to nobody's surprise, Eichel failed his physical and began the season on injured reserve. To make matters worse, Adams stripped Eichel of his captain designation. It was now only a matter of time that a break-up was inevitable. Finally, on Nov. 4, the Eichel saga ended as the Sabres traded him to the Las Vegas Golden Knights. Buffalo received center Peyton Krebs, winger Alex Tuch, a 2022 first-round pick and a 2023 third-round pick in return.

After all the turmoil, the Sabres, playing with primarily young players, finished the 2021–22 season out of the playoffs for the 11th consecutive year, an NHL record for futility. In addition, the Sabres reached an all-time low with their fans. Attendance cratered as the new rebuild began. For the first time (not including the pandemic season when fans were not allowed for most of the season) since their inaugural season, Buffalo averaged less than 10,000 fans per game. For a team that was used to playing to at least 95% capacity and that lost more than half its season ticket-holders in less than two years, it was shocking how far the franchise had fallen.

There were a few highlights during the season that included a 3–1 win over the Golden Knights on Eichel's return to Buffalo on March 10. Both Krebs and Tuch scored for Buffalo and Eichel was shutout, while also turning over the puck to Tuch that led to the game clinching goal. Eichel was dismayed after the game at all the booing he received and took a cheap shot at Sabres fans in the process, saying in the postgame locker room ,"Yeah, this is about the loudest I've heard this place ever. Really. After it took seven years, and me leaving to get into the game."

The Sabres followed that game with a 5–2 defeat of the Toronto Maple Leafs in the Heritage Classic played at Tim Horton's Field in Hamilton, Ontario in front of a sold-out crowd of 26,119. It was one of the most complete games the Sabres played during the season. Vinny Hinostroza and Krebs each scored twice in the impressive victory.

As the Sabres face this next rebuild, they have an array of young talent including six top ten draft picks on the roster with the likes of Rasmus Dahlin and Owen Power, both No. 1 picks overall, and Casey Mittelstadt, Dylan Cozens and Jack Quinn. They also have some other promising young players in Rasmus Asplund, Henri Jokiharju, Krebs, Mattias Samuelsson, Tage Thompson, Tuch and goalie Ukko-Pekka Luukkonen while veteran Jeff Skinner seems to be rejuvenated.

That's a start, but novice general manager Adams is still staring at a large hill to climb if they hope to be a playoff team in the near future. This talent needs to be developed, and more talent needs to be acquired for that to happen. Any thoughts of a Stanley Cup appear to be far off into the future as this new rebuild takes shape. Sabres fans can only hope this one goes better than the tank rebuild. And the Pegulas can only hope that Adams and Granato are up to the task and that the fans will come back to support the team.

CONCLUSION

In the previous chapters, 32 stories or examples have shown that there may be a case for calling this a sports curse. There is too much evidence to disregard, and some might even suggest that a paranormal event has occurred.

Not only have I listed examples and stated facts, but other writers have also expressed similar thoughts about some type of sports curse in Buffalo. Perhaps it is not a question of if, but rather a question of when the Curse started and how long has it lasted. To some, the overwhelming evidence dates back to 1901.

Here are a few of the Western New York newspaper reporters who have written articles implying the existence of a sports curse in Buffalo:

- Leo Roth interviewed Thurman Thomas for a piece in the Democrat and Chronicle and quoted Thomas as saying, "I mean, how much bad luck can one city take? Ever since that guy sold the Buffalo Braves — I wasn't here for it — but he had Randy Smith and Bob McAdoo. That's not a team you want to trade away. Ever since he sold that team, Buffalo's been cursed, like The Bambino." Roth jokingly referred to it as The Curse of Paul Snyder, the former owner of the Buffalo Braves basketball team.
- In a 2007 column headlined, "Buffalo is Number One in something," Buffalo News reporter Bucky Gleason wrote: "Look around the country, and there's no city that can stake quite the same claim when it comes to losing. … Please, enough about the AFL titles from the 1960s, when it was considered the NFL's little stepbrother. Perhaps no team in NFL history will reach four straight Super Bowls, so long as we concede no team will ever again lose four straight."
- Sean Kirst is a native of Dunkirk, New York whose journalism career would lead him to become a Buffalo News columnist. In 2006, he wrote a column in the Syracuse Post-Standard headlined, "Curses: In

title-starved Buffalo, blame it on Ban Johnson." His claim comes close to the position this book has taken regarding the birth of the Curse. He wrote, "In 1900, Buffalo had a franchise in Johnson's Western League, which he was already positioning to become the newest major league in baseball. Buffalo at that time was a muscular, artsy 'boom town,' easily among the largest handful of cities in the nation, and Johnson promised the Buffalo interests they'd have a place in his new American League."

"Then he screwed them, royally. … At the last minute, when some land opened up to build a new ballpark in Boston, he gave that city the team that was supposed to go to Buffalo." Kirst continued, "Johnson's shafting of Buffalo was no small thing. Let's face it: The presence of Major League Baseball lends a city the intangible status of the elite." The original eight teams in the American League in 1901 all have a major league team today. "What Johnson did was beyond insidious: It turned into prophecy," Kirst concluded.

After Buffalo lost its baseball team to Boston on Jan. 28, 1901, less than nine months later the president of the United States lay dying in a home on Delaware Avenue, where he eventually succumbed. And less than three months after that, Buffalo baseball owner James Franklin dropped dead at the age of 51.

Since those startling events in 1901, over the next 121 years Buffalo professional sports teams lost two runs to the Stanley Cup (1975, 1999), two NHL conference championship games (1980, 1998, 2006, 2007), four Super Bowls (1991, 1992, 1993, 1994), two AFC title games (1989, 2020), an AFL championship game for the right to participate in the first Super Bowl (1967), and an AAFC championship match (1948). In addition, as a result of the Staley Swindle in 1921, Buffalo was deprived of an NFL title; countless playoff games and series were lost throughout the decades; eight franchises moved away, folded or failed to materialize after much promise (1901, 1915, 1929, 1941, 1949, 1960, 1978, 1990); and Buffalo sports teams endured "Wide Right," "No Goal," "Home Run Throwback," and "Agony at Arrowhead." After all these years and with innumerable opportunities, still no universally recognized championship. The Buffalo Sports Curse was born in 1901 and is still alive and well! Yet the most passionate fans in sports have hope that each season brings a title and the chance to let go of the Curse. If that day comes, what a celebration it will be.

ABOUT THE AUTHOR

Greg Tranter is a prominent Buffalo sports historian, curator and collector with expertise in Buffalo Bills history. He has written two books, "Makers, Moments & Memorabilia: A Chronicle of Buffalo Professional Sports" (2019) and "RELICS: The History of the Buffalo Bills in Objects and Memorabilia" (2021). He is also the author of numerous articles on both the Bills and Buffalo sports history that have appeared in The Buffalo News, Gridiron Greats magazine, The Coffin Corner, Sports Collectors Digest, Shout! and Western New York Heritage magazine. He is the Assistant Executive Director of the Pro Football Researchers Association and in 2018 received its Bob Carroll Memorial Writing Award and in 2022 its Nelson Ross Award for "outstanding recent achievement in pro football research and historiography."

BIBLIOGRAPHY

Abramoski, Eddie, and Milt Northrop. *Tale of the Tape: A History of the Buffalo Bills from the Inside*. Buffalo: Western New York Wares, 2002.

Abrams, Roger I. *First World Series and the Baseball Fanatics of 1903*. Boston: Northeastern University Press, 2005.

AlBaroudi, Wajih, "Jack Eichel, Sabres saga explained: How a medical disagreement led to the star's trade to Vegas." www.CBSSports.com, November 5, 2021.

Armour, Mark and Dan Levitt. "A History of the MLBPA's Collective Bargaining Agreement: Part-2." *The Hardball Times*, November 8, 2016. https://tht.fangraphs.com/a-history-of-the-mlbpa-collective-bargaining-agreement-part-2/.

Armour, Mark and Dan Levitt. "A History of the MLBPA's Collective Bargaining Agreement: Part 3." *The Hardball Times*, November 9, 2016. https://tht.fangraphs.com/a-history-of-the-collective-bargaining-agreement-part-3/.

Associated Press. "All-Americans Only Pro Team Undefeated Now." *Buffalo Sunday Times*, November 27, 1921.

Associated Press. "Browns Edge Buffalo Bills 31–21, In All-America Conference Playoff." *Democrat and Chronicle*, December 5, 1949.

Associated Press. "Buffalo Baseball Bidder: Expansion Criteria Ignored." *Des Moines Register*, June 12, 1991.

Associated Press. "Buffalo Needs Another Miracle." *Asheville Citizen-Times*, June 4, 1991.

Associated Press. "Buffalo Pros Held Champs to Tie Score." *Buffalo Evening Times*, December 6, 1920.

Associated Press. "Buffalo's Rich: NL Ignored Own Criteria." *Democrat and Chronicle*, June 12, 1991.

Bailey, Budd. *Celebrate the tradition, 1970–1990: The History of the Buffalo Sabres*. Tonawanda, NY: Boncroft, 1989.

Bailey, Budd. "This Birthday in Buffalo Sports History: Connie Mack." *Buffalo News*, December 22, 2012.

Bailey, Budd. *Today in Buffalo Sports History: 366 Days of Milestones*. Buffalo: Western New York Wares, 2013.

Baker, Jim. *The Buffalo Bills: O.J. Simpson, Rushing Champion*. Englewood Cliffs, NJ: Prentice-Hall, 1974.

Baker, Jim. *O.J. Simpson*. New York: Grosset & Dunlap, 1974.

Baker, Jim. *O.J. Simpson's Most Memorable Games*. New York: Putnam, 1978.

"Ban Johnson's Newest Move." *Buffalo Evening News*, January 14, 1901.

Bisco, Jim. *A Greater Look at Greater Buffalo*. Northridge, CA: Windsor Publications, 1986.

Bonfatti, John, "Rich Insists Buffalo Is a Viable NL City." *Ithaca Journal*, December 19, 1990.

Bowles, Mark D. *The First NFL Season: 1920*. Cuyahoga Falls, OH: Belle History, 2019.

Brewitt, Ross. *A Spin of the Wheel: Birth of the Buffalo Sabres*. New York: Vantage Press, 1975.

Brown, Richard Carl, and Bob Watson. *Buffalo, Lake City in Niagara Land: An Illustrated History*. Woodland Hills, CA: Windsor Publications, 1982.

Brulia, Tim. "A Chronology of Pro Football on Television: Part 1." *The Coffin Corner*, Vol. 26, No. 3 (2004).

Buffalo Bills. *Bills Gamebooks, 1978, 1980, 1981, 1988, 1989, 1990, 1991, 1992, 1993, 1995, 1996, 1998, 1999, 2017, 2019, 2020, 2021*. National Football League, Inc.

Buffalo Bills. *Bills Media Guide, 2001*. Buffalo Bills, Inc., 2001.

Buffalo Bills. *Bills Media Guide, 2005*. Buffalo Bills, Inc., 2005.

Buffalo Bills. *Bills Media Guide, 2019*. Buffalo Bills, Inc., 2019.

Buffalo Bills. *Bills Media Guide*, 2021. Buffalo Bills, Inc., 2021.

Buffalo Braves. *Braves Media Guide, 1971–72*. Buffalo Braves, Inc., 1971.

Buffalo Braves. *Braves Media Guide, 1974–75*. Buffalo Braves, Inc., 1974.

Buffalo Braves. *Braves Media Guide, 1976–77*. Buffalo Braves, Inc., 1976.

Buffalo Braves. *Braves Media Guide, 1977–78*. Buffalo Braves, Inc., 1977.

"Buffalo Pros Beat Canton and Play Akron for Title." *Buffalo Courier*, December 5, 1920.

"Buffalo Pros Held Champs to Tie Score." *Buffalo Evening Times*, December 6, 1920.

Buffalo Sabres. *Sabres Media Guide, 1998–99*. Buffalo Sabres Inc. 1998.

Buffalo Sabres. *Sabres Media Guide, 2006–07*. Buffalo Sabres Inc., 2006.

Buffalo Sabres. *Sabres Media Guide, 2007–08*. Buffalo Sabres, Inc., 2007.

Buffalo Sabres. *Sabres Media Guide, 2013–14*. Buffalo Sabres, Inc., 2013.

"Buffalo Thrown Down." *Buffalo Morning Express and Illustrated*, January 29, 1901.

Carroll, Bob. "The American Football League Attendance, 1960–69." *The Coffin Corner*, Vol. 13, No. 4 (1991).

Carroll, Bob. *When the Grass Was Real: Unitas, Brown, Lombardi, Sayers, Butkus, Namath, and All the Rest: The Best Ten Years of Pro Football*. New York: Simon & Schuster, 1993.

Cohen, Rich. *The Chicago Cubs: Story of A Curse*. New York: Farrar Straus and Giroux, 2017.

Crippen, Kenneth R. *The Original Buffalo Bills: A History of the All-America Football Conference Team, 1946–1949*. Jefferson, NC: McFarland & Co., 2010.

Davis, Jeff. *Rozelle: Czar of the NFL*. New York: McGraw-Hill, 2008.

Esmonde, Donn. " 'The Curse' Finally Ends for Buffalo." *Buffalo News*, September 11, 2014.

Fisher, Jack C. *Stolen Glory: The McKinley Assassination*. La Jolla, CA: Alamar Books, 2001.

"Franklin a Sore Man." *Buffalo Morning Express and Illustrated*, January 29, 1901.

"Franklin Uneasy." *Buffalo Evening News*, November 20, 1900.

Gallagher, Robert C. *Ernie Davis, the Elmira Express*. Silver Spring, MD: Bartleby Press, 1999.

Gleason, Bucky. "Buffalo Is Number One in Something." *Buffalo News*, November 5, 2007.

Goldman, Ivan. "A New Look at Joe Mesi, From the Future Rocky to a Rocky Future." *The Ring*, Summer 2004.

Graham, Tim. "After Latest KO, Mesi Ponders Next Move." *Buffalo News*, September 29, 2003.

"Hal Chase Injunction is Vacated." *Buffalo Evening News*, July 21, 1914.

Harrington, Mike. "In midst of woeful season at the gate, Sabres have no choice but to look ahead." *Buffalo News*, February 27, 2022.

Jaworski, Ron, Greg Cosell, and David Plaut. *The Games That Changed the Game: The Evolution of the NFL in Seven Sundays*. New York: Ballantine Books, 2010.

Kirst, Sean. "In Buffalo, the Curse of Ban Johnson Trumps Even Cleveland's Losing Record." *Buffalo News*, June 22, 2016.

Kirst, Sean. "In Title-starved Buffalo, Blame It on Ban Johnson." *Syracuse Post-Standard*, May 13, 2006.

Kilgore, Ed. *As I've Seen It: Wide Right, No Goal and Other Buffalo Sports Sagas*. Buffalo: Western New York Wares, 2012.

Kondracke, Morton, and Fred Barnes. *Jack Kemp: The Bleeding-Heart Conservative Who Changed America*. New York: Sentinel, 2015.

Kritzer, Cy. "Pros are Gone but Not for Long; Back to Stay in 3 years at Latest." *Buffalo News*, September 14, 1953.

Lazarus, Adam. *Super Bowl Monday: From the Persian Gulf to the Shores of West Florida: The New York Giants, the Buffalo Bills and Super Bowl XXV*. Lanham, MD: Taylor Trade Publishing, 2011.

Levitt, Daniel R. *The Battle That Forged Modern Baseball: The Federal League Challenge and Its Legacy*. Chicago: Ivan R. Dee, 2012.

MacCambridge, Michael. *America's Game: The Epic Story of How Pro Football Captured a Nation*. New York: Random House, 2004.

MacCambridge, Michael. *Lamar Hunt: A Life in Sports*. Kansas City, MO: Andrews McMeel Publishing, 2012.

Maiorana, Sal. *Buffalo Bills: The Complete Illustrated History*. Minneapolis, MN: MVP Books, 2010.

Maiorana, Sal. *Relentless: The Hard-Hitting History of Buffalo Bills Football*. Lenexa, KS: Quality Sports Publications, 1994.

Marren, Joe. "Indians Occupy Faded Spot in Buffalo's Football Scrapbook." *The Coffin Corner*, Vol. XIX (1997).

McGillicuddy, Connie. "When the Indians Roamed Buffalo's Gridiron." *The Coffin Corner*, Vol. 22, No. 6 (2000).

Miller, Jeffrey. *Buffalo's Forgotten Champions: The Story of Buffalo's First Professional Football Team and the Lost 1921 Title*. Philadelphia, PA: Xlibris, 2004.

Miller, Jeffrey. *Rockin' the Rockpile: The Buffalo Bills of the American Football League*. Toronto: ECW Press, 2007.

Murphy, Dan. *Western New York 101: The 101 Greatest Moments in Buffalo History*. Buffalo: Western New York Wares, 2007.

Nowlin, Bill, Maurice Bouchard, Len Levin, and Dan Desrochers. *New Century, New Team: The 1901 Boston Americans*. Phoenix, AZ: Society for American Baseball Research, 2013.

"Organized Baseball Is Breaking Anti-Trust Law, Argues Lawyer for Chase." *Buffalo Evening News*, July 9, 1914.

Orr, Jack. *We Came of Age: A Picture History of the American Football League*. New York: Lion Press, 1969.

Overfield, Joseph M. *The 100 Seasons of Buffalo Baseball*. Kenmore, NY: Partners Press, 1985.

Page, Joseph S. *Pro Football Championships before the Super Bowl: A Year-by-Year History, 1926–1965*. Jefferson, NC: McFarland & Co., 2011.

Pitoniak, Scott. *Buffalo Bills Football Vault, The First 50 Seasons*. Atlanta, GA: Whitman Publishing, LLC., 2010.

Ratterman, George, *Confessions of a Gypsy Quarterback*, *Inside the Wacky World of Pro Football*. New York: Coward-McCann, 1962.

Roth, Leo, "Doubting Thomas' doesn't believe much in current Bills." *Democrat and Chronicle*, June 11, 2006.

Rubin, Bob. *All-Stars of the NFL*. New York: Random House, 1976.

Russert, Tim. *Big Russ and Me: Father and Son, Lessons of Life*. New York: Miramax Books, 2004.

Ruzzo, Bob. "Fate and the Federal League." *The Baseball Reference Journal*, Vol. 2, No. 2 (Fall 2013).

Salgado, Paul. "Closing In on the Heavyweight Elite, Joe Mesi Is No Longer Taking Baby Steps." *Boxing Magazine*, March 2004.

"Schlafly Hopes to Shake Jinx in Game Today." *Buffalo Evening News*, May 20, 1915.

Shapiro, Michael. *Bottom of the Ninth: Branch Rickey, Casey Stengel, and the Daring Scheme to Save Baseball from Itself*. New York: Times Books, 2009.

Shaughnessy, Dan. *The Curse of the Bambino*. New York: Penguin Books, 2004.

Simpson, O. J., and Pete Axthelm. *O.J.: The Education of a Rich Rookie*. New York: The Macmillan Company, 1970.

Starr, Daniel P. *The Golden Age of Buffalo Sports, 1845–1950*. Buffalo: Buffalo Heritage Unlimited, 2009.

Swados, Robert O. *Counsel in the Crease: A Big League Player in the Hockey Wars*. Amherst, NY: Prometheus Books, 2006.

Tranter, Greg D. "Ban-ing the Bisons, The Backhanded Maneuvering that Deprived Buffalo of an A.L. Franchise and Created the Boston Red Sox." *Western New York Heritage*, Vol. 21, No. 4 (Winter 2019).

Tranter, Greg D. *Makers, Moments & Memorabilia: A Chronicle of Buffalo Professional Sports*. Cheektowaga, NY: Western New York Heritage, 2019.

"Undefeated All-Americans Win Championship of A.P.F.A." *Buffalo Evening News*, November 28, 1921.

University of Southern California, *USC 1968 Media Guide*. University of Southern California, 1968.

Warchocki, Tim. *Buffalo Bisons, Before the Blade: The Complete Story of Buffalo's First Professional Hockey Team*. Buffalo: Rama Publishing, 1999.

Warrington, Bob. "John Shibe – A Biographic Sketch." Philadelphia Athletics Historical Society, May 8, 2006.

Wendel, Tim. *Buffalo, Home of the Braves*. Traverse City, MI: Sun Bear Press, 2009.

Wiggins, Robert Peyton. *The Federal League of Base Ball Clubs: The History of an Outlaw Major League, 1914–1915*. Jefferson, NC: McFarland & Co., 2009.

"Will Care for Franklin, May Be Given a Piece of Boston Club." *Buffalo Morning Express and Illustrated*, January 20, 1901.

Winfield, Mason. "Is This NFL Franchise Really Star-Crossed? Red Jacket's Revenge." BuffaloRising.com, February 5, 2016. https://www.buffalorising.com/2016/02/is-this-nfl-franchise-really-star-crossed-red-jackets-revenge/.

Wolcott, Bill. "Buffaloed, Bison Owner Rich Has Answers." *Ithaca Journal*, June 11, 1991.

Wolf, Jason. "Was Buffalo Robbed of the First Two NFL Championships?" *Buffalo News*, January 31, 2020.

Woods, Michael. "Here Comes Mesi." *Boxing Digest*, February 2004.

Woolever, Phil. "Gourmet Appetizers." *Boxing Digest,* May/June 2004.

Newspapers

Asheville Citizen-Times, Asheville, NC

Atlanta Journal-Constitution, Atlanta, GA

Baltimore News, Baltimore, MD

Boston Globe, Boston, MA

Buffalo Courier-Express, Buffalo, NY

Buffalo Evening News, Buffalo, NY

Buffalo Express, Buffalo, NY

Buffalo Evening Times, Buffalo, NY

Buffalo Morning Express and Illustrated, Buffalo, NY

Buffalo News, Buffalo, NY

Buffalo Sunday Times, Buffalo, NY

Democrat and Chronicle, Rochester, NY

Des Moines Register, Des Moines, IA

Detroit Free Press, Detroit, MI

Ithaca Journal, Ithaca, NY

Ledger, Lakeland, FL

Los Angeles Times, Los Angeles, CA

Star Tribune, Minneapolis, MN

New York Times, New York, NY

Ottawa Citizen, Ottawa, ON

Tampa Tribune, Tampa, FL

USA Today, McLean, VA

Valley News, Woodland Hills, CA

Vancouver Sun, Vancouver, BC

Websites

The Athletic — https://theathletic.com

Baseball Reference — https://www.baseball-reference.com/

Buffalo Bills — https://www.buffalobills.com

Buffalo Bisons — https://www.milb.com/buffalo/

Buffalo Indians/Tigers — https://americanfootballdatabase.fandom.com/wiki/
    Buffalo_Tigers

Buffalo Sabres — https://www.nhl.com/sabres

Buffalo Sports Page — https://www.buffalosportspage.com

Hockey Reference — www.hockey-reference.com

L.A. Clippers — https://www.nba.com/clippers

National Football League — https://www.nfl.com

National Hockey League — https://www.nhl.com

Newspapers.com — https://www.newspapers.com

Professional Football Researchers Association — www.profootballresearchers.org

Pro Football Archives — www.profootballarchives.com

Pro Football Reference — https://www.pro-football-reference.com/

United States Holocaust Memorial Museum — https://www.ushmm.org/

INDEX

Page numbers in italics indicate illustrations.

A

Abrams, Roger, 1
Abruzzese, Ray, 66
Adams, Bud, 64
Adams, Kevyn, 258, 260, 261
Adams Division, 98, 105
Addington, Keene H., 25
Afinogenov, Maxim, 223–25, 232
African Americans, 51, 65, 182, 183
Agler, Joseph, 22
Aikman, Troy, 151, 153
Alexander, Charles, 131–33, *132*
Alfredsson, Daniel, 232, 233, *234*
All-American Football Conference (AAFC), 3, 53–56, 58, 63, 64, 66; founding of, 50–51; NFL merger with, 57
Allen, Doug, 80
Allen, Josh, 244, 245–46, 248–51, *249*, 253–56
American Football League (AFL) (1940–41), 3, 45; Buffalo Sports Curse and, 46–48; founding of, 41–43; NFL and, 43
American Football League (AFL) (1960–69), 1, 43, 63–75, 77, 178
American League (baseball), 2, 8–10, 12–17, 21, 22, 264
American Legion (Buffalo, NY), 43, 45
American Professional Football Association (APFA), 8, 33–35, 37–39
Amole, Morris "Doc," 10
Anderson, Derek, 241
Anderson, Dick, 78
Anderson, Fred, 24

Anderson, Ken, 181
Anderson, Ockie, 34, 37, 38
Anderson, O. J., 138, 142
Andreychuk, Dave, 216
Arbanas, Fred, 73
Archibald, Nate, 119
Asplund, Rasmus, 261
Audette, Donald, 203, 204, 206

B

Babych, Dave, 205
Bahr, Matt, 141, 142, 188
Bailey, Carlton, 145
Bailey, Garnet, 95
Baker, Stephen, 142
Baldwin, Al, 52, 53
Ball, Phil, 30
Baltimore Colts, 53–54, 56–58, 70, 129, 142
Baltimore Ravens, 242–43, 250
Baltimore Terrapins, 23
Banas, Steve, 43, 45
Barger, Carl, 166–67
Barnaby, Matthew, 205, 206
Barnes, Chuck, 178, 182
Barnes, Stu, 210–12
Barrett, Monte, 219–20
Barth, Gene, 85
Bass, Glenn, 69–71
Bass, Tyler, 248
Bassett, Maurice, 64
Beane, Brandon, 239, 242, 245, 256
Beasley, Aaron, 193
Beasley, Cole, 245

Bedient, Hugh, 28

Beebe, Don, 149, 151

Belfour, Ed, 211–13

Béliveau, Jean, 96

Bell, Bert, 57–58, 60

Bellows, Brian, 208

Benirschke, Rolf, 126, 128

Benjamin, Kelvin, 243

Bennett, Cornelius, 137, 138

Bennett, William, 50

Bentley, Albert, 186

Bentley, Ray, 137

Berezin, Sergei, 210

Bettman, Gary, 215

Bichette, Bo, 169

Biggio, Cavan, 169

Bills Mafia, 4, 254

Bing, Dave, 120

Biron, Martin, 224

Bissell, Herbert P., 25

Black Sox scandal (1919), 31

Blair, Walter, 22, 28

Bledsoe, Drew, 192, 195–96, 239–40

Bogacki, Henry, 43

Bondra, Peter, 206, 207

Boone, Aaron, 1

Borchardt, Jon, 88

Bortles, Blake, 243–44

Boston Americans, 2, 14–16

Boston Bruins, 209–10

Boston Celtics, 109–12, *110*, *114*,
    115–17, 119–21

Boston Patriots, 64–69, 72. *See also* New
    England Patriots

Boston Red Sox, 1, 2, 16

Bouye, A. J., 243

Bowman, Scotty, 105, 106

Boyd, Tyler, 243

Brace, Bill, 34

Brady, Tom, 239

Brammer, Mark, 89, 123, 133

Braxton, Jim, 80, 81, 85–88

Bresnahan, Tom, 137

Breuil, Jim, 50–52

Briere, Daniel, 223, 226–28, 230, 231,
    233, 235, 256

Brind'Amour, Rod, 228, *229*

Brockington, John, 179

Brohm, Brian, 241

Bromley, Gary, 98

Brown, Jim, 70

Brown, John Y., 118–21

Brown, Paul, 66

Bryant, Emmette, 108

Buffalo All-Americans, 3, 33–40, *36*

Buffalo Bandits, 1

Buffalo Bills (AAFC), 52–61; Baltimore
    Colts and, 53, 54, 57, 58; Cleveland
    Browns and, 53–57, *55*; creation of,
    52; New York Yankees, 52, 53; San
    Francisco 49ers, 57; Sports Curse on, 58

Buffalo Bills (AFL/NFL), 1–5, 64–75,
    185–202, 239–42; Arizona Cardinals,
    248; Baltimore Ravens, 242–44, 250;
    Boston Patriots, 64, 68, 69, 71, 72;
    Cincinnati Bengals and, 131–34, *132*,
    137, 178, 181, 186–88, *187*, 242–43;
    Cleveland Browns and, 70, 138, 188–89;
    creation of, 63–64; Dallas Cowboys
    and, 151–56, *152*, *155*, 245; Denver
    Broncos and, 65, 138, 145; Detroit
    Lions and, 181; Green Bay Packers
    and, 75, 179; Houston Oilers and, 138,
    149–50, 177, 186; Houston Texans and,
    241, 245–47; Indianapolis Colts and,
    186, 192, 194, 197–98, 248, *249*, 255–56;
    Jacksonville Jaguars and, 192–94,
    243–44, 251; Kansas City Chiefs and,
    3, 68, 72–75, *74*, 77, 143, 145, 153, 192,
    250–55, *252*; Los Angeles Chargers
    and, 244; Los Angeles Raiders and, 138,
    140–41, 153; Los Angeles Rams and, 87,
    124, 125; Miami Dolphins and, 77–91,
    84, 123, 130, 134, 150–51, 181, 190,
    196–97, 242; Minnesota Vikings and,
    247; New England Patriots and, 123,

125, 129–30, 181, 192, 195–96, 239, 247, 251–53; New Orleans Saints and, 89; New York Giants and, 72, 138–43, *144*; New York Jets and, 67, 71, 72, 130, 131, 179, 185, 192; New York Titans and, 65, 67; Oakland Raiders and, 81, 129, 176, 177, 241; Philadelphia Eagles and, 138, 176, 177; Pittsburgh Steelers and, 82–83, 124, 150, 179, 181, 190–92, 240, 245, 251; San Diego Chargers and, 66–71, 126–30, *127*; San Francisco 49ers and, 125, 126, 181, 186; Seattle Seahawks and, 248; Simpson and, 177–81, *180*; Sports Curse on, 3, 58, 69, 72, 75, 77, 78, 83, 91, 125, 134, 143, 147, 151, 156–57, 202, 247, 250, 255; Super Bowl runs of, 137–57, 185; Tampa Bay Buccaneers and, 185–86; Tennessee Titans and, 3, 198–202, *201*, 239, 251; Washington Redskins and, 145–47, *148*, 153

Buffalo Bisons (AAFC), 3, 50–52

Buffalo Bisons (baseball), 1, 2, 10–14, 160–62, *163*, *165*, 166, 169, 170

Buffalo Bisons (NFL), 40

Buffalo Blues, 3, 21–31, *26*, *29*

Buffalo Braves, 100, 107–21, *114*, 263

Buffalo Indians/Tigers, 3, 43–46, *47*

Buffalo Pan Ams, 14

Buffalo Rangers, 40

Buffalo Sabres, 2, 4–5, 93–106, *102*, 203–16, *214*, 223–37, *229*, *234*, 256–61, *259*; Sports curse on, 104–5, 208, 216, 223, 228, 230, 257

Buffalo Sports Curse, 5–7, 87; All-Americans and, 39, 40; American Football League and, 46–48; Buffalo Bills and, 58, 72, 75, 77, 78, 83, 91, 125, 128, 134, 135, 143, 147, 151, 156–57, 192, 194, 202, 247, 250, 255; Buffalo Bisons and, 167, 168; Buffalo Blues and, 28; Buffalo Braves and, 121, 263; Buffalo Sabres and, 104–5, 208, 215, 216, 223, 228, 230, 235, 237, 257; Flutie and, 239; Mesi and, 222; origins of, 2–3, 20, 28, 31, 263–64; Simpson and, 173, 183, 264

Bulaich, Norm, 85

Bumgardner, Rex, 54

Burke, Sean, 204

Burris, Jeff, 190, 193

Burroughs, Derrick, 188

Butker, Harrison, 254

Butler, Jerry, 88, 124

Byner, Earnest, 146

Byrd, Butch, 71

C

Cabana, Oliver, Jr., 22

Campbell, Brian, 224, 228

Campbell, Calais, 243

Campbell, Clarence, 94, 95

Canisius College, 108

Cappelletti, Gino, 68

Carolina Hurricanes, 209, 226–28, *229*

Carr, Joe, 37

Carrier, William, 257

Carriere, Larry, 97, 100

Carroll, Richard T. "Dick," 22, 25

Carter, DeAndre, 246

Cason, Dwane, 218

Cater, Greg, 89

Cesare, Fiore, 45

Chandler, Bob, 82

Chandler, Chris, 186

Charles, Ken, 113, 116, 118

Chase, Hal, 24–28, *26*, 31

Chenier, Phil, 113

Cheyunski, Jim, 81

Chicago Bears, 38, 40, 140

Chicago Cubs, 16

Chicago Federals, 24

Chicago Staleys, 38, 39

Chicago White Sox, 24–25, 31

Christie, Steve, 149, 150, 154, 190, 194, 195, 199–200

Cincinnati Bengals, 131–34, *132*, 178, 181, 185–88, *187*, 242–43

Clark, Gary, 145, 147

Clark, Mario, 126

Clarke, Bobby, 101

Clay, Charles, 244

Clay-Bey, Lawrence, 218

Clement, Bill, 104

Clements, Nate, 240

Cleveland, Grover, 7

Cleveland Browns, 188–89

Cleveland Indians, 12, 16

Coates, Ben, 196

Colclough Ricardo, 240

Collier, Joel, 72

Collins, Gary, 70

Collins, Jimmy, 15

Collins, Todd, 193

Collinsworth, Cris, 133

Comiskey, Charles, 8, 24

Conlan, Shane, 137, 188

Connolly, Tim, 224, 225, 227

Continental Baseball League, 159–61, 168

Cooper, Earl, 126

Cordovano, Sam, 49–51

Corvo, Joe, 233

Cournoyer, Yvan, 97, 99

Cousineau, Tom, 88

Covid-19 pandemic, 168–70, 247, 258

Cox, William B., 46

Cozens, Dylan, 261

Cribbs, Joe, 89, 123, 128, 130, 133, 134

Crippen, Kenneth, 58

Crockett, Bobby, 73

Crosby, Sidney, 235

Crotty, Peter, 107

Crowe, Clem, 56

Crowley, Jim, 50

Crowley, Thomas F., 14

Crozier, Joe, 95, 97, 98, 100, 103

Crozier, Roger, 95

Csonka, Larry, 79, 82, 88

Curse of the Bambino, 1, 263. *See also*
    Buffalo Sports Curse

Czolgosz, Leon, 18

D

Dafoe, Byron, 210

Dahlin, Rasmus, 261

Daley, Joe, 94, 96

Dallas Cowboys, 151–56, *152*, *155*, 245

Dallas Stars, 211–15, *214*

Dalton, Andy, 243

Dalton, Frank, 41

Danforth, Doug, 162–67

Dantley, Adrian, 118, 119

Darby, Matt, 153, 191

Dareus, Marcell, 242

Dart, Joseph, 7

Davis, Ernie, 65–66

Davis, Gabriel, 253–54

Davis, Kenneth, 138, 143, 149, 150

Davis, Mike, 108

Davis, Robert, 219

Dawson, Len, 73

Dawson, Red, 51

Day, Tom, 64

Deadspin (sports blog), 5

Del Greco, Al, 199

DeLamielleure, Joe, 88, 178

DeLeon, Juan, 218

Dempsey, Tom, 89

Demske, James M., 108, 121

Denver Broncos, 65, 138, 145, 177

Desjardins, Gerry, 98–100

Diggs, Stefon, 247, *249*, 250, *252*, 253

DiGregorio, Ernie, 109, 111–14, *114*, 116–20

Dinneen, "Big Bill," 15

Dobler, Conrad, 89

Dodd, Bobby, 175

Dolan, John, 45

Draisaitl, Leon, 257

Drane, Dwight, 137

Drobnitch, Alex, 44, 45

Drury, Chris, 223–27, 230–33, 235, 256

Dryden, Ken, 97, 99, 100

Dubenion, Elbert, 68, 69, 71

Dudley, Rick, 99

Dumont, J. P., 224, 225, 227

Dunn, Francis W., 51
Duper, Mark, 139
Dyson, Kevin, 200, *201*

E

Early, Quinn, 192
Eastern Association, 10
Edwards, Brad, 146
Edwards, Glen, 128
Edwards, Trent, 241
Eichel, Jack, 257, 258–61, *259*
Ekblad, Aaron, 257
Elway, John, 138, 145
Emery, Ray, 225–26, 233
Engebretsen, Paul "Tiny," 45
Enos, Laurens, 22
Erie Canal, 7
Erving, Julius, 118
Ervins, Ricky, 146
Esche, Robert, 224
Esiason, Boomer, 188

F

Fairbairn, Ka'imi, 247
Falcon, Guil "Hawk," 38
"fandemonium," 150, 185
Federal League of Base Ball Clubs, 3,
        21–31, 159, 169
Feeney, Al, 34
Feliciano, Jon, 245
Felser, Larry, 200
Ferguson, Charley, 67
Ferguson, George, 105
Ferguson, Joe, 78, 81–83, 87, 90, 123–30, 133
Fernandez, Manny, 79
Fillmore, Millard, 7
Fisher, Mike, 225, 232
Fitzpatrick, Rory, 227
Fitzpatrick, Ryan, 241
Fitzsimmons, Cotton, 119, 121
Fleming, Marv, 80
Flutie, Doug, 194–99, 202, 239
Foley, Dave, 178

Foley, Tim, 79, 88
Ford, Cody, 245, 247
Ford, Russell, 22, 27, 28
Forsberg, Peter, 224
Fournette, Leonard, 243
Fouts, Dan, 126, 128
Franklin, James, 2, 10–15, *11*, 264
Franks, Sheldon H., 41
Frazee, Harry, 16
Freeman, Steve, 124, *127*, 131
Fuhrmann, Louis P., 23
Fuller, Mike, 128

G

Gaffney, Derrick, 131
Gant, Reuben, 80, 88
Gardner, Milton, 38
Gare, Danny, 98–100, 103
Garretson, Darell, 112, 117, 121
Garrett, Dick, 108
Garrett, Mike, 73, 75
Garron, Larry, 68
Gault, Willie, 138
Gaustad, Paul, 223
Gianelli, John, 119
Gilbert, Steve, 43, 44
Gilchrist, Cookie, 66, 67, 69, 70
Gilles, Clark, 105
Gillman, Sid, 140–41
Gilmore, James A., 23, 27
Girgensons, Zemgus, 258
Gleason, Bucky, 263
Gogolak, Pete, 68, 69, 72
Golisano, Tom, 223, 235
Gompers, Bill, 54
Goodell, Roger, 256
Gore, Frank, 245
Gouveia, Kurt, 147
Goyette, Phil, 95
Granato, Don, 260, 261
Gray, Chummy, 10
Great Depression, 40
Green, Donnie, 178

Green, Johnny, 65
Greene, Tony, 79, 82
Griese, Bob, 78, 82, *84*, 87
Griffin, James D., 161, 166
Griffith, William D., 41
Grošek, Michal, 204–6
Guerrero, Vladimir, Jr., 169
Guman, Mike, 124
Gurriel, Lourdes, Jr., 169
Guy, Charlie, 38

H

Hagg, Robert, 260
Hajt, Bill, 96, 103
Halák, Jaroslav, 257
Halas, George, 38, 39, 58, 60
Haley, Charles, 151
Hall, Taylor, 258
Hanford, Charles, 22, 23, 27
Hardman, Mecole, 250–51
Harmon, Ronnie, 137–38, 189
Harper, Bruce, 130
Harris, Franco, 124, 179
Harris, George M., 41
Harris, James, 78, 177
Harrison, Dwight, 81
Harrison, James, 240
Hasek, Dominik, 203–16, *214*
Haslett, Jim, 88, 125
Hatcher, Derian, 212
Hauschka, Stephen, 245–46
Havlicek, John, 109–11, 120
Hay, Ralph, 33
Hayes, Elvin, 113, 115
Heard, Garfield, 109, 111, 118
Heatley, Dany, 233
Hecht, Jochen, 223, 225, 228, 232, 257
Hernández, Teoscar, 169
Hickerson, Gene, 70
Hill, J. D., 81, 82, 85
Hilton, Barron, 64
Hilton, Fred, 108
Hinostroza, Vinny, 261

Hirsch, "Buckets," 52
Hogeboom, Gary, 186
Holcomb, Kelly, 241
Holden, Tony, 220
Holling, Tom, 43
Hollis, Mike, 193
Holmes, Darick, 190
Holzinger, Brian, 205, 209
Hooks, Roland, 87, 129–30
Hopkins, DeAndre, 248
Horning, Clarence "Steamer," 38
Horton, Tim, 97, 98
Hostetler, Jeff, 141–43
Hotel Lafayette (Buffalo, NY), 41, *42*, 48
Houston Astros, 162
Houston Colt .45s, 161
Houston Gamblers, 189
Houston Oilers, 67, 68, 138, 149–50, 177, 186
Houston Texans, 245–47
Howsam, Bob, 64
Hrycyszyn, Steve, 43, 45, 46
Hudson, Chris, 193
Hughitt, Tommy, 34, 38
Huizenga, Wayne, Sr., 166
Hull, Brett, 3, 211, 213, *214*
Hull, Kent, 137, 143
Humm, David, 125
Hummer, John, 108
Hunt, Bobby, 75
Hunt, Lamar, 60, 61, 63, 64
Hutchinson, Scott, 128
Hyde, Carlos, 246
Hyde, Micah, 248

I

Imlach, George "Punch," 93–98, 101, 105
Indianapolis Colts, 186, 192, 194, 197–98, 248, *249*, 255–56
Ingram, Mark, 142
International League, 10
Iraq war, 141
Izon, David, 219

J

Jackson, Lamar, 250

Jacksonville Jaguars, 192–93, 243–44, 251

Jacobs, Harry, 67

Jacobs, Louis M., 159–61

Jaeger, Jeff, 140

James, Robert, 82

Janik, Doug, 227

Janik, Tom, 73

Jauron, Dick, 241

Jaworski, Ron, 200

Jeanneret, Rick, 226

Jefferson, Shawn, 195

Jessie, Ron, 89

Jillson, Jeff, 227

Jirov, Vassiliy, 217, 220–22, *221*

Johnson, Ban, 2, 8–10, *9*, 12–14, 17, 24, 263–64

Johnson, Curtis, 86

Johnson, Harvey, 78, 178

Johnson, Pete, 131

Johnson, Rob, 194, 198–99, 202, 239

Johnson, Taron, 250

Joiner, Charlie, 126

Jokiharju, Henri, 261

Jones, Bobby, 130

Jones, Edgard "Special Delivery," 54, *55*

Jones, Henry, 149, 153, 190, 195

Jones, Ken, 128

Jones, Taiwan, 247

Joseph, Curtis, 210, 211

Juneau, Joe, 206, 208, 211, 215

K

Kalinin, Dmitri, 225, 227

Kane, Evander, 257

Kansas City Chiefs, 3, 67, 72–75, *74*, 77, 143, 145, 153, 192, 250–55, *252*

Kansas City Royals, 168

Karp, Joe, 43, 45

Karpus, Andy, 45, 46

Kauffman, Bob, 108, 109

Kearse, Jevon, 198

Kelly, Bob, 103

Kelly, Jim, 91, 135, 137–43, 145–47, 149–51, 153, 154, 156, 188–94

Kemp, Jack, 66, 68–71, 73, 75

Kerbawy, Nick, 60

King, Dana, 41

King, Fay, 52

Kirst, Sean, 263–64

Klitschko, Vitali, 217

Knight, Billy, 119

Knox, Chuck, 78, 87–90, 124, 125, 128–31, 133, 134

Knox, Dawson, 246, 250

Knox, Northrup, 93, 203

Knox, Seymour H., III, 64, 93, 94, 96

Knox brothers, 203

Kocourek, Dave, 69

Kolen, Mike, 80

Kölzig, Olaf, 206

Korab, Jerry, 98, 101, 103

Kosar, Bernie, 188, 189

Kotalik, Ales, 223, 226, 231

Koyack, Ben, 244

Krapp, Gene, 23, 24, 27

Krebs, Peyton, 260, 261

Kritzer, Cy, 60

Kroft, Tyler, 248

Krueger, Ralph, 258, 260

Kruse, Paul, 207

Krygier, Todd, 207

Kubiak, Gary, 145

Kuehl, Ray "Waddy," 38

Kulbitski, Vic, 51

Kunnert, Kevin, 109

Kush, Rod, 88

L

Lackawanna Steel Company, 7

Lafleur, Guy, 99

Lageman, Jeff, 193

Lahr, Warren, 57

Lamonica, Daryle, 67

Landis, Kenesaw Mountain, 27, 31

Langenbrunner, Jamie, 212
Larkin Administration Building, 7
Leach, Reggie, 103
Leaks, Roosevelt, 89, 90, 124, 133, 134
LeClair, John, 204
Lee, Ken, 79
Lehtinen, Jere, 212, 213
Leino, Ville, 236–37
Leitch, Will, 5
Lemaire, Jacques, 97, 99, 100
Leonard, "Sugar Ray," 218
Lepper, Barney, 33
Levi, Devon, 260
Levin, Irving, 120
Levitt, Daniel R., 28
Levy, Marv, 135, 137–39
Lewis, Frank, 90, 123, 124, 126, 128–30, 134
Lewis, Thaddeus, 241
Leypoldt, John, 79–81, 83, 85
Lincoln, Keith, 69
Lindros, Eric, 204
Lingner, Adam, 190, 191
Linton, Jonathan, 199
Little, Lou, 37
Littlefield, Carl, 43–45
Locke, Tates, 117, 119
Lofton, James, 139, 140, 142, 146, 149, 151, 189
Lombardi, Vince, 71
Long, Howie, 140
Long, Kevin, 131
Lord, Harry, 28
Lorentz, Jim, 99, 101, 103, 104
Los Angeles Angels, 161
Los Angeles Raiders, 138, 140–41, 153
Los Angeles Rams, 124, 125
Losman, J. P., 240–41
Louden, William "Baldy," 22, 24
Lowe, Paul, 71
Lucas, Richie, 64, 65
Luce, Don, 96
Luckett, Phil, 200
Lundqvist, Henrik, 230–32
Luukkonen, Ukko-Pekka, 261

Lydman, Toni, 224, 227, 231, 232
Lynch, Marshawn, 242

M

MacCambridge, Michael, 60
Mack, Connie, 13
MacKinnon, Bob, 119
MacLeish, Rick, 103
Maddox, Mark, 190
Maddox, Tommy, 240
Maguire, Paul, 68
Mahomes, Patrick, 250–51, 253–55
Mahovlich, Peter, 99
Maiorana, Sal, 4, 65, 73
Major League Baseball (MLB), 159, 162, 164, *165*, 166–68, 170
Malone, Moses, 118, 121
Manucci, Dan, 125, 126
Manuel, E. J., 241
Mara, Paul, 231
Marangi, Gary, 82
Marchibroda, Ted, 138
Marin, Jack, 109, 111, 118
Marino, Dan, 91, 139–40, 150, 196
Marlowe, Dean, 248
Marrone, Doug, 241–42
Marshall, Bert, 104
Marshall, Don, 95
Marshall, George Preston, 57–58, 60
Martin, Rick, 96–100, 103–5
Mason, Derrick, 198
Mathieu, Tyrann, 250
Maxwell, Clayton, 50
May, Don, 108
Mays, Carl, 16
McAdoo, Bob, 109–13, *110*, 115–19, 121, 263
McCabe, Jake, 258
McClanahan, Randy, 88
McDavid, Connor, 256–57
McDermott, Sean, 239, 242–45, 247, 255, 256
McDole, Ron, 67, 75
McGahee, Willis, 240, 242
McGinnis, George, 115, 116

McGroder, Pat, 57

McKay, John, 176

McKee, Jay, 215, 226, 227

McKenzie, Reggie, 134, 178

McKinley, William F., 2, 17–18, *19*, 264

McKnight, Keith, 219

McMillen, Tom, 115, 119

McMillian, Jim, 109, 111, 113, 115, 118

McMullen, John, 162

McNab, Peter, 100

McNair, Steve, 198

McNally, Johnny "Blood," 45

McNeil, Frank J., 33–39

Means, Natrone, 193

Meehan, Gerry, 95

Meredith, Dudley, 73

Mesi, "Baby Joe," 3, 217–22, *221*

Metcalf, Eric, 189

Metzelaars, Pete, 153

Miami, 63, 164, 166

Miami Dolphins, 77–91, *84*, 123, 130, 134, 139–40, 150–51, 181, 190, 196–97, 242

Miami Marlins, 167, 169–71

Middleton, Ron, 189

Mike-Mayer, Nick, 89, 124, 126, 128, 130, 134

Mikita, Stan, 99

Milburn, John, 17

Miller, Heinie, 34, 37

Miller, Ryan, 223–28, 231, 233, *234*, 257

Miller, Shannon, 222

Miller, Van, 150, 185

Mittelstadt, Casey, 258, 261

Modano, Mike, 211, 212

Mohr, Chris, 191

Monk, Art, 145

Montana, Joe, 125–26, 153

Montler, Mike, 178

Montoyo, Charlie, 170

Montreal Canadiens, 95–101, 205–6, 258

Montreal Expos, 168

Montreal Junior Canadiens, 95

Moody, Keith, 89

Moog, Andy, 205

Moon, Warren, 149, 150

Moore, Earl, 22, 23

Morrall, Earl, 79

Morris, Mercury, 79–81

Morse, Mitch, 245

Motley, Marion, 51, 56

Moulds, Eric, 192, 194–97, 199, 239–40

Mueller, Jamie, 137

Mularkey, Mike, 240

Mullaney, Joe, 119

Mullen, Walter, 22, 25

Muncie, Chuck, *127*

Murray, Kyler, 248

Mutryn, Chet, 52, 53, 56

N

Namath, Joe, 71, 72, 183

Nash, Robert "Nasty," 37

Nater, Swen, 120

Nathan, Tony, 89

National Baseball Hall of Fame (Cooperstown, NY), 15

National Baseball League, 8, 43; American League's agreement with, 21; expansion of, 162, 164; Federal League's agreement with, 30

National Basketball Association (NBA), 3, 107–8, 121

National Football Association, 8

National Football League (NFL), 8, 40, 43; AAFC merger with, 57; AFL and, 70, 72, 178; American League players from, 43; forerunner of, 33

National Hockey League, 8, 93, 94, 104

Neal, Lorenzo, 200

Nelson, Don, 116

Nelson, Shane, 126

Nesmith, Orlando, 43

Neville, Paul, 63

New England Patriots, 123, 125, 129–30, 181, 192, 195–96, 239, 247, 251, 253

New Jersey Devils, 226

New York Americans, 45

New York Giants, 138–39, 141–43, *144*, 153, 245

New York Islanders, 104–5, 230

New York Jets, 71–72, 123, 130–31, 177, 179, 185, 251

New York Mets, 161, 162

New York Rangers, 230–32

New York Titans, 65. *See also* New York Jets

New York Yankees, 16, 17

Niagara Falls hydroelectric plant, 7

Nicolau, Nick, 137

Nieuwendyk, Joe, 211, 212

Nikolishin, Andrei, 207

Nixon, Jeff, 88, 124

Norwood, Scott, 3, 137, 139, 141–43, *144*, 157, 185, 189

Nottingham, Don, 82, 83, 85

Novacek, Jay, 151

Nsekhe, Ty, 245

Numminen, Teppo, 224, 226, 227

Nylander, Michael, 230

O

Oakland Raiders, 81, 123, 129, 176–77

Oates, Adam, 206

O'Brien, Jim, 142

O'Brien, Larry, 118

O'Connell, Tommy, 65

Odomes, Nate, 137, 150

O'Donnell, Neil, 190, 191

O'Donoghue, Neil, 86

Okposo, Kyle, 258

Oliphant, Elmer, 37

Oliver, Ed, 245

Olofsson, Victor, 257

Olsavsky, Jerry, 191

O'Reilly, Ryan, 257

Orton, Kyle, 241

Ott, Steve, 257

Ottawa Senators, 208–9, 225–26, 232–35, *234*

Owens, Terrell, 242

P

Padlo, Walt, 43

Paetsch, Nathan, 223, 227

Paille, Daniel, 223

Pan-American Exposition (1901), 2, 7, 12, 17–18, *19*

Parcells, Bill, 192

Parent, Bernie, 101–4, *102*

Parilli, Babe, 68

Parker, Ervin, 89

Pascal, Zach, 248

Patton, Jerry, 79–80

Peace, Larry, 44

Peca, Michael, 203, 205–7, 209, 210, 216

Pegula, Kim, 235–37

Pegula, Terry, 235–37, 241–42

Perreault, Gilbert, 95–97, 99, 100, 103–5

Peterman, Nathan, 241, 244

Philadelphia Athletics, 13

Philadelphia Eagles, 176

Philadelphia Flyers, 101–4, *102*, 204–5, 224, 235

Philadelphia Phillies, 16

Philadelphia 76ers, 108, 115–16, 118–19

Phillips, Wade, 195, 198–200

Piccone, Lou, 126, 128, 133

Pike, Mark, 137

Pitoniak, Scott, 64

Pittsburgh Penguins, 94–96, 105, 216, 235

Pittsburgh Pirates, 13, 15, 162

Pittsburgh Steelers, 82–83, 124, 150, 179, 181, 190–92, 240, 251

Plante, Derek, 203

Players' League, 2–3, 13

Polian, Bill, 4, 135, 137

Pominville, Jason, 224, 226, 230, 232, 257

Pothier, Brian, 226

Power, Owen, 261

Powers, John, 21

Poyer, Jordan, 248

Pratt, Tracy, 95

Prescott, Dak, 245

Price, Peerless, 199, 239–40

Primeau, Wayne, 204, 210, 212
Pronovost, Marcel, 105
Prudhomme, Remi, 79
Pyeatt, Johnny, 65

Q

Quinn, Jack, 261
Quinn, John, 23

R

Rabb, Warren, 65
Ramsay, Craig, 96, 100
Ramsay, Jack, 108–9, 112–13, 115, 117, 121
Ramsey, Buster, 64, 65
Ramsey, Jalen, 243
Ranney, Art, 35
Rashad, Ahmad, 80, 81, 86
Rasmussen, Erik, 209, 211
Ratica, Joe, 45
Ratterman, George, 52–54, 56–57
Rauch, John, 78, 177–78
Ray, Rob, 203
Redden, Wade, 226, 232
Reed, Andre, 138–40, 145–50, *148*, 186, 188,
    195–97, 202
Reeves, Dan, 58
Regier, Darcy, 203
Reich, Frank, 139, 149–50
Reid, Del, 4
Reinhart, Sam, 257, 260
Renney, Tom, 230–31
Reynolds, M. C., 65
Rich, Bob, Jr., 162, 164–66, 168
Rich, Mindy, 164–66
Richards, Brad, 236
Rickey, Branch, 159–61
Rigas, John, 203, 216, 223
Riggs, Gerald, 146
Ringo, Jim, 78, 86
Ristolainen, Rasmus, 260
Ritcher, Jim, 89
Rivers, Philip, 248
Robert, René, 96–100, 103, 104

Robertson, Isiah, 90, 134
Robertson, William E., 22
Robinson, Eugene, 186
Robinson, Jackie, 51
Robinson, Johnny, 73, *74*
Robitaille, Mike, 96, 100–101
Rockne, Knute, 49
Roloson, Dwayne, 210
Romes, Charles, 86, 88, 126, 130
Rooney, Art, 58
Roosevelt, Franklin D., 46
Roosevelt, Theodore, 17, 18
Rote, Tobin, 69
Roth, Leo, 230, 263
Roy, Derek, 223, 225, 227, 233, 257
Rozsíval, Michal, 231
Rubin, Bob, 178
Ručinsky, Martin, 205
Rudolph, Mendy, 112
Ruff, Lindy, 203, 208, 211, 215–16,
    228, 235, 237
Russert, Tim, 4
Ruth, George Herman "Babe," 16
Rutkowski, Ed, 176–77
Ryan, Frank, 70
Ryan, Philip, 107
Ryan, Rex, 242
Rypien, Mark, 145–47
Ryu, Hyun Jin, 169

S

Saban, Lou, 66–67, 72, 78, 83; Gilchrist
    and, 70; Patton and, 80; resignation of,
    85–86; Simpson and, 178
Saimes, George, 67
Samuelsson, Mattias, 261
San Diego Chargers, 66–72, 126–29, *127*
San Diego Clippers, 120
San Francisco 49ers, 125–26, 181
Sanders, Emmanuel, 253
Sanders, Ricky, 145
Sanderson, Geoff, 205, 210, 212–13
Sanford, Lucius, 126

Satan, Miroslav, 203, 204, 206, 209, 211

Schafrath, Dick, 70

Schayes, Dolph, 107

Schlafly, Larry, 22–23, 28

Schoenfeld, Jim, 97, *102*

Schreckengost, Ossee, 14

Schulz, Al, 28

Schulz, Kurt, 190

Scott, Charlie, 117

Scott, Jake, 80

Scott, Johnny, 37

Seals, Leon, 137, 145

Sedita, Frank, 160–61

Seick, Earl "Red," 41, 43

Sestak, Tom, 66

Seymour, Paul, 178

Shack, Eddie, 96

Shanahan, Brendan, 230

Shannon, Darryl, 207

Shaw, Dennis, 78–80

Shea, William, 159–61

Shellogg, Alex, 43, 46

Shonta, Chuck, 69

Shula, Don, 77, 78, 190

Shuler, Mickey, 130, 131

Shumate, John, 115, 116, 118, 119

Silas, Paul, *110*

Simmons, Clyde, 192

Simpson, Bill, 124, 126–29, *127*

Simpson, O. J., 78, 80, 81, 83, 85–87, 173–83; acting career of, 182; as broadcaster, 182–83; as Buffalo Bill, 177–81, *180*; as Heisman Trophy winner, 176; murder trial of, 173–74; as San Francisco 49er, 181; at University of Southern California, 174–76

Singletary, Devin, 245, 246, 250, 253

Skinner, Jeff, 258, 261

Skorupan, John, 85

Slaughter, Webster, 149, 188, 189

Smerlas, Fred, 88, 125

Smith, Antowain, 199

Smith, Bruce, 141, 143, 186, 190

Smith, Don, 141

Smith, Elmore, 108, 109

Smith, Emmitt, 156

Smith, Floyd, 96, 98, 103

Smith, Leonard, 138

Smith, Malcolm, 222

Smith, Randy, 108–9, 113, 115–17, 119–20, 263

Smith, Sherry, 16

Smolinski, Bryan, 225

Smythe, Stafford, 96

Snyder, Paul, 107–8, 112, 117–19

Somers, Charles, 12, 13

Sonju, Norm, 119, 120

Spagna, Butch, 37

Spencer, Brian, 98

Spezza, Jason, 225, 233

Spielman, Chris, 192

Spiller, C. J., 242

Staal, Eric, 258

Stanfield, Fred, 99

Sternaman, Ed, 38

Stewart, Chris, 257

Stiglmeier, John, 159

Still, Jim, 54

Stillman, Cory, 227

Straka, Martin, 230–31

Stratton, Mike, 66, 69

Strock, Don, 85, 90

Sullivan, Billy, 64

Sullivan, Haywood, *165*

Sundin, Mats, 210

Super Bowl, 5, 72, 75, 91, 123, 129, 134, 137–57, 185, 191, 200, 247, 251, 255, 264; of 1967, 186; of 1973, 80; of 1974, 83; of 1989, 186; of 1990, 190; of 1991, 3, 141–43, *144*, 190; of 1992, 145–47, *148*, 190; of 1993, 190; of 1994, 154–56, *155*; of 1996, 192; of 2001, 239

Swacina, Harry, 23

Swados, Robert O., 93, 159, 161

Sweeney, Don, 209

Szpylman, Mike, 211

Szur, Joe, 43, 44

T

Tallinder, Henrik, 224, 226, 227
Tampa Bay Buccaneers, 185–86
Tasker, Steve, 4, 190
Taylor, Otis, 73
Taylor, Reginald B., 159–61
Taylor, Tyrod, 241, 243, 244
Tellez, Rowdy, 169
Tennessee Titans, 3, 198–202, *201*
Terlep, George, 51–52
Thalman, Budd, 88
Théodore, José, 206
Thomas, Steve, 210
Thomas, Thurman, 137, 139, 140, 142, 146–47, 150, 153–56, *155*, 188–92, 194, 196, 202, 263
Thompson, Deonte, 244
Thompson, Tage, 261
Thorpe, Jim, 33–35
Tikkanen, Esa, 206
Tindale, Tim, 190
Tittle, Y. A., 53
Todd, Richard, 130–31
Toomay, Pat, 85
Toronto Blue Jays, 168–70
Toronto Maple Leafs, 93, 96, 210–11, 210–11, 261
Tuch, Alex, 260, 261
Tuel, Jeff, 241
Tuten, Rick, 141
Twilley, Howard, 82
Tyson, Mike, 217

U

Umberger, R. J., 224
Unitas, Johnny, 70
Unseld, Wes, 113, 115

V

Valley, Wayne, 64
Van Pelt, Alex, 191, 239
Vanek, Thomas, 223, 230, 231, 257
Varad'a, Václav, 206, 209, 210

Verducci, Tom, 166
Villapiano, Phil, 89
Villar, Jonathan, 169
von Schamann, Uwe, 88–89
Voss, Walter "Tillie," 38

W

Wagner, Honus, 15
Wallace, Levi, 254
Walsh, Bill, 125
Ward, Arch, 49, 50
Ward, Cam, 227
Ward, Dixon, 205, 210–13
Ward, Robert Boyd, 30, 31
Warfield, Paul, 70, 78, 81, 82
Warlick, Ernie, 66, 69
Warrener, Rhett, 210, 215
Washington, Dave, 82
Washington Bullets, 113, 115
Washington Capitals, 206–8
Washington Nationals, 168
Washington Redskins, 145–47, *148*, 153
Washington Senators, 161
Watkins, Sammy, 242
Watson, Deshaun, 246
Watson, Jim, 95
Webster, Tom, 95
Weeghman, Charley, 27, 30
Weight, Doug, 228
Weiss, Bob, 112
Weldon, Bodie, 34
Whaley, Doug, 242
Wheeler, Ernie, 45
White, Bill, 162
White, Jo Jo, 109, 112, 116
White, Sherman, 88, 134
White, Tre'Davious, 248
Wichita Aeros, 162
Wilcox, Ansley, 18
Williams, Darryl, 251
Williams, Gregg, 240
Williams, J. D., 147
Williams, Mario, 242

Williamson, DaVarryl "Touch of Sleep," 219

Willis, Bill, 51

Wilpon, Fred, 162

Wilson, Jerrel, 73

Wilson, Ralph C., Jr., 4, 63–65, 85, 86, 90,
    160, 177, 196; Hunt and, 61; on Miami
    Dolphins, 88; Pegulas and, 236

Wilson, Russell, 248

Winfield, Mason, 1

Wismer, Harry, 64

Witten, Jason, 245

Wolford, Will, 137, 139, 141

Woods, Ickey, 186–88, *187*

Woolley, Jason, 207, 209, 212

World Series, 21; of 1903, 2, 8; of 1915, 30; of
    1916, 16; of 1918, 16; of 1919, 31; of 1997,
    167; of 2003, 167; of 2015, 168

World War II, 44, 46, 48–49

Wray, Lud, 37

Wright, Frank Lloyd, 7

Wycheck, Frank, 200, 201

Y

Yepremian, Garo, 79, 81

Young, Cy, 15

Young, George, 54

Youngstrom, Swede, 34, 35

Z

Zhitnik, Alexei, 203, 204, 210, 212

Zimmer, Justin, 248

Zimmerman, Paul B., 175

Zubov, Sergei, 211

COLOPHON

DESIGN

Marnie Soom

PRINTING AND BINDING

More Vang
Alexandria, Virginia

PAPER

Endurance Silk

TYPEFACES

Minion Pro
URW DIN and DIN Condensed
ATF Poster Gothic Condensed
Look Script Bold

This book was made possible, in part,
through the generosity of More Vang.